DEDICATION

I WOULD LIKE TO DEDICATE THIS BOOK TO THE STUDENT WHO ANSWERED THE FOLLOWING QUESTION BY SKETCHING THIS DIAGRAM WHILE OBSERVING A LIGHTED LIGHT BULB PROTRUDING FROM THE TOP OF A BLACK BOX. THE QUESTION, "What do you think is inside the black box causing the light to light?" THE RESPONSE:

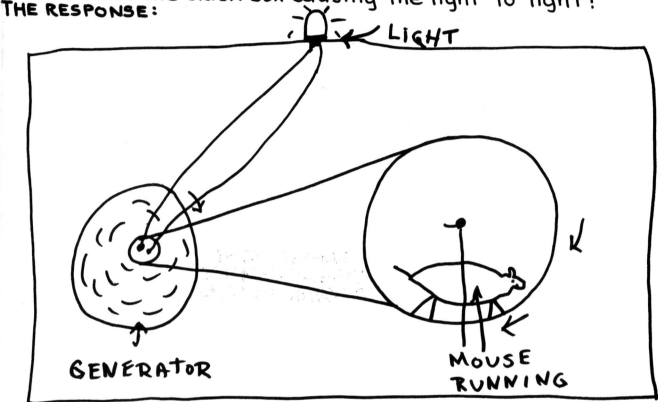

LIGHT

GENERATOR

MOUSE RUNNING

I WOULD ALSO LIKE TO DEDICATE THIS BOOK TO ALL PEOPLE WHOSE HANDS REACH OUT AND TOUCH CHILDREN IN HOPES THEY WILL CHERISH THE FOLLOWING WORDS WRITTEN BY KATHLEEN KELLY.

REMEMBER MY HANDS?

Long ago they welcomed you into a
    heart so full.
Never again to be empty; oh, the
    strings you'll pull.
They put food into your mouth and
    held unto you so,
Wondering where and when they'd
    have to let go;
They picked you up and let you
    down,
Caressed your face when there
    was a frown.

When your hair in braids they put,
    remember the pulling and tugging?
But don't forget the wiped-off tears
    and all that kissing and hugging!
The fatal day came to release you,
    as they opened up the door;
They watched you walk away, never
    to touch you any more.
These hands still remember, with
    burning desire aglow;
Can you still feel them, though it
    was so long ago?

                              - KATHLEEN KELLY

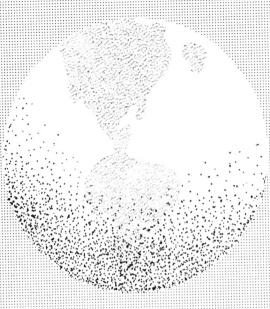

IT IS A LAW OF
HUMAN LIFE, AS
CERTAIN AS
GRAVITY; TO
LIVE FULLY, WE
MUST LEARN
TO USE THINGS
AND LOVE
PEOPLE —
NOT LOVE
THINGS AND
USE
PEOPLE.

CONTENTS

CONTENTS

CONTENTS

CONTENTS

PREFACE

The early morning sun glistens on droplets of rain that had settled on the grass overnight. A nine-year-old boy, with pitchfork over shoulder, heads down a long lane toward the back forty. His job is to turn windrows of hay that have become soaked from the previous evening's storm. Throughout the morning the boy is curious how the white hot sun burns the tiny droplets from the hay and wonders what happens to the moisture.

Noon comes. Mom arrives at the field with tasty sandwiches and a jug of lemonade. The boy quickly notices the tiny droplets of water on the outside of the jug and wonders how it is possible for the water to move from inside the jar, through the thick glass to the outside of the jar. Years later he learned that the tiny droplets resulted from the condensation of water vapor in the air onto a cold surface but on this day he merely lay on his back, looking at the sky and just wondering. He wonders why the sky is blue, what causes the clouds to move ever so gently and about how the universe began.

The boy continues his work in the afternoon. He turns a clump of hay and hears an object clang against the tine of his fork. He rustles through the prickly stubbles with his bare hands and finds an Indian arrowhead. He wonders about how these people lived long ago and how they hunted. His thoughts turn to other farm experiences including different types of rocks and soil, how chickens get rocks in their gizzards, how a calf can exit such a small opening in its mother and what the long cord that attaches the calf to its mother is used for. He finishes his day even more curious and wonders why the setting sun is so red and so much larger than the rising sun he had seen only hours before.

Throughout the years the boy grew to adulthood and gained in knowledge of himself, others and the world around him. The older he became, the more he understood but he fully realized how little he actually knew. One day while the man was teaching, a three-year-old child, holding a glass of lemonade in one hand, squeezed his hand and asked what caused the water on the outside of his glass of lemonade. The man smiled and squeezed the child's hand in return. He gathered ice cubes and containers and together they experimented. Both were curious. Eventually, both clearly understood what was happening when the water quickly formed on the outside of the container. History did repeat itself. A record of events was made.

The man continued his work as a "teacher" for a number of years and kept further notes of his experiences. He learned that youngsters seemed to be most excited, and learned more, when they physically touched materials, especially free and inexpensive materials, found in their own, real world. After a great deal of thinking, wondering and discovering, the man decided to write a book and share his findings and feelings with others. This is his book. Like the squeeze of hands, this book is written to touch and be used not only with the head but with the heart as well.

Creative, Hands-On Science Experiences is written for people of all ages and for those in any occupation. Classroom teachers, administrators, youth leaders, camp guides and parents will hopefully find it useful. The book focuses on the use of *common, everyday materials,* some of which can be obtained free or purchased rather inexpensively, or found around the home, school or in the community. Major emphasis is placed on *starter activities;* activities designed to prompt children to ask "Why" or "What would happen if" type questions about science events.

These starter activities are intended to have children explore rather than memorize facts and are cross-referenced, using animal characters, to the NOTES section in the back of the book. For example, the starter activity Rock Exchange on page 169 has a butterfly with the page number 237. The reader can turn to page 237 where a butterfly with page 169 will designate extending activities for the starter activity, in this case sources of information for pen pals. The references offer a variety of extending activities that can be done after the starter activity is completed. A similar cross reference system is used for the "meditators" identified by the small Buddahs found throughout the book.

The book uses customary English measurements, with metric measurements in parentheses and focuses on *interdisciplinary activities* via *webbing*. Activities generally incorporate the use of all academic disciplines. Finally, the book emphasizes *touching* and *valuing* activities. People using the book are encouraged to touch materials, investigate their properties by trial and error learning and then reflect on the value of these activities in their everyday lives. This reflection can be accomplished by using the science diary and log sheets found in the back of the book on pages 240 and 241.

The contents of *Creative, Hands-On Science Experiences* include a suggested SCOPE AND SEQUENCE for a K-6 ELEMENTARY SCIENCE PROGRAM in Chapter One. The frog is a symbol for Biological Science concepts, the chemist for Physical Science concepts and the rocket for Earth and Space Science concepts. Sample activities found in the book, with appropriate page numbers, are noted for each concept and level in the SCOPE AND SEQUENCE.

Chapter Two, WHEEL OF FOURTHS, identifies four major functions of teaching: planning, implementation, evaluation and communication. Tips, hints, and concrete examples for each function are given in this chapter.

SCIENCE SAFETY hints and charts for the teacher and student are included in Chapter Three. Examples that show how to MAKE YOUR OWN SCIENCE MATERIALS using free and inexpensive materials are found in Chapter Four.

Chapters Five, Six and Seven include over 100 hands-on science activities for teachers and students in BIOLOGICAL, PHYSICAL and EARTH AND SPACE SCIENCES respectively. MY MINI BOOK OF SCIENCE ACTIVITIES found in Chapter Eight contains hundreds of starter activities and can be run off for enrichment purposes. Chapter Nine gives you another 100 STARTER IDEAS using free and inexpensive materials. You are encouraged to do a bit of STRETCHING in Chapter Ten which includes information on science organizations, science periodicals, science catalogs, science curriculum projects, textbook series and how to evaluate the latter. Notes, sample log sheets, and reference material including a periodic table of the elements and the Handy Metric/ Customary Conversion Chart are also included.

In the end, *Creative, Hands-On Science Experiences* is only a beginning. It is hoped that its contents touch many minds, hearts and hands and that much growth is experienced by all who come in contact with its contents. One is encouraged to remember the words spoken by Alice in *Alice in Wonderland*, "What is the use of a book without pictures or conversations?" Keep in touch. I'd like to spin a few yarns with you.

EARTH AND SPACE

PHYSICAL

1

SCOPE AND SEQUENCE

BIOLOGICAL

Here are some big ideas in Biological Science that you may want your kids to become familiar with.

1. All living things depend on each other and their environment.

2. Any living thing is a product of its heredity and environment.

3. All living things are in constant change.

BIOLOGICAL SCIENCE

	MAJOR TOPIC	CONCEPT(S)	ACTIVITY PAGE #
K	Myself	Senses	56
	Animals	Baby, adult	83
	Plants	Leaves	86, 87
		Flowers	85
1	You and Me	Similarities and differences	55
	Mammals	Differences	80, 84
	Plants	Parts of and function	76
	Senses	Five and more	88, 89
2	Living Things	Groups and subgroups	69
	Nonliving Things	Dinosaurs	174
	Insects	Life cycles	73
	Plants	Reproduction and photosynthesis	86, 87
	Human Body	Systems, general	57
	Health	Dental	14
3	Ecology	Balance of nature	76
	Birds	Nests, types, habits	81
	Insects	Harmful, nonharmful	70
	Endangered Species	Extinction	30
	Trees	Kinds, growth, uses	93
4	Animals	Behavior of, reproduction	81
	Water	Life in water	78
	Mammals	Kinds	70
	Cells—Plant and Animal	Differences with microscope	75
	Diseases	Kinds and effects	93
5	Environmental Science	Conservation, pollution	71
	Human Body	Systems, care of	57
	Health	Drugs, smoking, nutrition	58, 63
	Insects	Habits and habitats	140
	Microscopic Plants and Animals	Tissues, organs and systems	75
6	Plants and Animals	Life cycles, dissection of	85
	Algae, Fungi, Microbes	Kinds of and differences	75
	Human Body	Basic genetics, sex education	54, 60, 61
	Food Chains and Nutrient Cycles	Photosynthesis, solar energy	76
	Careers in Science	Exploration of	94, 95, 96

Here are some big ideas in Physical Science that you may want your kids to become familiar with.

1. The total amount of ENERGY remains unchanged when ENERGY changes from one form to another.

2. The total amount of MATTER remains unchanged when MATTER changes from one form to another.

PHYSICAL SCIENCE

MAJOR TOPIC	CONCEPT(S)	ACTIVITY PAGE #
K		
Changes in State of Matter	Causes	132
Magnets	Push and tug	130
Colors	Types of and mixing	104
Energy	Awareness	124, 125, 126, 127
1		
Sounds and Music	Kinds of	119
Electricity	Types of	124
Simple Machines	Work	129
Energy	Kinds of	124
2		
Matter	States of solids, liquids and gases	137
Energy	Conservation	125, 126, 127
Models	How and why things work	121
3		
Heat and Temperature	Changes and effects	112
Magnets and Electricity	Uses of	131
Energy	Sources and shortage of	30
Sounds	Effects of	68
4		
Physical Forces—small	Molecular	96
Physical Forces—large	Work	123
Energy	Uses	129
Matter	Molecules, atoms and subatomic particles	100, 101
5		
Electricity and Magnetism	Use of in motors, engines	131
Chemical and Physical Changes in Matter	Basic reactions, identification of	103
Sounds	Kinds of and location of	119
Light	Behavior and composition	122
6		
Forces—Natural vs Man-made	Gravity, mass, acceleration	160, 161
Solids, Liquids, and Gases	Behavior and effects of	114
Energy	Types of and value-laden issues	30
Great Names in Science	Inventions and effects of	112
Careers in Science	Investigation of	109, 180

1. The entire universe is in constant change.

2. Our galaxy, the Milky Way, is only part of a much larger universe.

EARTH AND SPACE SCIENCE

In an effort to understand and communicate with others, one must first understand and communicate with oneself.

	MAIN TOPIC	CONCEPT(S)	ACTIVITY PAGE #
K	Our World	Day, night	154
	Weather	Air, wind	134, 135
	Water	Snow, fog, ice	137
1	Sun and Earth	Seasons	153
	Weather	Records of	136
	Rocks and Sand	Time awareness	168
	Space	Near, far	146
2	Moon	Size, shape, position and changes	163
	Oceans and Rivers	Effects of change	170, 171
	Rocks and Soil	Changes in state	164, 165
	Space and Beyond	Atmosphere and UFO's	144, 145
3	Sun, Moon, Stars	Simple relationships and constellations	152
	Weather and Climate	Observing and recording	134, 135
	Motions of Earth	Causes of	160, 161
	Science Fiction	A look to the future	181
4	Basic Geology	Identify rocks and minerals and products made from these	172
	Natural Disasters	Causes of, prevention and control	141
	Fossils	Prehistoric life	176
	Planets	Extraterrestrial life	150
5	Solar System and Universe	Differences, make up and origin	173
	Atmosphere	Forces in and effects of	137
	Seasonal Changes	Observing and recording changes	153
	Oceans	Uses of: energy, life support	170, 171
	Science Fiction	A look to the future	181
6	Past	Big bang, steady state	175
	Weather and Climate	Predicting, satellites, etc.	134, 135
	Space	Living in and exploration of	146
	Earth	Composition of and changes in	174
	Future	Red giants, black holes, white dwarfs	182
	Careers	Investigation of	180

WHEEL OF FOURTHS

PLANNING
COMMUNICATION
EVALUATION
IMPLEMENTATION

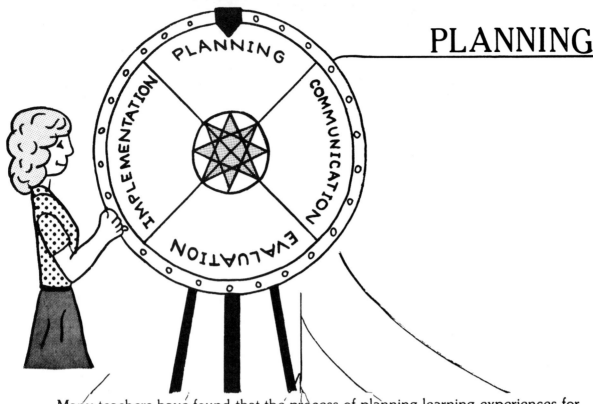

Many teachers have found that the process of planning learning experiences for children is similar to a spider spinning a web. Thinking in this way helps you as a teacher with both everyday and long-range planning. A web starts with any activity, idea, topic, or object that gets children excited about learning. You or your children merely choose a topic from something in which you and your students are interested. Write it down in the center of a large piece of paper and circle it. Then mark the paper with each academic discipline representing an extension or spoke off the central topic. You and your children can then think of a learning activity that could be developed from the original idea in that discipline. Then write this down next to the original idea by connecting it with an arrow or line. Each idea you attach to the central idea becomes another idea and the process is continued over and over again. Some ideas will overlap. Hence, from one idea flows many others in an interdisciplinary manner. A web is never complete. You and your children can always add at least one more idea.

Once you have a fairly extensive web, you and your students can hang the web up in the classroom for all to use. Anyone can suggest ideas. You may also want to keep a copy at your desk so you can suggest future activities to children. Used in this way, the web becomes a type of lesson plan or can be used as a guide to extend learning. You and your students need only to remember that all the ideas do not have to be studied and if an idea or activity develops that wasn't on the original plan, that's okay too.

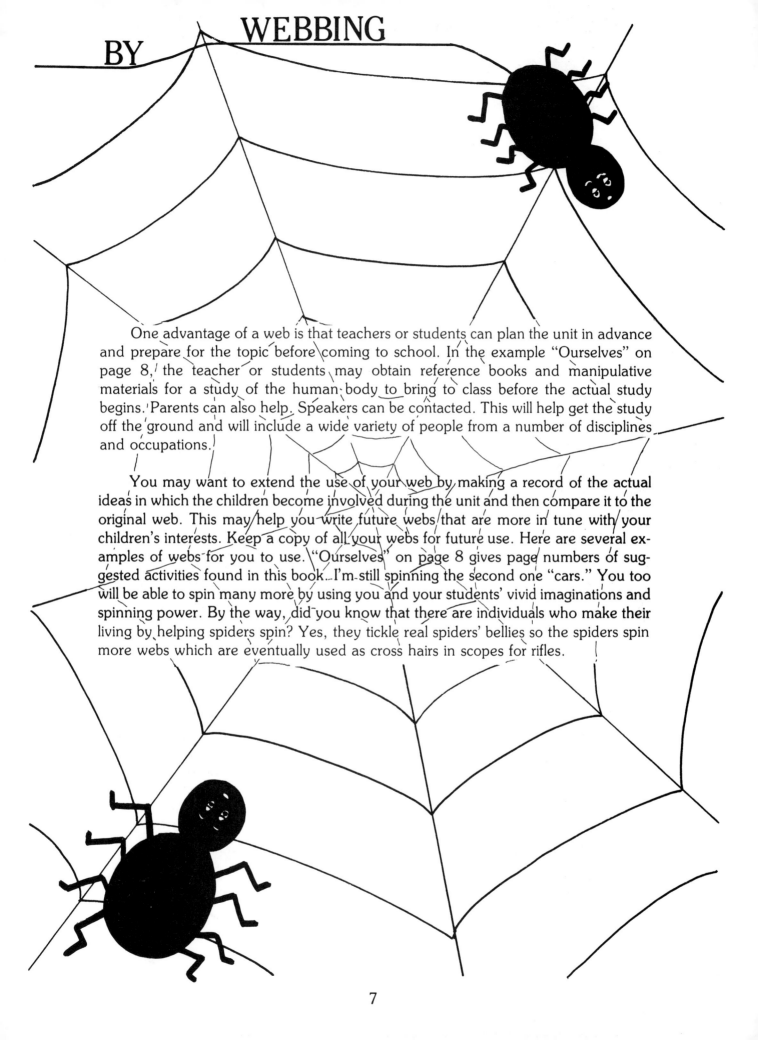

BY WEBBING

One advantage of a web is that teachers or students can plan the unit in advance and prepare for the topic before coming to school. In the example "Ourselves" on page 8, the teacher or students may obtain reference books and manipulative materials for a study of the human body to bring to class before the actual study begins. Parents can also help. Speakers can be contacted. This will help get the study off the ground and will include a wide variety of people from a number of disciplines and occupations.

You may want to extend the use of your web by making a record of the actual ideas in which the children become involved during the unit and then compare it to the original web. This may help you write future webs that are more in tune with your children's interests. Keep a copy of all your webs for future use. Here are several examples of webs for you to use. "Ourselves" on page 8 gives page numbers of suggested activities found in this book. I'm still spinning the second one "cars." You too will be able to spin many more by using you and your students' vivid imaginations and spinning power. By the way, did you know that there are individuals who make their living by helping spiders spin? Yes, they tickle real spiders' bellies so the spiders spin more webs which are eventually used as cross hairs in scopes for rifles.

AN INTERDISCIPLINARY PLANNING WEB

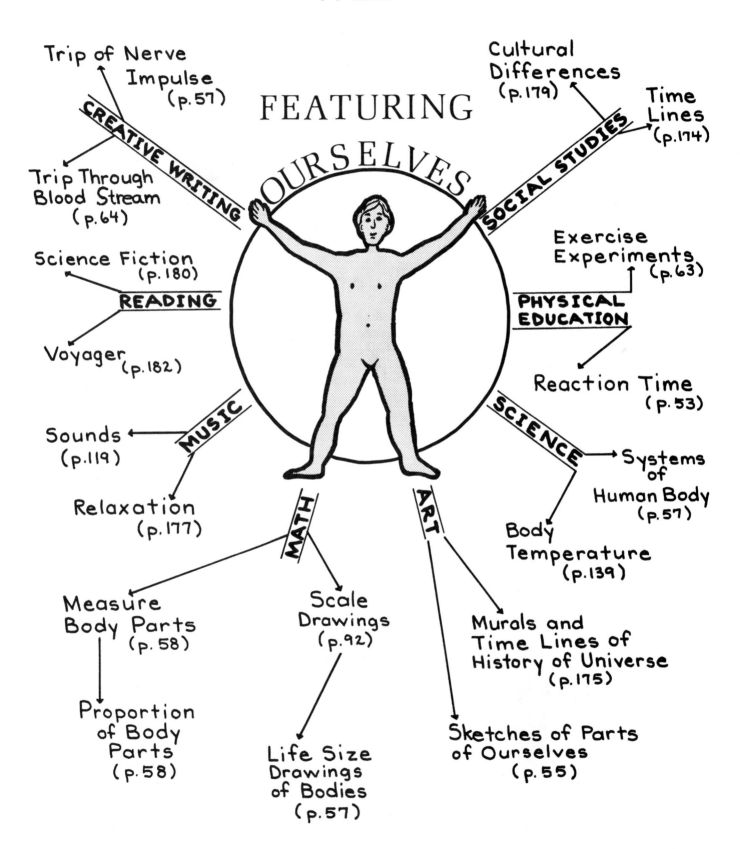

FEATURING OURSELVES

Trip of Nerve Impulse (p.57)

CREATIVE WRITING

Trip Through Blood Stream (p.64)

Science Fiction (p.180)

READING

Voyager (p.182)

MUSIC

Sounds (p.119)

Relaxation (p.177)

MATH

Measure Body Parts (p.58)

Proportion of Body Parts (p.58)

Scale Drawings (p.92)

Life Size Drawings of Bodies (p.57)

ART

Murals and Time Lines of History of Universe (p.175)

Sketches of Parts of Ourselves (p.55)

Cultural Differences (p.179)

SOCIAL STUDIES

Time Lines (p.174)

Exercise Experiments (p.63)

PHYSICAL EDUCATION

Reaction Time (p.53)

SCIENCE

Systems of Human Body (p.57)

Body Temperature (p.139)

A Car Web

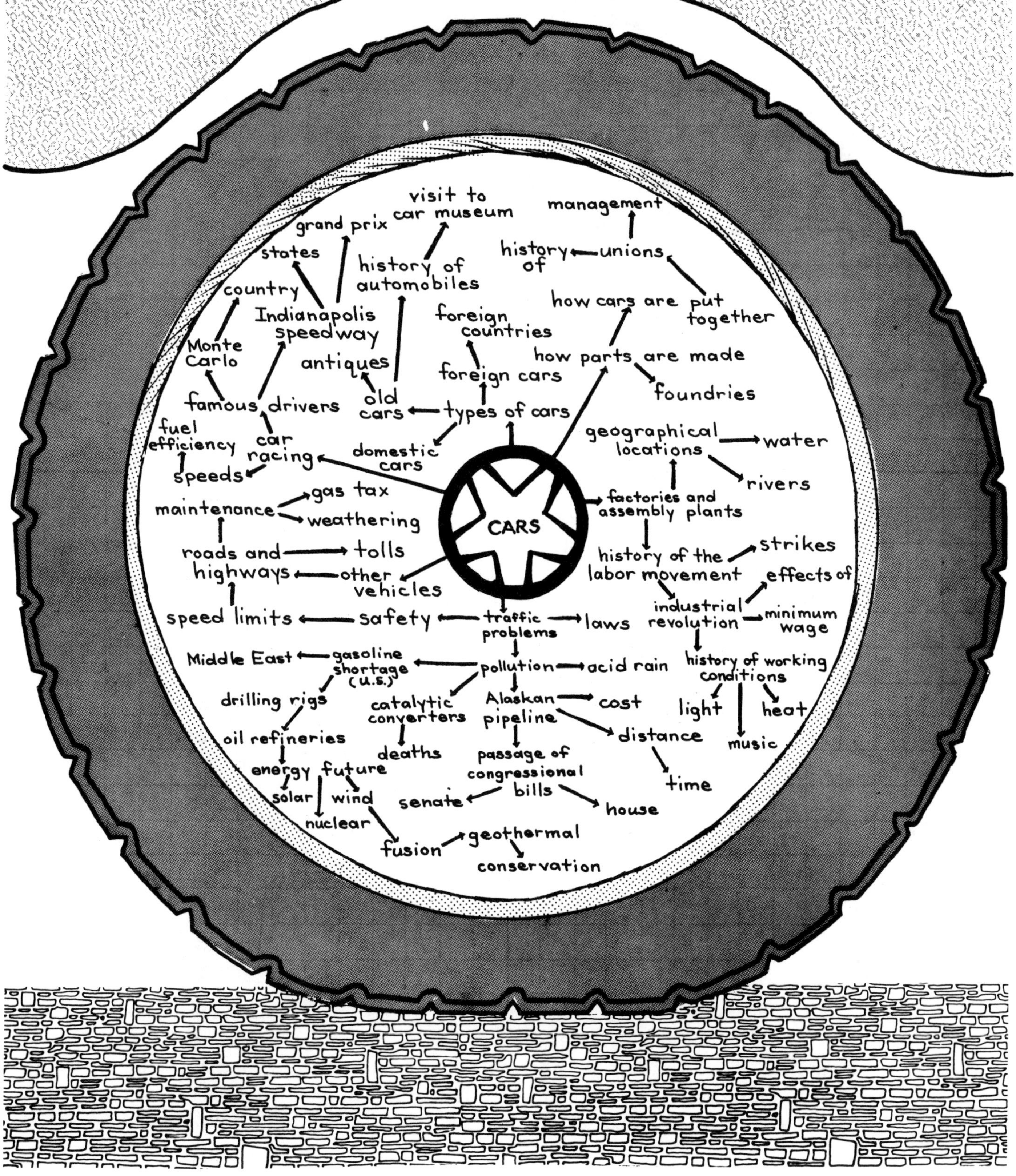

visit to car museum

grand prix

states

country

history of automobiles

Monte Carlo

Indianapolis speedway

antiques

famous drivers

old cars

fuel efficiency

car racing

speeds

maintenance

gas tax

weathering

roads and highways

tolls

other vehicles

speed limits

safety

traffic problems

gasoline shortage (u.s.)

Middle East

drilling rigs

catalytic converters

pollution

oil refineries

deaths

energy future

solar

wind

nuclear

fusion

Alaskan pipeline

senate

passage of congressional bills

geothermal

conservation

house

management

history of

unions

how cars are put together

foreign countries

how parts are made

foreign cars

types of cars

domestic cars

foundries

geographical locations

water

rivers

factories and assembly plants

history of the labor movement

strikes

effects of

industrial revolution

minimum wage

laws

acid rain

cost

distance

time

history of working conditions

light

heat

music

CARS

IMPLEMENTATION BY LEARNING CENTERS

What Are Learning Centers?

Teachers know that children are unique human beings. We know that children learn at different rates, have different styles, need a variety of experiences to learn and some need more experiences than others. Most importantly, we know, from experience, that children seem to be most interested in their learning and learn most effectively when they are actively involved in their learning. One way to get children actively involved is through the use of manipulative materials in learning centers. As teachers teaching science, it is important for us to put into action the following Chinese proverb by using manipulative materials: I Hear and I Forget

I See and I Remember

I Do and I Understand

Learning centers are specific places in space that contain activities which help children understand specific science concepts. They supply welcome and wholesome alternatives to seatwork. They emphasize an active, self-selecting and problem-solving approach to learning which is carried out by individual or small groups of children. Learning centers free the teacher from large group instruction and allow the teacher to work with individual children in a more personalized manner. In summary, learning centers can be used to:

- help children develop independent and self-directed learning skills
- introduce new concepts and skills for children to learn
- reinforce skills and concepts previously taught by the teacher
- provide enrichment experiences for *all* children
- help children develop self-motivation and self-discipline through tools of self-assessment and personal satisfaction
- individualize instruction so more attention can be given to specific children; to those who need that extra help in the form of remedial activity and for those who need those extra enrichment activities for further development of the self

Write the goals that you'd like to teach on a sheet of paper.

> Ex: I would like my kids to learn about an open circuit, closed circuit, series circuit, parallel circuit, etc.

 Decide on a sequence of concepts that you'd like to teach, usually having simple to complex levels of difficulty.

> Ex: open circuit
> closed circuit
> series circuit
> parallel circuit

 Decide on a sequence of activities that will help teach the sequence of concepts in the centers.

> Ex: Using one dry cell, one wire and one light bulb, make the bulb light. Keep a record, including drawings of ways that you tried to make the bulb light. Include both those ways that the bulb didn't light and those that did light (concepts: open and closed circuits).

> Ex: Using one dry cell, two wires, two light bulbs, and two bulb holders, make two bulbs light such that if you unscrew one bulb the other remains lit (concept: parallel circuit) and if you unscrew one bulb the other goes out (concept: series circuit).

 Communicate your goals and concepts to the students by using activity cards, charts, tapes, etc. These act as springboards into the learning activities for your centers. Make at least one activity card per concept that you would like to teach. Put name of concept on back of the activity card and laminate for durability.

Ex: Card 1   Reverse Side

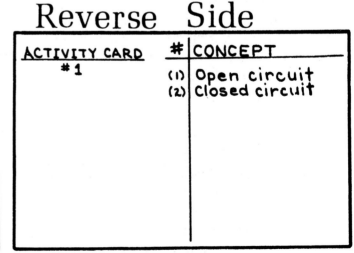

Make two bulbs light using only 1 dry cell and two bulb holders. You may use more than one wire. Find a way that if you unscrew one bulb the other will remain lit and another way if you unscrew one bulb the other will go out. Make a drawing of these two ways in your science notebook.	**ACTIVITY CARD #2**

EX: CARD 2 (front)   EX: CARD 2 (back)

☞ Construct a self-assessment record keeping system and teacher record keeping system for each center. These record keeping systems can be keyed to the order in which concepts are taught.

Ex: See Record Keeping System for Students and Parents on page 19.

☞ Gather all manipulative materials needed for the centers.

Ex: 1.5v dry cells, wires, bulbs, bulb holders, etc.

☞ Identify designated spaces for the location of your centers and begin building them. (Put plastic on floor for water and sand centers. Put newspapers on desks for messy experiments.) Your room may look like this if you are teaching a unit on basic electricity and magnetism.

Here is the ACTIVITY CARD #2 concept list:

#	CONCEPT
(3)	Series circuit
(4)	Parallel circuit

Plan to manage the centers effectively. You may want to color code each learning center using a different color Con-Tact paper on a large sheet of cardboard (see diagram on page 12). Color code coffee cans, one per center, with the same color Con-Tact paper used on the cardboard in the center. Place matching color-coded sticks in the cans. (Popsicle sticks or tongue depressors work well for this.) Put only the number of sticks that are equivalent in number to the number of manipulatives you have in the center for each can. This will permit each child to work in the center effectively and avoid overcrowding. Place cans on your desk. Children must choose center and have appropriate color-coded stick to work in the center. If there are no sticks left in the can, this means that the center is full and no more children can work in the center.

Ex: See diagram on page 12.

Discuss with children proper behavior for centers. Make a transparency of pages 14 and 15 for this purpose.

Do a trial run and actually teach children how to use the centers. Write down rules with the children for the centers including safety rules on pages 34, 35 and 36. Remember that children need time to learn how to learn.

Start slowly. You may want to do a large group lesson first to get the unit underway then gradually introduce the centers as children become more familiar with the topic.

Have students check their own progress using a self-checking record keeping system.

Ex: See sample on page 19.

Have children record their observations and findings in their science log books using copies of pages 240 and 241 in this book.

Give students immediate feedback using Communication Cards found on page 23 or by using self-checking devices.

Have students build their own activities and learning centers to share with others. Some truly great discoveries have been made when using this technique.

Communicate results of learning center activity to parents with the use of the Record Keeping System for Students and Parents on page 19. Staple this to weekly Stretch-O-Gram found on pages 24 and 25.

Share ideas with others including other teachers, special area personnel, parents, principal, custodial staff, *et. al.* Sharing does help.

Continue to grow in knowledge and understanding of yourself and others.

APPROPRIATE BEHAVIOR
FOR
SCIENCE CENTERS

Teacher's Desk

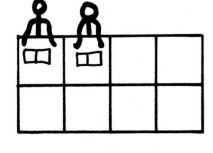

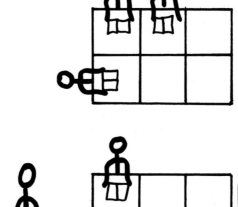

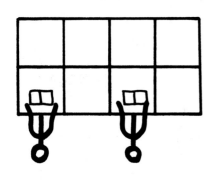

Bookshelf

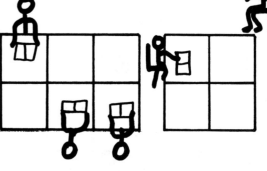

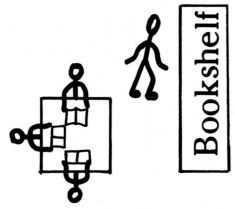

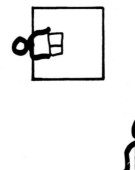

INAPPROPRIATE BEHAVIOR
FOR
SCIENCE CENTERS

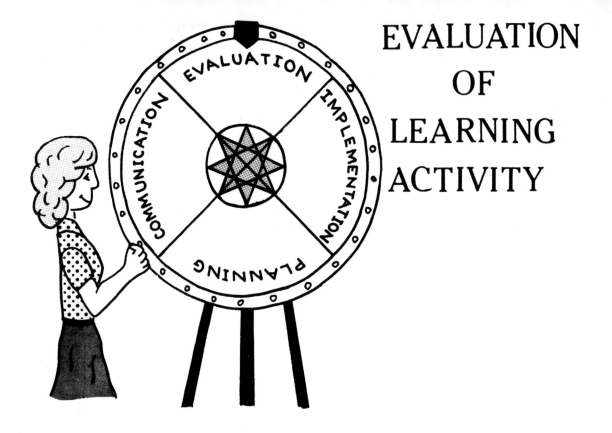

EVALUATION OF LEARNING ACTIVITY

There are many different paths that one can follow to evaluate both teacher and student progress. Some teachers use *COGNITIVE* oriented evaluation tools like paper and pencil tests that feature fill in the blank, matching, true-false questions, etc., (a fun example of this is found on page 18). Others focus on *PSYCHOMOTOR* skills such as having students actually strip a piece of wire, prepare a slide, or focus a microscope. Still others focus on *AFFECTIVE* measures like trying to find out how students *feel* about themselves, about their work and about others (see page 17). All three methods of evaluation should be used in an effort to help individuals grow in understanding the world about them and feelings toward themselves and others. In the latter case, smiley faces, personal letters, interviews, individual conferences, student questionnaires and checklists can be used. Both you and your children should be encouraged to do these activities and develop a daily self-evaluation of progress through science logs or diaries (see sample pages 240 and 241). Give the instrument on page 21 before, in the middle of, and after a unit of study to learn if student attitudes have increased, decreased or remained the same. Point values can be assigned to questions and you can record student attitude scores, calculate changes in attitudes over a period of time and note changes in such attitudes.

SAMPLE AFFECTIVE EVALUATION

Example: Circle the number to indicate whether you:

1. Strongly Agree
2. Agree
3. Disagree
4. Strongly Disagree

STATEMENT	REACTION				
	Strongly Agree	Agree	Disagree	Strongly Disagree	Points
1. I am a curious person.	1	2	3	4	_____
2. I like science.	1	2	3	4	_____
3. Making new inventions is fun.	1	2	3	4	_____
4. My teacher allows us to make suggestions about what we study.	1	2	3	4	_____
5. Being a scientist would be neat.	1	2	3	4	_____
6. My teacher seems excited about teaching science.	1	2	3	4	_____
7. This class is very worthwhile.	1	2	3	4	_____
8. I can do science without knowing much about the topic.	1	2	3	4	_____
9. I can talk with the teacher as a person.	1	2	3	4	_____
10. My teacher seems interested in what I have to say.	1	2	3	4	_____
11. I can trust the teacher and the teacher trusts me.	1	2	3	4	_____
12. This class is often boring.	1	2	3	4	_____
13. We seem to have a choice in what we want to discover.	1	2	3	4	_____
14. I like what goes on in this class.	1	2	3	4	_____
15. The activities we do are interesting.	1	2	3	4	_____
16. Not having science would be okay with me.	1	2	3	4	_____

Total Points _____

★ SAMPLE COGNITIVE EVALUATION

Directions: Write the letter in the blank of the answer in column B that best matches the term in column A.

COLUMN A

1. _____ $BaNa_2$
2. _____ Fisson
3. _____ Half Reaction
4. _____ Mole
5. _____ Weak base
6. _____ HIOAg
7. _____ Barium
8. _____ $CoFe_2$
9. _____ Specimen
10. _____ CH_2O
11. _____

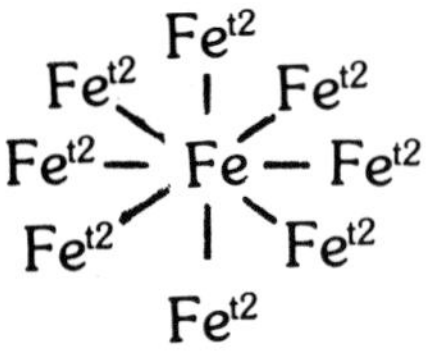

$$Fe^{t2} - \underset{\underset{Fe^{t2}}{|}}{\overset{\overset{Fe^{t2}}{|}}{Fe}} - Fe^{t2}$$

with Fe^{t2} groups at corners

12. _____ Dipoles
13. _____

(structure of fused rings with CH_3 groups: CH_3 CH_3 at top, CH_3 at right, CH_3 at left, CH_3 CH_3 at bottom)

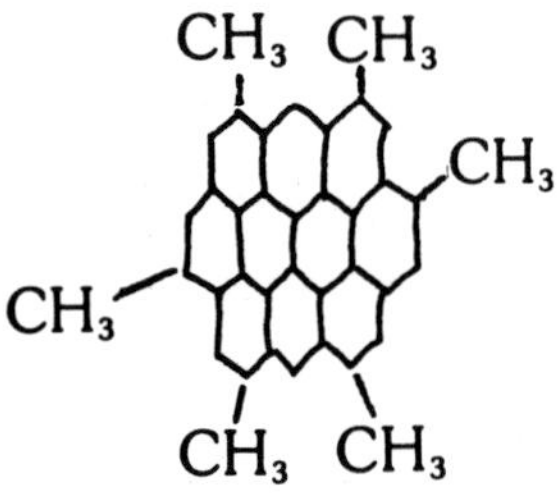

14. _____ Zn
15. _____ H_2O (not a liquid)
16. _____ $Br + Br + Br + Br \rightarrow Br_4$
17. _____ $Ba + Au + H_2O \rightarrow$
18. _____ Nitrogen
19. _____ NO_3^{-1}
20. _____ Holiday Greeting

COLUMN B

A. Two Europeans
B. A place to wash one's hands
C. A breakfast beverage
D. Very powerful alcoholic drink
E. Found at an amusement park
F. Hexamethyl chicken wire
G. $NaHCO_3$
H. Tropical fruit
I. $MeRe_2$ KRISMAS
J. Written when you don't know the whole reaction
K. A reaction that goes to the right
L. HIJKLMNO
M. Small burrowing animal
N. Associated with Tonto's partner
O. What they do with dead people
P. Used to support an unwanted vase
Q. A cold weather reaction
R. A sport or summer relaxation
S. Italian astronauts
T. Found in the Mediterranean
U. Night club dancer
V. House + H_2O =?
W. A purple people eater
X. Charge when you call after 6 p.m.
Y. Presidential candidate in 1964

SOME HINTS

Ag = silver

NO_3^{-1} = nitrate

$NaHCO_3$ = Sodium bicarbonate

Sample Record Keeping System for Students and Parents

The following is a sample record keeping system that you can give to children to help them evaluate their own progress in electricity and magnetism. This could eventually be attached to Stretch-O-Gram and sent home to parents at the end of the unit.

Name_____

STUDENT PROGRESS REPORT

Unit: Basic Electricity and Magnetism

Concept Number	Activity/Concept/Skill	Yes	No	Student Self-Evaluation (1-5) of Concept or Learning Center	Comments
Ex:	Drawing of contents inside black box (See page i of this book.)	9/14/86		5	I liked this activity especially the mouse inside the black box.
1	Open circuit using one dry cell, one wire and one bulb				
2	Closed circuit using one dry cell, one wire and one bulb				
3	Series circuit				
4	Parallel circuit				
5	Short circuit				
6	Electrical circuits using dry cell holders				
7	Drawing of contents inside broken bulb				
8	Electrical circuits using many bulb holders				
9	Drawing of contents inside dry cell				
10	Strip insulation from wire using a wire-stripper				
11	Study of objects in home using electricity				
12	Construct paper clip switch				
13	Construct toilet paper roll flashlight				
14	Construct coil motor with drawing (See page 131.)				
15	Construct buzzer with drawing				
16	Rings bells. Includes drawing of bell with appropriate parts				
17	Other: Student devised activities/projects/skills				

A Sample Class Record Keeping System for the Teacher

The following is a sample record keeping system that you can use to note children's progress in electricity and magnetism. Merely ask student to perform the indicated task (concept) and check "yes," "no." Add comments as needed. You can easily match your goals, concepts, learning center activities, and this evaluation of progress checklist by numbering concepts sequentially.

Unit: Basic Electricity and Magnetism

NAME	SKILL OR CONCEPT NUMBER																COMMENTS
	1	2	3	4	5	6	7	8	9	10	11	12	13	14	15	16	

Sample Affective Evaluation of a Science Unit

For each of the paired items listed below, place an (x) on the line that best represents your feelings about the unit on _____.

Example: The unit on _____ will be (before unit) is (mid-unit) was (end of unit)

Hot ___: ___: ___: ___: ___: ___: ___: Cold

1.	Interesting	___: ___: ___: ___: ___: ___: ___: Boring
2.	Important	___: ___: ___: ___: ___: ___: ___: Useless
3.	Informative	___: ___: ___: ___: ___: ___: ___: Worthless
4.	Complete	___: ___: ___: ___: ___: ___: ___: Incomplete
5.	Mixed Up	___: ___: ___: ___: ___: ___: ___: Smooth
6.	A Downer	___: ___: ___: ___: ___: ___: ___: An Upper
7.	Selfish	___: ___: ___: ___: ___: ___: ___: Unselfish
8.	Enough Time	___: ___: ___: ___: ___: ___: ___: Not Enough Time
9.	Light	___: ___: ___: ___: ___: ___: ___: Dark
10.	Negative	___: ___: ___: ___: ___: ___: ___: Positive
11.	High	___: ___: ___: ___: ___: ___: ___: Low
12.	Bad	___: ___: ___: ___: ___: ___: ___: Good
13.	Liked	___: ___: ___: ___: ___: ___: ___: Disliked
14.	Black	___: ___: ___: ___: ___: ___: ___: White
15.	Fast	___: ___: ___: ___: ___: ___: ___: Slow

_____ Total Points

Things I like(d) best about the unit.

Things I like(d) least about the unit.

Things we can do to change the unit to make it better.

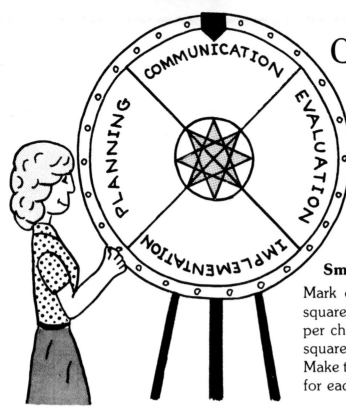

COMMUNICATION

Open communication that fosters relationships based on mutual trust and respect is important in any classroom. To keep communication lines open with children, yourself and parents you may want to use Communication Board, Communication Cards and Posters and develop a Stretch-O-Gram.

Smiley Face Communication Board

Mark off a piece of wood or triple wall into squares using magic marker. Have one square per child and one for yourself. Print names in squares. Screw cup hook into each square. Make three smiley faces out of tagboard like this for each person including yourself.

Cut out. Laminate. Punch hole in upper part of face. You and your students place the smiley face on the hook that best represents your/their feelings when arriving at school in the morning and upon dismissal at the end of the day. This will generate communication and will hopefully develop respect for the other person's feelings both in and out of school.

COMMUNICATION BOARD							
How Are You Feeling Today?							
JOHN	SUE	BILL					

Computer cards that are laminated work well to increase communication between you and your children. Obtain some cards, then laminate. Write message on card using erasable pen. Give message to child who in turn can write message to you. Messages can be exchanged also among students and you as a result of interesting discoveries or outstanding work.

Communication
Cards

Communication want ad posters can be used effectively in the classroom. Give each child a sheet of paper and have students write their names on their posters. Students then write about things "for sale" or "want ad" wanted material or help. Display posters. Add necessary features that come up. For example, a for sale ad may include, "I have ability to help in math for sale" or "I need help in science" may be a want ad for help. These make excellent support systems for the teacher and students and help all concerned to work together.

Want Ad Posters

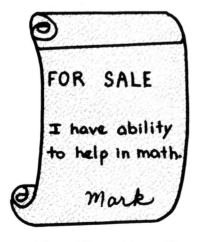

Use this handy Stretch-O-Gram on a ditto to send home each week to parents. At the end of each day, write a few sentences with your children about that day. Check smiley face feelings. Include student sketches and artwork. Use the following page, A Peek at Next Week, as a ditto and run on back of this sheet for a single page Stretch-O-Gram.

Best Happening This Week	**Phase of Moon**	**Weekly High**	**Weekly Low**	**For the Week of** _____

Day	Our Feelings About the Day
Monday	😊 😐 ☹️
Tuesday	😊 😐 ☹️
Wednesday	😊 😐 ☹️
Thursday	😊 😐 ☹️
Friday	😊 😐 ☹️

A PEEK AT NEXT WEEK

★

NEXT WEEK WE WILL BE STUDYING:	JUNK MATERIALS WE WILL NEED:
_____	_____
_____	_____
_____	_____
_____	_____
_____	_____
_____	_____
_____	_____

REMINDERS for PARENTS:	REMINDERS for PARENTS:
1. _____	4. _____
2. _____	5. _____
3. _____	6. _____
Write questions and comments here.	Tear off and return to teacher.

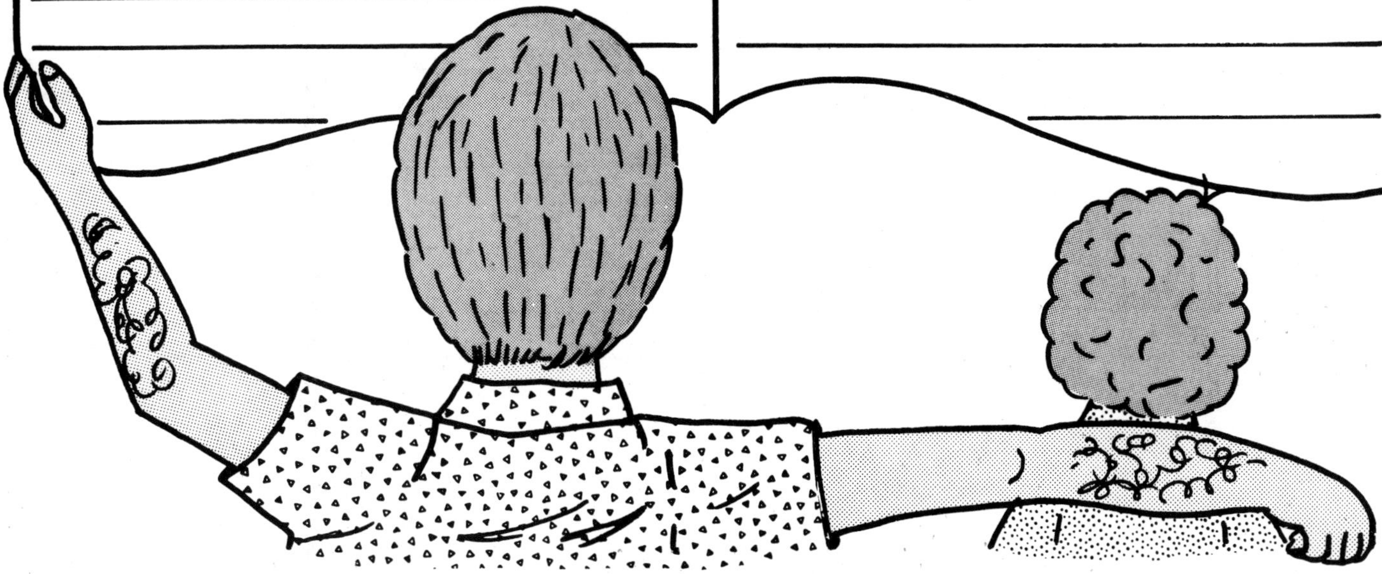

- -

_____ _____

_____ _____

_____ _____

_____ _____

Do this Top Secret Message and staple to Stretch-O-Gram to help increase communication between you, kids, and their parents. Obtain some lemon juice  from a couple of lemons from and these will lead you to your of understanding SCIENTIFIC CHANGE and how change can lead to increased COMMUNICATION. You will also need a *lamp or flatiron, white paper* and some *pipe cleaners* or *Q-tips*. Have each child send a secret message to himself, to each student, and to his parents. Using a Q-tip, draw or print messages on white paper using lemon juice. Allow to dry. Put over light bulb or iron the paper. What happens? Why? Paste a copy of this message in your science notebook. Then make another message for members of your family but do *not* place over light bulb or iron. Staple to Stretch-O-Gram. Take home and have family members use an iron or light bulb to decipher the top secret message from you to them. Good luck.

COMMUNICATION CANDLE!

After a few months into the school year and after you and your students have gotten a chance to know each other better, you may want to use COMMUNICATION CANDLE to open up communication lines even further. You will need a fairly large *candle* for each member of the group and a *match*. Have children sit comfortably in a circle. Darken room. Light your candle. Then light first person's candle with your candle. Touch the two flames together while saying something positive to that child. For example, "Happy Birthday, Julie, I am hoping you have an enjoyable day." Eye contact under candlelight is important. (Comments from others are accepted at any time.) In turn, Julie lights candle of student next to her while saying something positive about that person. This continues until all candles are lit and all comments are given. Some children may choose not to say anything but merely light the next person's candle. That's okay too, as a great deal is said nonverbally. You may want to talk about the significance of candles and what they represent, e.g., the Torch used in the Olympics, the making of a candle, how a candle flame burns, the hottest part of the flame, or about the "scratch the flame" test given out by the gas companies so you can smell gas in your home. Better yet, make a candle web. Continue your study even further by making candles in the classroom.

5 SQUARES

28

Five Squares will facilitate COMMUNICATION among you and your kids. It will lead to a great deal of GROUP COOPERATION and UNDERSTANDING and get your new school year off on the right foot. Obtain some *single-layered cardboard* or *triple-wall* from refrigerator boxes. You will also need a *scissors*, or *utility knife*, and a *marking pen* to make the pieces on the opposite page and some large *envelopes* for storing the pieces. Five Squares is a nonverbal group game used to develop the process of group cooperation when trying to solve a problem. Make your five squares from triple-wall or single-layered cardboard by cutting shapes as shown. Put each set of pieces in envelopes. This will give you enough for one group of five people so you may want to make more. Color code, paint, or label each set of pieces in each envelope.

Directions are simple. Each group is given a box containing five envelopes, one envelope per person. The task is to form five squares so that each person has a square the same size. There must be no talking, pointing, or communicating, and the players must not ask for assistance or take pieces from others. The only action allowed is to *give* pieces to others by handing the pieces and establishing eye contact. It's important not to touch another person's puzzle except to receive pieces. The game is over when each person has the same size square in front of him. When all groups are finished, a large group discussion focusing on feelings concerning the game and its application to real-life situations should be held. Your five squares should look like these when the game is finished:

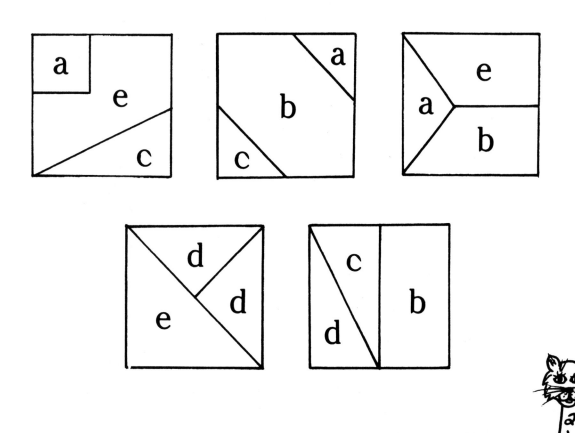

Communication in the classroom can be enhanced even further when students voluntarily state their views on contemporary scientific issues. This activity helps students to question and clarify their own values. This can be done by having students design and write their own bumper sticker that deals with a contemporary issue. (Run off copies of blank bumper stickers on page 31.) Below are several contemporary bumper stickers with the scientific issues they represent in parentheses. Always remember that students have the option to pass anytime. Do not impart your value system upon the students; rather, discuss the issues and allow students to formulate their own basic beliefs and values.

PULL THE PLUG.
(mercy killing)

EXTINCT IS FOREVER.
(endangered species)

TIRED OF TV?
WATCH AN AQUARIUM.
(effects of television)

SPLIT WOOD, NOT ATOMS.
(nuclear power development)

WHEN GUNS ARE OUTLAWED, ONLY OUTLAWS WILL HAVE GUNS.
(regulation of guns and effects on populations)

RECYCLE YOURSELF: SIGN A KIDNEY DONOR CARD.
(transplants)

AND ON THE SEVENTH DAY, HE CLOSED ALL THE GAS STATIONS.
(energy crisis)

I BELIEVE IN MIRACLES; I AM ONE.
(first test tube baby and genetic engineering)

SLOW DOWN: INSULATE SAVE ENERGY.
(energy crisis)

IF YOU ARE OUT OF A JOB AND HUNGRY, EAT AN ENVIRONMENTALIST.
(environmental regulations)

DEAF CHILDREN ARE LEARNING TO TALK.
(technological advancements)

H_2O: IF YOU CAN READ THIS, THANK YOUR SCIENCE TEACHER.
(importance of science and education)

CAUTION: I GIVE ANIMALS A BRAKE.
(use of animals for scientific research purposes)

A FINAL WORD ON COMMUNICATION: focus on VALUES by using BUMPER STICKERS.

I TOOK A STAND TO SAVE THE LAND.
(land use for real estate or farming; also, pesticide control)

AREN'T YOU GLAD YOUR MOTHER DIDN'T HAVE AN ABORTION?
(zero population growth)

ARGUE IT

ROAMING PETS CAUSE REGRETS.
(dognapping)

55 MPH: IT'S A LAW WE CAN LIVE WITH.
(energy crisis)

BUTTERFLY GARDEN

31

FOCUS ON CREATIVITY

Run this picture off for your students to test their degree of creativity. Stare at the dot between the two noses for 60 seconds and count the number of reversals, first seeing the vase and then the two faces. Keep accurate records of the number of reversals over a period of time to find out if you can increase your creativity. Some people think that the more reversals, the more creative a person actually is. What is your creativity quotient?

A TEACHER'S GUIDE

As a teacher of science, you will want to provide a safe and healthful working environment for your students. Here are some tips that will help you reach this goal.

GENERAL TIPS

+ Provide adequate working space that will permit the proper conduct of science activities. Spread learning centers out to allow a free flow of children between centers.
+ Keep floor free of equipment, refuse, and spilled materials.
+ Provide adequate heating, ventilation and lighting. Know where your thermostat is, electrical outlets, circuit breakers, shades, and light switches. Some experiments require darkness.
+ Provide adequate space for storing science materials. Label each box. Discard unknown substances after checking with proper authorities.
+ Have a fire extinguisher in your classroom and learn how to use it.
+ Have a First Aid Kit in your classroom and learn first aid safety.
+ Have a propane torch, hot plate, alcohol burner or sterno can in your classroom.
+ Instruct students on how to use these safely.
+ Sterilize used, free and inexpensive materials that have been obtained from a hospital, etc.
+ Instruct students that all accidents should be reported immediately to the teacher — no matter how minor.
+ Goggles should be worn if there is any potential for splashing, rocks chipping, etc. Orient students to the need for and use of these safety devices. Keep goggles sterile.
+ Instruct students to never taste or touch chemicals unless specifically told to do so.
+ Instruct students to roll long and baggy sleeves up above the elbows before doing science experiments.
+ Remind students that they should be alert and proceed with caution when doing science experiments. Try not to bump into others and stay at the center until all activities are completed.
  Liquid, nonflammable and biodegradable wastes can generally be poured down the drain. Be sure to flush well with water. Do not put solid wastes down drain, e.g., plaster of Paris. Punch small holes in bottom of detergent bottle. This can be used as a screen to filter out solid wastes thus keeping them from going down the sink.
+ Instruct children to put newspapers down over desks for messy experiments. This helps make cleanup faster and easier.
+ Instruct children to wear old shirts for messy experiments. This will save wear and tear on children's clothing.
+ Instruct children when removing an electrical plug from its outlet, to pull the plug, not the electrical cord.
+ Have a thorough understanding of potential hazards in *all* activities by actually doing the activity first before doing the activity with children.
+ Post a set of safety rules in several places in the classroom and discuss these rules with your students. These rules should deal with eye and face protection, fire hazards, the use of the fire extinguisher, the handling of laboratory animals, etc. Remind students of safety precautions before each class session or before each experiment is conducted. Encourage them to wash hands thoroughly before and after each day's work.

TO SCIENCE SAFETY

SPECIFIC TIPS

Glassware

+ Be sure to tape all edges of glassware with masking tape to eliminate cuts from burrs of glass.
+ If you must use glass, instruct students on the use and care of glass in the classroom. Glassware should never be used for eating or drinking purposes.
+ Great care should be taken when inserting glass tubing into stoppers. Use *plastic* containers and *plastic* tubing whenever possible to avoid breakage, injury, etc.
+ Never point a test tube at yourself or point it at others or look directly into a test tube while heating a mixture, etc.

Fire

+ Instruct students to tie long hair back especially when working with fire.
+ Instruct students to tie up baggy sleeves above the elbows.
+ Remind students to strike match away from them when lighting a match. Close cover before striking match if using nonwooden matches. Use wooden matches whenever possible.
+ Remind students to always strike match before turning gas on when lighting propane torch. Alcohol burners or sterno cans can also be used but need to be preceded by proper safety precautions.
+ Instruct students to dip lighted matches into a container of water to extinguish flame.

Plants and Animals

+ Instruct students on the regular cleaning of aquaria, cages, water bottles and feed containers. Involve them in these activities as such involvement leads to accepting responsibility.
+ Be aware of children who are allergic to plants or animals. Check cumulative records for this.
+ Carefully inspect all animals that children bring to the classroom. Make sure the principal is aware of the presence of such animals also.
+ Caution students and visitors about the dangers of sticking fingers into animal cages.
+ Instruct students to wear heavy rubber or leather gloves when handling classroom animals.
+ Handle gerbils, rats, mice, guinea pigs and other animals gently so as not to excite them.
+ Instruct students that there are over 700 poisonous plants such as poison ivy, poison oak, poison sumac, etc. Have children become familiar with poisonous plants in your locale. Some important rules for the handling of plants are:
  1. never eat unknown leaves, berries, seeds or fruit; e.g., do not chew acorns or use stems of elderberries for blowguns.
  2. never rub any sap or fruit juice into or on the skin of an open wound.
  3. never inhale or expose your skin or eyes to smoke coming from a burning plant.
  4. never pick any strange wildflowers or cultivated plants unknown to you.
  5. scrub your hands thoroughly before and after handling plants and before eating.
  6. always thoroughly wash any fruit before eating.

Other

+ Wash hands thoroughly before and after each day's work.
+ Never drink or eat off or from lab glassware or containers.
+ Never suck up a liquid chemical with your mouth.
+ Avoid contacting skin and eyes with dry ice. Use tongs instead.
+ Avoid inhaling alcohol, etc., vapors. If students must smell, have them wave hand in vapor toward face, then smell.

A STUDENT'S GUIDE TO SCIENCE SAFETY

Name _____

I will:

+ Use patience and common sense when working with science equipment and materials.

+ Report all accidents to the teacher no matter how minor they are or seem to be.

+ Never taste or touch chemicals unless specifically told to do so by my teacher.

+ Roll up long and baggy sleeves above the elbows before doing an experiment.

+ Tie long hair behind my head before beginning experiments.

+ Place newspapers on desks or tables before doing science experiments.

+ Wear old shirts for very messy experiments but will be careful that they are not too baggy.

+ Be alert and proceed with caution when doing a science experiment.

+ Try not to bump into others. I will go to the learning center and stay there until all tasks are completed.

+ Do my share to clean up all materials after completing activities in the centers.

+ Never drink or eat from lab glassware such as bottles, etc.

+ Never "suck up" a liquid chemical with my mouth.

+ Never point a sharp object or a test tube at anyone or look directly into such test tube when mixing or heating chemicals.

+ Keep the floor and the centers free of spilled materials.

+ Observe the safety precautions listed and posted by my teacher regarding the use of fire, handling of animals, using electricity, etc.

+ Keep accurate records of my results in my science notebook and share these promptly with my teacher.

+ Accept responsibility for the cleaning of aquaria, terraria, etc., in the classroom.

MAKE YOUR OWN SCIENCE EQUIPMENT

37

YARDSTICKS AND METER STICKS

MAKE YARDSTICKS (METER STICKS) for your classroom. You will need a piece of *wood* from a lumber company or from the bottom of an old window shade and *marking pens.*

HOW: Cut piece of wood 36" long and 1½" wide for yardstick, 100 cm long and 3 cm wide for meter stick. Glue 4" (10 cm) length of doweling (broom handle) to midpoint for handle. Make graduations on stick with marking pen.

USE your yardstick (meter stick) to measure objects in your environment especially when you "stake your claim" found on page 73. Use also for making straight lines on chalkboard and for numerous other activities.

CUSTOMARY AND METRIC TAPES

MAKE A TAPE for your classroom. You will need some *adding machine tape, masking tape, yardstick (meter stick)* made above, and *marking pens.*

HOW: Measure 39 inches (1 meter) of both adding machine tape and masking tape. Fold over both edges of adding machine tape lengthwise leaving space in center.

Lay masking tape over space. Use yardstick (meter stick) made above to mark inches and/or centimeters on tape. Laminate for lasting durability.

USE your tape to measure parts of your body as found on page 59 and other objects in the environment. Mount tape vertically to wall. Move paper clip upward on tape to measure height of plants each day. Keep a record of plant growth. Be sure to use your tape and measure you and your kids' heights at least four times per year using the charts found on pages 60 and 61.

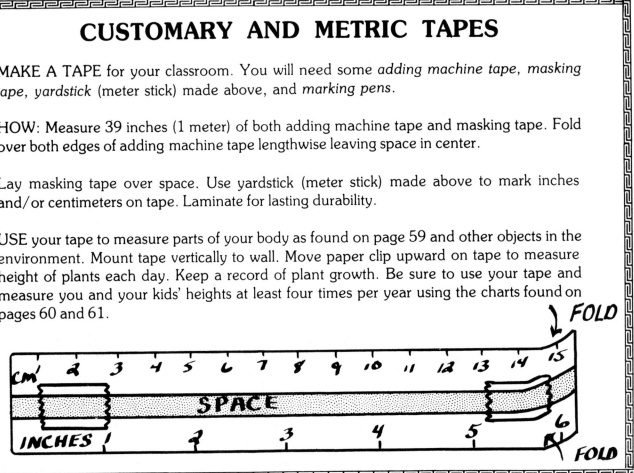

YARDSTICK/METER STICK HOLDER OR WALL DIVIDER FOR SPECIAL SCIENCE AREA

MAKE A HOLDER for yardsticks (meter sticks) and for large science charts or posters. Visit businesses that do printing and copy work. Ask them for leftover tubes found in empty rolls of paper used in copy machines. You will need these *tubes,* some *glue* and a *board* or *piece of triple-wall* for the base.

HOW: These tubes are very sturdy and will make excellent holders or chart stands merely by gluing them end to end to desired height. Glue to base of wood or triple-wall.

USE: Place yardsticks (meter sticks) rolled-up charts, posters, etc., into tubes for storage purposes. You may want to calibrate the outside of the tubes in inches (cm) for a handy reference system of measurement. You may also want to glue a number of tubes end to end, Con-Tact paper them using wood grain Con-Tact paper and build a wall to section off part of your classroom for a special science area. See page 152 for another use of these tubes.

SPECIAL
SCIENCE
AREA

SMALL ITEM ORGANIZER

COLLECT and SAVE styrofoam hamburger containers from fast food places. These make excellent containers for keeping small items organized in your classroom. You will need a *board* or *piece of triple-wall* and some *glue*.

HOW: Cut base to desired size from board or triple-wall. Glue styrofoam containers to base. Some teachers cut off lids of the containers for easier access. A copier tube that you used to build your yardstick (meter stick) holder, cut in half horizontally and glued to the base, also works well for this organizer.

USE: Keep washers, nuts, bolts, paper fasteners, paper clips, tacks, etc., in separate containers. Use also for classification tasks such as those found on page 75, place value in math, and for energy related experiments on page 125.

EGG CARTON HOLDER

COLLECT and SAVE egg cartons from home or grocery stores. If you want to mount these egg cartons, you will need a *board* or *piece of triple-wall* and some *glue*.

HOW: Cut base to desired size from board or piece of triple-wall cardboard. Glue egg carton upside down to base. Some teachers cut off lids for easy access and push carton tightly together. Tip over and punch holes in raised parts of egg carton to store test tubes, scissors, nails, thermometers, etc.

USE: In addition to using as a test tube holder, etc., your egg cartons can be used to deaden sound when affixed to walls and to classify and store rocks and fossils such as those on page 176. Children can also find ways to classify individual cartons according to color, size, shape, etc. Have children carefully observe the cartons for color, types of letters used in printing, cost of eggs, expiration date, etc. Have them try to tear an egg carton, measure its dimensions and size of egg cups, weigh and 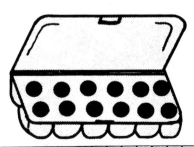 calculate amount of volume in each cup. Use in ice cube melting experiments similar to those found on page 138. Try to have children find out how far each egg carton has traveled and keep a record similar to the record found on page 169. This could lead to egg hatching unit on page 83. Then make a flag out of egg cartons to display in your classroom.

WEIGHTS

COLLECT and SAVE discarded 35mm film cans from a photo processing center. Then, make your own set of WEIGHTS for your classroom. You will also need some *glue, sand* or *shot* and a *balance scale.*

HOW: Fill film cans with appropriate amounts of sand for desired weights. Weigh carefully on scale. Each film can filled with sand weighs approximately 2 ounces (60 grams) with cover. Glue on cover. Make a number of .5 oz. (15 gms), 1 oz. (30 gms), 1.5 oz. (45 gms) and 2 oz. (60 gms) weights for your weight collection.

USE your weights to weigh various substances using the balance below. Film cans also work well for making and stringing mobiles and for collecting water samples on a nature hike as found on page 68. NOTE: Read the March 1984 issue of *The Good Apple Newspaper* for other ideas on how film cans can be used to teach science.

BALANCES

BUILD your own BALANCES for your classroom. You will need some *scrap pieces of lumber* or *triple-wall* (3 layers of cardboard glued together), a *saw, knife, paper punch, meat skewer, string* and some *plastic containers.*

HOW: Cut one base, two supports, and one arm of desired size. Cut hole in base. Insert supports and glue. Make a hole in center of supports and arm. Push meat skewer into hole to hold arm in place. Make holes in ends of arm. Use paper punch to make holes in plastic containers. Tie on plastic containers. Add piece of clay to arm (left or right of center) to calibrate balance.

USE your balance often to determine the weight of various objects in the environment. Then do Rock 'N Balance found on page 166.

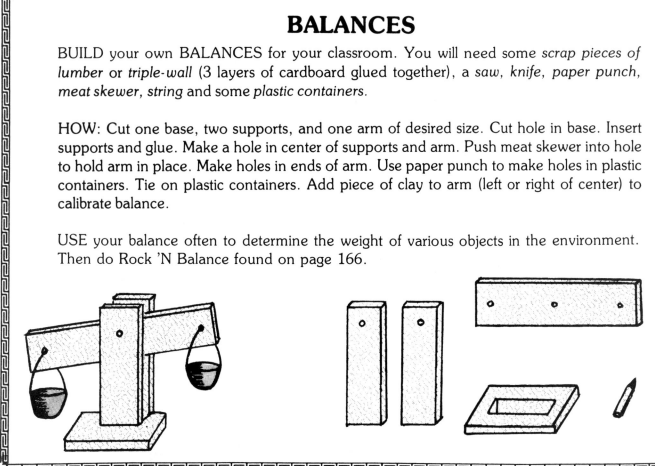

TEMPERATURE SCALE

BUILD A TEMPERATURE SCALE for your classroom. You will need a *piece of cardboard* or *triple-wall* from discarded appliance boxes, *red and black magic markers* and *elastic*.

HOW: Cut scrap piece (of cardboard) 48″ (120 cm) in length by 8″ (20 cm) in width. Make a 2″ (5 cm) slit 4″ (10 cm) from each end. Calibrate scale with ½″ (1 cm) graduations representing each degree Fahrenheit (Celsius). Cut elastic 39″ (1 m) long and 1½″ (4 cm) wide. Color one-half length of elastic red with marker. Thread through slits and sew ends of elastic together to form a loop.

USE each day. Have kids set morning and afternoon temperature by sliding elastic up and down. Keep a record of your results over an extended period of time and complete My Daily Weather Record found on page 136 of this book.

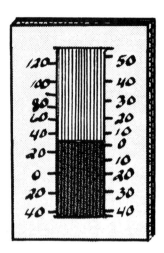

BAROMETRIC PRESSURE SCALE

BUILD A BAROMETRIC PRESSURE SCALE for your classroom.

HOW: Follow the same steps when building a temperature scale but calibrate the two scales in inches (0-35) and centimeters (0-87.5).

USE: Have kids use this every day. Set morning and afternoon barometric pressure by sliding elastic up and down. Note that a rising barometer generally indicates fair weather. A falling barometer indicates stormy weather. Record barometric pressure for each on My Daily Weather Record on page 136. Then build your own barometer.

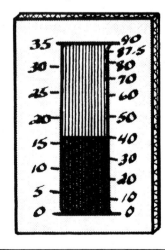

SCIENCE FLASH CARDS

COLLECT *COMPUTER CARDS* from a data processing center and make your own *flash cards*. You'll need some *marking pens* and a *laminating machine* if you have access to one.

HOW: Develop collection of flash cards showing the elements on page 242 with the symbol of each element on one side and the name of the element on the other side. Pictures of rocks, birds, etc., can also be glued to one side with the appropriate name on the reverse side. Then laminate.

USE: Flash cards are excellent for games and drill work in science. Have students make their own sets featuring chemical symbols, animals, plants, etc. Then use blank laminated cards with erasable markers so students can write their own messages to you and vice versa. These can also be used for rewards for good work and to check out specific science equipment as found on page 23.

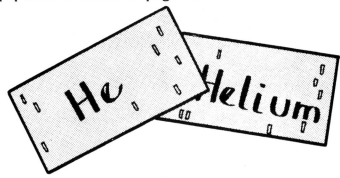

PERIODIC TABLE OF THE ELEMENTS

MAKE your own PERIODIC TABLE OF THE ELEMENTS for your classroom from a *pull down window shade*. You will also need the Periodic Table of the Elements found on page 242 and some *marking pens*.

HOW: Transfer information from the Periodic Table of the Elements to window shade by using marking pens. Hang in classroom for all to see and study from.

USE: Use for reference when studying about atoms, molecules, atomic weights, etc. Similar charts showing laboratory safety, laboratory equipment, etc., can be made by using a simple window shade.

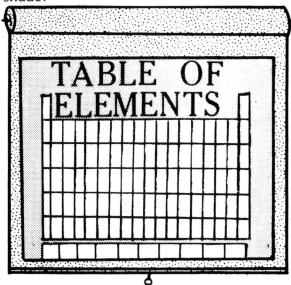

Metric Wind Chill Chart

WIND SPEED (Kilometers per hour)	8	4	0	-4	-8	-12	-16	-20	-24	-28	-32	-36	-40	-44
Calm	8	4	0	-4	-8	-12	-16	-20	-24	-28	-32	-36	-40	-44
10	5	0	-4	-8	-13	-17	-22	-26	-31	-35	-40	-44	-49	-53
20	0	-5	-10	-15	-21	-26	-31	-36	-42	-47	-52	-57	-63	-68
30	-3	-8	-14	-20	-25	-31	-37	-43	-48	-54	-60	-65	-71	-77
40	-5	-11	-17	-23	-29	-35	-41	-47	-53	-59	-65	-71	-77	-83
50	-6	-12	-18	-25	-31	-37	-43	-49	-56	-62	-68	-74	-80	-87
60	-7	-13	-19	-26	-32	-39	-45	-51	-58	-64	-70	-77	-83	-89

TEMPERATURE (°C)

Customary Unit Wind Chill Chart

WIND SPEED (Miles per hour)	35	30	25	20	15	10	5	0	-5	-10	-15	-20	-25	-30	-30	-40	-45
Calm	35	30	25	20	15	10	5	0	-5	-10	-15	-20	-25	-30	-30	-40	-45
5	32	27	22	16	11	6	0	-5	-10	-15	-21	-26	-31	-36	-42	-47	-52
10	22	16	10	3	-3	-9	-15	-22	-27	-34	-40	-46	-52	-58	-64	-71	-77
15	16	9	2	-5	-11	-18	-25	-31	-38	-45	-51	-58	-65	-72	-78	-85	-92
20	12	4	-3	-10	-17	-24	-31	-39	-46	-53	-60	-67	-74	-81	-88	-95	-103
25	8	1	-7	-15	-22	-29	-36	-44	-51	-59	-66	-74	-81	-88	-96	-103	-110
30	6	-2	-10	-18	-25	-33	-41	-49	-56	-64	-71	-79	-86	-93	-101	-109	-116
35	4	-4	-12	-20	-27	-35	-43	-52	-58	-67	-74	-82	-89	-97	-105	-113	-120
40	3	-5	-13	-21	-29	-37	-45	-53	-60	-69	-76	-84	-92	-100	-107	-115	-123

TEMPERATURE (°F)

GRADUATED CYLINDERS

Make your own GRADUATED CYLINDERS for your classroom from clear glass or clear plastic bottles. Coffee cream jars work well for this. You will also need some graduated measure of some type to be used as a standard for measurement.

HOW: Attach strip of masking tape vertically to outside of jar. Measure out 100 mL of water. Pour (water) into jar and mark height (of water) on tape. (Read level of water at the meniscus.) Label this 100 mL. Continue this for other graduations to desired height of liquid. Rubber bands can also be placed around graduated cylinder to show different amounts of liquid. Your graduated cylinder may look like the one below.

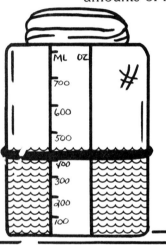

USE: Use these graduated cylinders for measuring quantities of liquids for science experiments and to get to know your children through Bottles of Fun found on page 67.

COLLECT and save plastic baby bottles from a local hospital. These bottles are used only once to feed premature babies and then often discarded. The baby bottles are usually graduated in English and metric measurements and make excellent GRADUATED CYLINDERS.

HOW: Be sure to sterilize bottles before using. Remove and save nipples. Use nipples for connectors when making a stream table found on page 170.

USE: Use plastic part of baby bottle for graduated cylinder. Measure various amounts of liquids in the cylinders. Also use your graduated cylinders to study Boyle's Law on page 112.

TWO-PISTON CONVERTER

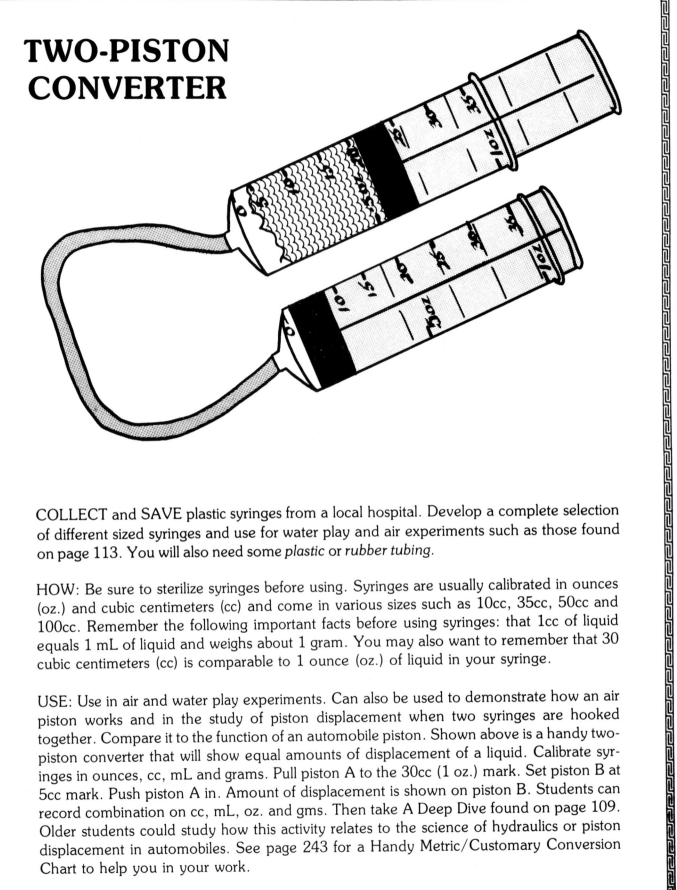

COLLECT and SAVE plastic syringes from a local hospital. Develop a complete selection of different sized syringes and use for water play and air experiments such as those found on page 113. You will also need some *plastic* or *rubber tubing*.

HOW: Be sure to sterilize syringes before using. Syringes are usually calibrated in ounces (oz.) and cubic centimeters (cc) and come in various sizes such as 10cc, 35cc, 50cc and 100cc. Remember the following important facts before using syringes: that 1cc of liquid equals 1 mL of liquid and weighs about 1 gram. You may also want to remember that 30 cubic centimeters (cc) is comparable to 1 ounce (oz.) of liquid in your syringe.

USE: Use in air and water play experiments. Can also be used to demonstrate how an air piston works and in the study of piston displacement when two syringes are hooked together. Compare it to the function of an automobile piston. Shown above is a handy two-piston converter that will show equal amounts of displacement of a liquid. Calibrate syringes in ounces, cc, mL and grams. Pull piston A to the 30cc (1 oz.) mark. Set piston B at 5cc mark. Push piston A in. Amount of displacement is shown on piston B. Students can record combination on cc, mL, oz. and gms. Then take A Deep Dive found on page 109. Older students could study how this activity relates to the science of hydraulics or piston displacement in automobiles. See page 243 for a Handy Metric/Customary Conversion Chart to help you in your work.

ACTIVITY CARDS

COLLECT and save RECTANGULAR CARDS that come from the inside of a transparency frame. These cards are often left over when punched out from the frame. These make excellent activity cards when laminated. Visit graphic arts places and collect these. Then make activity cards such as those found on pages 58 and 71. NOTE: Panty hose containers also contain these cards which make excellent activity cards for learning centers.

MOBILES / SEQUENCING DISCS

COLLECT and save CIRCULAR PLASTIC DISCS used as test strip discs at local chemical companies. These come in various sizes and shapes and are often discarded.

USE: Clean thoroughly. Make groove lengthwise in 2″ by 4″ block of wood or a piece of triple-wall. Print information on discs, e.g., stages of man's evolution, etc., found on page 173, or the order of the planets on page 150. Then stand discs upright in groove to show stages or periods in chronological order. Also these can be used for mobiles like the solar mobile on page 147 and many other sequence activities in reading, etc.

COMPUTER CHECKOUT FORMS

COLLECT discarded COMPUTER CARDS from a data processing center. Then make your own checkout materials form to keep a record of materials checked out overnight for student use. Cut out sample below. Run off copies and glue to computer cards. Laminate. Have students complete with erasable marker. When materials are returned, merely erase and use again. NOTE: Do not erase if you are keeping a record of consumable materials used and also the types of science equipment checked out by your students. Laminated computer cards also make an excellent communication media such as found on page 23. Also, have students do a study of computers and what the numbers and columns on computer cards represent.

MATERIALS CHECKOUT FORM

Name: _____
Address: _____
Telephone Number: _____
Date Checked Out: _____
Date to Be Returned: _____
Materials: _____
_____
_____
X_____
Student Signature: _____
Teacher Initials: _____
Date Returned: _____

COMPUTERIZED

COLLECT discarded COMPUTER PRINT-OUT SHEETS from a data processing center. Blank pages make excellent booklets in which students can write their science observations and conclusions. See Where Are You, Moon? on page 157 for one such use of these handy print-out sheet record forms. Some teachers also use these discarded print-out sheets for ditto paper in their classrooms. This could also lead into a fascinating study of computers as some of your students may already have them in their homes or school.

SCIENCE BOOKLETS

PHASES OF MOON

Tonight I couldn't see the moon so it might be in new moon phase.

I saw a sliver of the moon tonight. It was about 3 fists (30°) above the horizon and is in a new crescent phase. The horns are pointing East when I'm facing South.

Today I saw the moon and it looked like this. This is first quarter and is found 90° above the horizon.

Collect discarded computer print-out forms and develop your own Guinness Book of Science Records in your classroom. Merely chart data concerning the number of times something happens, how many of such a quantity, etc., onto print-out booklets. For example, our record for Lofty Layers on page 104 is fifteen, the number of seconds that the diver in A Deep Dive on page 109 stays in the middle of the bottle *without* the person touching the bottle is 29 seconds, the number of regular waterdrops on the head side of a penny in Mission Impossible on pages 100 and 101 is 204, etc. Extend this activity into the real *Guinness Book of Records* and try to get your new record published in this book.

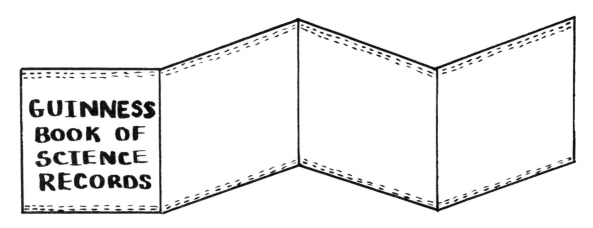

GUINNESS BOOK OF SCIENCE RECORDS

Many school systems spend a mere one percent of their budgets on instructional materials. The rest is spent on salaries, utilities and maintenance. Teachers have turned to free and inexpensive materials. This is an effective practice to follow, but you and your children should be aware of corporate industry promoting their brand names and vested ideologies. Children can perform their own tests on materials such as paper toweling found on pages 95 and 96. Encourage them to develop their own *Consumer Reports* featuring the advantages and disadvantages of each product. Study the motives of corporate industry. Be curious and question. The piece of AV equipment you get from saving soup labels is good, but how much does the company make in selling the soup? Is ice cream nutritious at breakfast? Is there a "generous measure" of vitamins in cereal and pickles as advertised? Yes, soft drinks contain 90% water which is healthful to the body but what about the 10% of sugar, artificial colors, additives, etc.? Yes, accept freebies but always question the ulterior motives by developing your own *Consumer Reports*.

Consumer Reports: A Word of Caution

Consumer Reports

This is a sample "**Scrounge and Save**" letter that you can send home or to local businesses, etc., requesting materials for your units of study.

Date_____

Dear Friend,

In the near future, our class will be studying (*Basic Electricity and Magnetism*) and how these ideas relate to our everyday lives. Some of the activities that we will be doing include setting up (*series and parallel circuits*) and constructing (*switches, electromagnets, motors, flashlights, electrical magnets, etc.*). Most of the projects can be completed by using materials found around the home. Some of these materials have already been collected. However, we would appreciate it if you could save and send to us (*toilet paper tubes, wire, magnets, dry cells, burned out light bulbs, flashlight bulbs, etc.*) for our study. Also, would you be willing, or do you know of anyone who has expertise in (*Basic Electricity and Magnetism*) who may be willing to come and visit our class and share that expertise with us?

We plan to start our unit on (*Basic Electricity and Magnetism*) on (*October 15, 1986*) and tentatively conclude our formal study by (*November 24, 1986*). We will communicate the results of our study to you in our weekly Stretch-O-Gram.

If you have any questions, feel free to contact me at your convenience. We appreciate your help and continued interest in our work.

Sincerely,

Name of Teacher

Name of School

School Address

5 BIOLOGICAL SCIENCE ACTIVITIES

Stake Your Claim

Sketch Pad

#Leaves

Sense a Friend

Terrarium

Sprouting Beans

Balloons from a local will lead you to the

of better UNDERSTANDING YOURSELF. You will also need a *pencil*, some *scrap paper* and some *helium* if you have some. (Check Yellow Pages under "bottled gas.") Students should find themselves a quiet space. First, think about and then make a list of all the things that are troubling you. Place the list in the balloon, blow up the balloon and release it into the air. Write a story in your science notebook about how you feel after doing this exercise. You will want to extend this activity by having children write their favorite science activities on postcards. Place return address on front of card, slip into plastic baggie and release it into the air. Keep a record of returns, where they came from, and activities received. Then do the recipient's suggested science activity. This exercise is similar to Rock Exchange found on page 169.

Feeling Good About Yourself

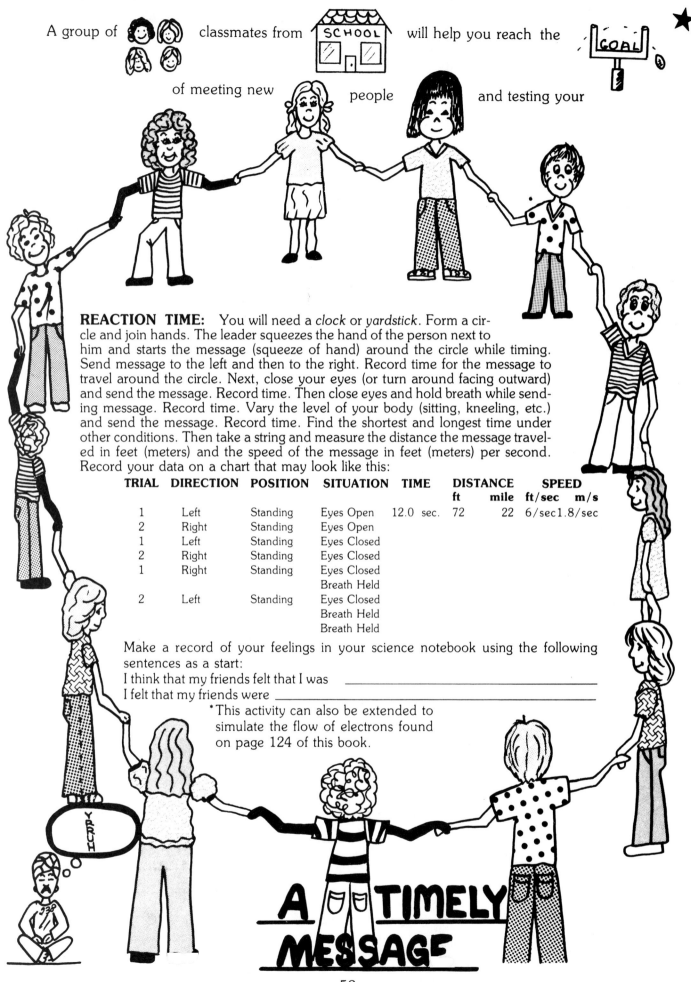

A group of classmates from SCHOOL will help you reach the ★ GOAL of meeting new people and testing your

REACTION TIME: You will need a *clock* or *yardstick*. Form a circle and join hands. The leader squeezes the hand of the person next to him and starts the message (squeeze of hand) around the circle while timing. Send message to the left and then to the right. Record time for the message to travel around the circle. Next, close your eyes (or turn around facing outward) and send the message. Record time. Then close eyes and hold breath while sending message. Record time. Vary the level of your body (sitting, kneeling, etc.) and send the message. Record time. Find the shortest and longest time under other conditions. Then take a string and measure the distance the message traveled in feet (meters) and the speed of the message in feet (meters) per second. Record your data on a chart that may look like this:

TRIAL	DIRECTION	POSITION	SITUATION	TIME	DISTANCE		SPEED	
					ft	mile	ft/sec	m/s
1	Left	Standing	Eyes Open	12.0 sec.	72	22	6/sec	1.8/sec
2	Right	Standing	Eyes Open					
1	Left	Standing	Eyes Closed					
2	Right	Standing	Eyes Closed					
1	Right	Standing	Eyes Closed Breath Held					
2	Left	Standing	Eyes Closed Breath Held Breath Held					

Make a record of your feelings in your science notebook using the following sentences as a start:

I think that my friends felt that I was _____

I felt that my friends were _____

*This activity can also be extended to simulate the flow of electrons found on page 124 of this book.

A TIMELY MESSAGE

A  classmate from  can help you reach the **GOAL**

of meeting a new friend at the beginning of the school year. Just the two of you can first close your eyes and relax a bit. Then open your eyes and find out how many different ways you can tell your partner something about yourself by using your five senses. You may use your finger or eyes to write your name, shake hands, exchange ID cards, etc. Complete the following in your science log book. Then ask your friend if you can share with the class something that your friend is most proud of in his life.

I wonder about how many different ways I can find out about someone and how that person can find out about me by using our five senses.

Seeing_____

Hearing _____

Feeling _____

Tasting _____

Smelling_____

My friend's name is_____

My friend's distinguishing characteristics are _____

The best thing that my friend is most proud of is _____

SENSE A FRIEND

"I wrote my name with my eyes and used the mirror writing technique."

"I wrote my name on my friend's arm using my finger."

STAND I

Hands  from a friend lead you to the **GOAL**

of becoming a keen observer and further understanding your friend's characteristics. Close eyes. Touch palms of your hands to palms of your friend's hands. Feel the skin. Describe what you feel.

Then open your eyes and carefully observe the fingerprints on your friend's hands. Make a sketch. Study how fingerprints can be used to identify people. Enter a sketch of your friend's fingerprints and your fingerprints in your science notebook. Then use various substances and assorted objects to make a print on a notecard. Tape to wall and have your friends guess what the object is that made the print. Extend this activity even further. Have one student hold palm of left hand of other student. Have students take index finger and thumb of free hand and rub fingers of free hand up and down on fingers of touching hands. Describe what you feel. Is the person dead? Write a story about your scary experiences.

BEING
A
DETECTIVE

55

A  from a local  can help you reach the

of developing a real feeling for such things as TEXTURE.

You will also need some *scrap pieces of cloth, carpeting, rugs, etc.* Cut 2 squares of each item. Glue one square of each of these to the top of the shoe box. Place other matching squares inside the shoe box. Cut a hole in the end of the shoe box so you can get your hand inside the box. Feel objects inside the box with your right hand. With your left hand, point to the matching square on top of the box. This is a self-checking activity and gives immediate feedback to the child. Next, do the same, but only vary the *shape* of each item. Then match *shapes, textures, etc.*

Some brown wrapping paper from home or school will lead you to the goal of UNDERSTANDING YOURSELF by measuring parts of your body and keeping a record of CHANGES. You will also need some *string, scissors,* and a *marking pen.*

Have students work in pairs. Have one student lie down on large sheet of wrapping paper. Have other student trace around the body with a black marker. Record measurements on the paper using record forms found on page 59. Do four times per year. Then have the students cover their bodies with sayings that represent the various parts of the body. Students sketch in actual parts of the human body. Some are done for you below. Extend this to creative writing and write a story of what paths you would follow if you were a red blood cell, neuron, etc., going through the body.

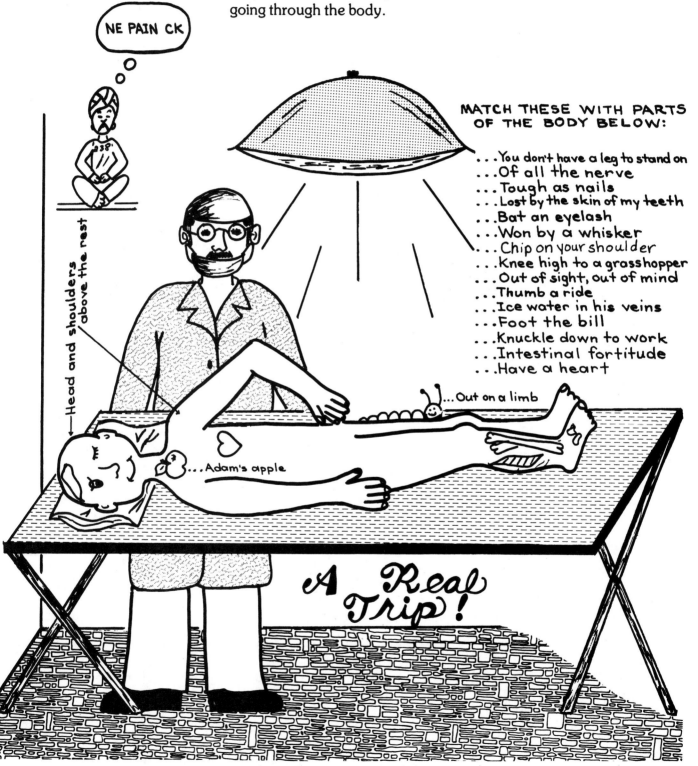

NE PAIN CK

MATCH THESE WITH PARTS OF THE BODY BELOW:

...You don't have a leg to stand on
...Of all the nerve
...Tough as nails
...Lost by the skin of my teeth
...Bat an eyelash
...Won by a whisker
...Chip on your shoulder
...Knee high to a grasshopper
...Out of sight, out of mind
...Thumb a ride
...Ice water in his veins
...Foot the bill
...Knuckle down to work
...Intestinal fortitude
...Have a heart

Head and shoulders above the rest

...Out on a limb

...Adam's apple

A Real Trip!

57

Some computer activity cards like the ones below from a **DATA CENTER**

will lead you to your **GOAL** of developing a feeling for BIOLOGICAL

CHANGES in your students over a period of time. Make up computer activity cards similar to the ones below and laminate. Place face down on table. Have children choose and complete the activities at least four times during the year and record their measurements each time to note changes in their growth and development. Use the sample recording form on page 59. Then use charts found on pages 60 and 61 and have children compare their height and weight with those of others found nationally.

A CHANGING YOU

1. With a piece of string or a tape measure, measure each classmate's neck size. Record the measurements. Make a graph of your results.

2. Measure the height of each of your classmates. Record the measurements. Find out the tallest and shortest members of the class.

3. Measure your classmates' right wrists. Record your measurements. Measure left wrists and find out how many students have larger right wrists than left wrists.

4. Measure the hand span (tip of thumb to tip of little finger when hand is outstretched) of each of your classmates. Make a record of the measurements.

5. Measure the distance around each classmate's head. Find out how the measurement corresponds to the person's hat size.

6. Using ½" (1cm) graph paper, find the surface area of each classmate's left hand. Trace around the hand, cut it out, and make a collection of hands. Have classmates try to identify each person's hand.

7. Trace around each person's right foot onto 1" (2.5cm) graph paper. Determine the surface area of each person's foot. Find out who has the smallest foot size. Is there any difference in right and left foot sizes?

8. Find out a way to measure the diameter of each of your classmates' heads. Then ... do it!

9. Measure each classmate's left ankle with a strip of paper. Glue paper strips to a large chart to show ankle size from largest to smallest.

10. Find out the "wing span" of each classmate by measuring from the tips of fingers on one hand to tips of fingers on other hand when arms are outstretched.

11. Find out the "squarest" member of the class by measuring height vs. arm span of each student. If both are equal, the person is square.

12. Measure wrist, neck and waist sizes of classmates to find out who is most nearly proportioned. The wrist will be one-half the neck size and the neck will be one-half the waist size for perfect proportions.

My name is _____ and my measurements are found in column one.

A CHANGING YOU DATA SHEET

CARD	PERSON #1: Yourself	PERSON #2:	PERSON #3:	PERSON #4:	PERSON #5:	PERSON #6:	PERSON #7:	PERSON #8:	PERSON #9:	PERSON #10:	PERSON #11:	PERSON #12:
CARD 1												
CARD 2												
CARD 3												
CARD 4												
CARD 5												
CARD 6												
CARD 7												
CARD 8												
CARD 9												
CARD 10												
CARD 11												
CARD 12	★											

59

HEIGHT and WEIGHT — GIRLS

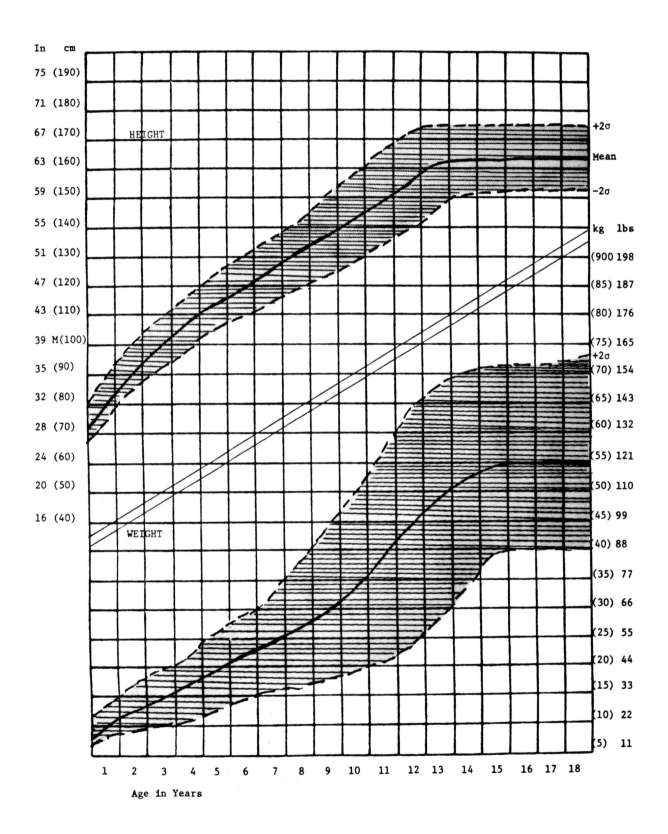

HEIGHT and WEIGHT—BOYS

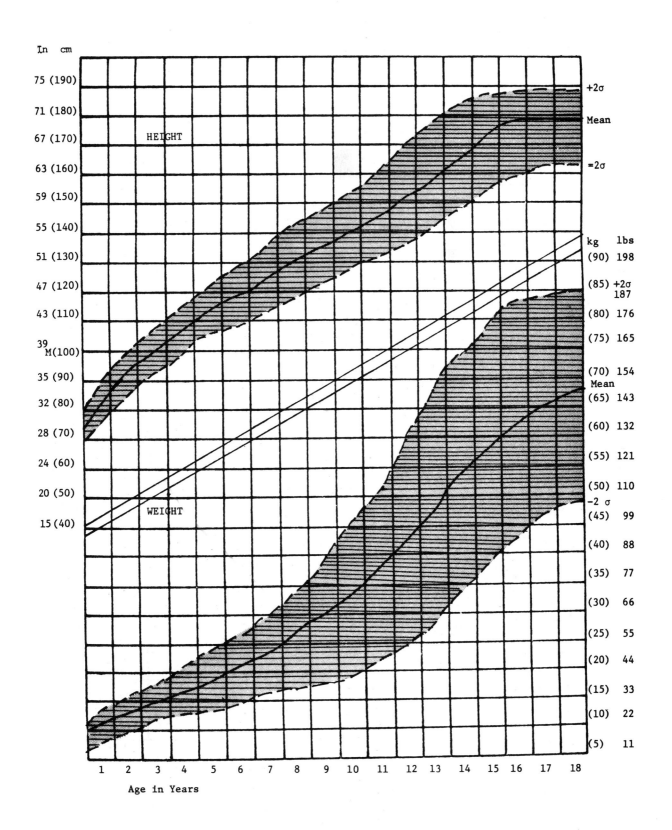

A clear glass  jar from a  or restaurant will lead

you to the 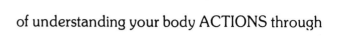 of understanding your body ACTIONS through

movement. You will also need some *water* and *food coloring.* Fill jar with clear tap water. Encourage students to physically make their bodies as small as possible like a drop of water. Drop one drop of food coloring into the container of water. Observe the drop of food coloring. Develop a vocabulary chart of words on what is seen. Some words may include a stream, stalactites, stalagmites, and crystals. Then have students act out what they would feel like if they were the drop of food coloring dropped into the water. Extend this activity further by having students develop one movement with their bodies. Add a sound to the movement and vary the movement's speed and level. Have them put all their movements together to make a machine. Join bodies together with appropriate movements to make the machine. Add music. Vary the machine's speed, sound, level and distance traveled. Students should record their feelings in their science logs using the starter sentences below. Extend this activity further by doing heart rate experiments on the next page.

My favorite movement was _____ because it made me feel _____.
The part I felt best about when we made our machine was _____.
If I operated a real machine, I'd probably feel _____.

MOVE YOUR BODY

A watch or 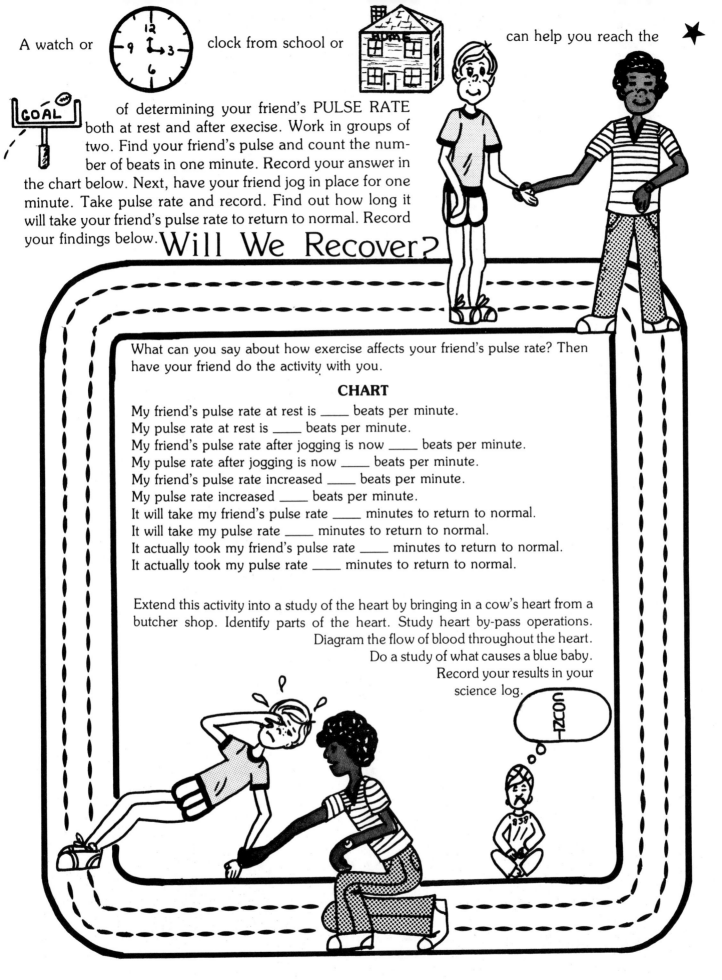 clock from school or can help you reach the

of determining your friend's PULSE RATE both at rest and after execise. Work in groups of two. Find your friend's pulse and count the number of beats in one minute. Record your answer in the chart below. Next, have your friend jog in place for one minute. Take pulse rate and record. Find out how long it will take your friend's pulse rate to return to normal. Record your findings below.

Will We Recover?

What can you say about how exercise affects your friend's pulse rate? Then have your friend do the activity with you.

CHART

My friend's pulse rate at rest is _____ beats per minute.

My pulse rate at rest is _____ beats per minute.

My friend's pulse rate after jogging is now _____ beats per minute.

My pulse rate after jogging is now _____ beats per minute.

My friend's pulse rate increased _____ beats per minute.

My pulse rate increased _____ beats per minute.

It will take my friend's pulse rate _____ minutes to return to normal.

It will take my pulse rate _____ minutes to return to normal.

It actually took my friend's pulse rate _____ minutes to return to normal.

It actually took my pulse rate _____ minutes to return to normal.

Extend this activity into a study of the heart by bringing in a cow's heart from a butcher shop. Identify parts of the heart. Study heart by-pass operations. Diagram the flow of blood throughout the heart. Do a study of what causes a blue baby. Record your results in your science log.

63

Some triple-wall cardboard or wood from a local lumber company will lead you to the goal of understanding the action of the HEART when pumping blood throughout the body. You will also need *some paint, glue, pieces of cardboard,* a *meat skewer* or so and some *marbles.*

 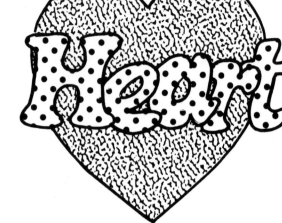

Build a model of the heart to show the path of blood throughout the heart.

Enlarge the heart model on the opposite page using opaque projector and cut out of triple-wall cardboard or wood. Glue to another piece of triple-wall to make a base. Color the right open portion of the heart red and the left open portion blue. Make and attach valves at indicated areas. Glue two triangular pieces of triple-wall or wood underneath model in the center of each side to act as a rocker.

TO OPERATE:

Place marbles in the open areas of the heart model. Tilt heart so marbles move downward showing the resting (relaxing) phase of the heart. Then tilt heart upward to show the pumping (contracting) phase of the heart.

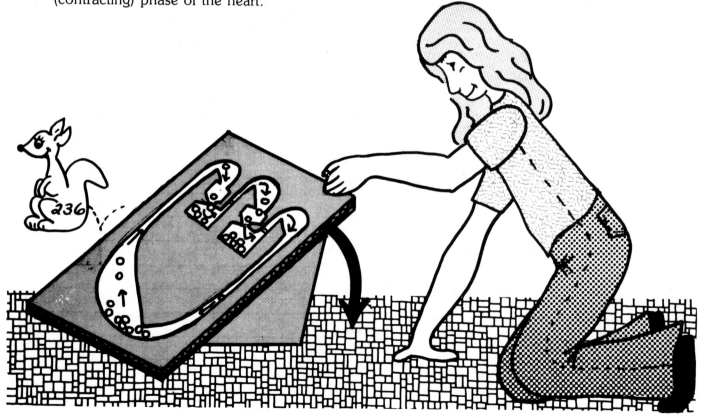

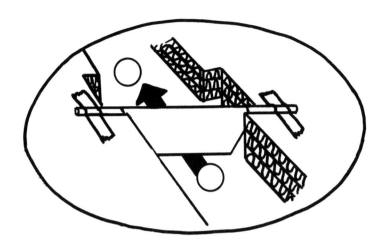

To make valves for circled areas, fold lightweight cardboard pieces over slim wooden skewers, thin doweling, or round lollipop sticks. Glue or tape sticks so cardboard hangs into path of the marbles. Trim triple-wall or wood so cardboard valves can swing only in the direction indicated by the arrow.

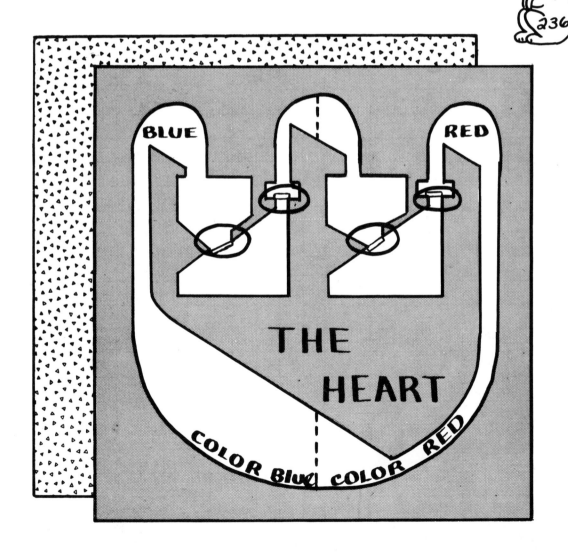

BLUE

RED

THE

HEART

COLOR BLUE COLOR RED

236

Some scrap  chipboard from a  will lead you to the

 of understanding the SURFACE AREAS and PRESSURE exerted by various PARTS of your BODY. You will also need some *paper towels*, a *pencil*, a *plastic grid* 1 inch (1 cm) x 1 inch (1 cm), *scale* and some *paper*. Wet the sole of your right foot with the paper towel. Place your right foot on the chipboard and stand on that foot only. Remove your foot from the chipboard and draw around the "wet" area, both areas if they are not connected. Use a plastic grid made from page 244 or 246 to determine the area by counting the number of square inches (centimeters) it takes to cover the "wet" area. Area = _____ in² (cm²)

Weigh yourself on a scale. Weight = _____ lbs. (kg)

Calculate the pressure in pounds per square inch (kilopascals or newtons per square meter).

$$P = \frac{lbs}{sq\ in} \quad \text{or} \quad P = \frac{newtons}{square\ meters} \quad \text{or} \quad P = kPa$$

Collect data from the class and determine the average pressure exerted by the feet of boys and girls. Or, go outdoors with the plastic grid and measure the surface area in square inches or (cm²) of leaves or other objects found in nature such as real BIG FOOT tracks. This activity works well when done in conjunction with those found on page 92. Can you think of a way to use your "pedal power" to help solve the energy crisis? Could spring mechanisms installed in sidewalks actually turn a generator? Make a record in your science log.

Going Further

Some  bottles from  will lead you to the  GOAL

of getting a feel for CONSERVATION of VOLUME and thus your students' level of cognitive development. You will also need some *graduated measures, food coloring, funnel,* and *rubber bands.*

This diagnostic activity is for the teacher who wants to diagnose a child's level of cognitive development based on the work of Piaget. Obtain a set of five differently shaped bottles. One bottle in the set should be tall and thin and another short and wide. Pour in equal amounts of water in the bottles and color with food coloring. Have students mark water level in each bottle with a rubber band and then put bottles in order from tallest to shortest. Not knowing each bottle contains the same amount of water, students should be asked if the bottles contain the same amount of water or if they have different amounts of water. Encourage the children to empty water from bottles into empty containers. Conservation of volume skill is developed with this activity and can be used with all age levels, including adults.

BOTTLES OF FUN!

TIPS ON TAKING A HIKE

This nature hike activity will help you develop many new skills that will enable you to help children learn a great deal by exploring an outdoor environment. These skills include:

(1) Looking vs. Seeing

We can all look. We have to learn to *see*. Seeing may be heightened by consciously searching for pattern, movement, color and irregularity by trying to locate differences in the way things are lighted, or by looking for reflections and shadows.

Seeing may become more vivid if you make a sketch with a felt-tipped pen or soft black pencil. If you become interested in detail, try using a hand lens. Try looking at an object through cupped hands, through a piece of cardboard with a pinhole in it and through a hand lens.

(2) Silence vs. Noise

Conversation may help or inhibit observation. You may like to be alone while you are out. You could try telling your companion you would prefer that! Remember, noise often obscures attention. It can also scare away creatures in a woods. It can prevent you or another from listening to a bird song, to the snapping of twigs, to the whisper of the wind, or to the bubbling of water.

(3) Doing Something You Have Never Done Before

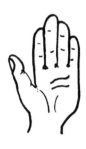

Try doing something that you have never done before. Have you looked at, sniffed and crushed in your fingers a piece of decaying bark? Have you pressed your hand against soft mud to make a print? Have you looked at a pattern of ripples in a stream and allowed your mind to wander? These activities may sensitize you to the excitement and wonder of the world around you and your children and will make life seem suddenly more worth living.

(4) Collecting Specimens and Samples

Pockets are not much good. Take plastic bags or cartons with covers (see page 41). If you are after water life, consider taking nets. Soil samples are easily collected by using a tongue depressor as a trowel. You rarely require a bagful of these for later examination under a hand lens or microscope.

It may be a good idea to label samples as you collect them or you will end up with a confusing array when you get back to the classroom.

With a tape recorder, you can extend your sampling to include sounds, on the spot commentaries, etc.

Forceps, string, a tape measure, trundle wheels, binoculars, materials for making bark rubbings, thermometers, light meters and cameras all extend the range of your inquiry. Now, go to it.

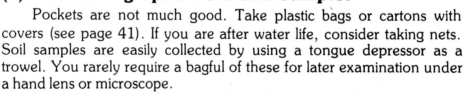

Some  from a cardboard  will lead you to the

of making a MINI SKETCH PAD to help you and your children understand the WORLD AROUND THEM. You will also need some *string*, a *pencil*, and a keen *ability to observe.* Cut a 6″ (15 cm) × 9″ (23 cm) sheet of cardboard. Staple a 20″ (51 cm) length of string to upper left corner along with sheets below. Tie a pencil to the end of string. Take students on an outdoor hike and have them do the activities on the cards below.

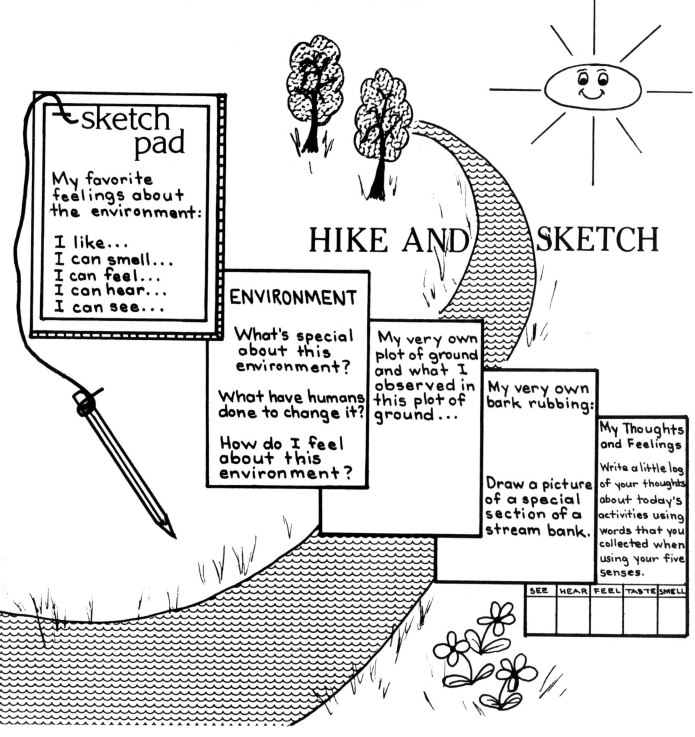

HIKE AND SKETCH

sketch pad

My favorite feelings about the environment:

I like...
I can smell...
I can feel...
I can hear...
I can see...

ENVIRONMENT

What's special about this environment?

What have humans done to change it?

How do I feel about this environment?

My very own plot of ground and what I observed in this plot of ground...

My very own bark rubbing:

Draw a picture of a special section of a stream bank.

My Thoughts and Feelings

Write a little log of your thoughts about today's activities using words that you collected when using your five senses.

SEE	HEAR	FEEL	TASTE	SMELL

NATURE HIKE TREASURE HUNT

You may want to ask for volunteers to collect a sample of each of the items below. These items will then act as springboards into other areas of study. For example, a student who brings back a track made by an animal may want to do a study of tracks; a person who finds a bone may want to save chicken bones and put a chicken skeleton together. Please remember though that children should *not* collect any item that in its absence would disrupt the ecological balance of the natural environment. Let's keep the natural environment as natural as possible. Hold a large group sharing session after the items are brought back into the classroom. Extend further by doing the Post Nature Hike Activities found on page 75.

Item	**Person(s) Responsible**
1. An acorn	
2. A rock containing two kinds of material	
3. Evidence that an insect has been at work	
4. Two kinds of seeds that travel	
5. A bark rubbing labeled with the tree name	
6. A piece of material used in making a nest	
7. A branch with the winter buds	
8. A wild flower	
9 A cocoon	
10. A silver maple leaf	
11. Evidence of erosion	
12. A weed found in a grassy area	
13. Evidence of a litter bug	
14. A birds's feather with proper identification	
15. An oak leaf	
16. A clover leaf	
17. Something destructive which was done by man	

Item	**Person(s) Responsible**
18. A leaf with insect eggs	
19. A leaf with spores	
20. Evidence that a predator has been at work	
21. Evidence of good conservation	
22. Evidence of poor conservation	
23. A dead tree branch with a fungus growth. Try to identify both.	
24. A frog or toad	
25. Evidence of dependency between two plants	
26. An animal track with proper identification	
27. Plant succession	
28. Five geometric patterns in nature	
29. Evidence of one way to measure the height of a tree	
30. A bone of some type	
31. A way to tell how fast a stream is running or the distance across a stream	
32. Your choice	

Here are some additional activities that can be put on cards to extend your nature hike even further. Run these off for kids to cut out. Staple together to make a Mini Book of Nature Hike Activity Cards for each student or each group of students. Be sure to leave some blank cards for students to develop their own activities.

My Mini Book of Nature Hike Activities

Measure the temperature of a stream at various depths in °F (°C). Keep a record of what you found.

Collect soil from the bottom of a stream and find out how many organisms you can identify in your soil. Make sketches of these creatures.

Collect water from a stream and identify winter/summer organisms found in the water. Make sketches of each.

Collect winter/summer specimens from tree bark. Identify them. Do research to find out their various stages for each time of the year.

Look for and record signs of mini-beast life in winter, summer, fall, and spring. Make a sketch of the sign that impressed you the most.

Chisel a hole in the ground. Measure the depth of the hole in inches (centimeters) and the temperature in °F (°C) at various depths. Keep a record of your results.

What are the largest and smallest tracks you can find? Measure the surface area of these tracks with a geoboard or on graph paper. Use both inch and centimeter grid paper or transparencies for this activity.

What is the greatest depth of snow/water that you can find? Measure in inches (centimeters). If snow, melt it down. Find out how many inches (centimeters) of snow equals how many inches (cubic centimeters) of melted water.

Use a sling psychometer and measure the relative humidity outside. Record the temperature in °F (°C) first and then find the relative humidity by using a chart found in your science book.

Use a light meter to measure how bright the sun is. Compare this to how a camera and your own eyes work. Make a record in your science log.

Do a bark rubbing of a number of trees. Write a poem about your rubbing.

Tape-record sounds found in nature and play them back to the class to identify.

Study predator/prey relationships and endangered species. Record your findings in your science log.

Collect soil samples from different regions for analysis and content. Study what pH means. Find out what types of soil yields what types of crops in your region.

HOW TALL IS TALL?

On your nature hike, you may want to involve your students in some INDIRECT MEASUREMENT ACTIVITIES. You will need a *pencil, tape measure, rulers* and *sticks*. You can easily help children find the height of a tree by using the stick and thumb methods.

STICK METHOD

For the stick method measure length of stick (9″) (22.5 cm) and drive into ground so 6″ (15 cm) shows. Measure length of shadow cast by stick (10″) (25 cm) and tree (360″). Then do this:

$$\frac{\text{Length of stick}}{\text{Stick shadow length}} = \frac{\text{Height of tree}}{\text{Shadow of tree}}$$

Therefore, Customary (in.)   Metric (cm)

$$\frac{6''}{10''} = \frac{x}{360''} \qquad \frac{15 \text{ cm}}{25 \text{ cm}} = \frac{x \text{ cm}}{900 \text{ cm}}$$

$$10x = 2160'' \qquad\qquad 25x = 13500$$
$$x = 216'' \qquad\qquad\quad x = 540 \text{ cm}$$

Height of tree = 216 in. or 18 ft.   Height of tree = 540 cm or 5.4 m

THUMB METHOD

For the thumb method, you'll need a student and a pencil. Measure height of student (60″) or (152 cm). Place student against trunk of tree or pole. Hold pencil vertically and slide thumb down pencil until person comes into view. This is 5 feet (152 cm). Now, move pencil upward counting each 5 feet (152 cm). If you moved the pencil upward four more times, the tree would be 25 feet (608 cm) tall.

HAND METHOD

Measure the distance across a stream without crossing it.

Place right hand to forehead in salute style until bottom of little finger comes in contact with opposite bank. Turn 90° holding a steady position. Have student walk away from you. Tell student to stop walking when out of your field of vision. Measure this distance with your tape measure. This is the approximate distance across the stream.

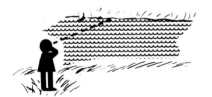

HOW WIDE IS WIDE?

236

A scrap piece of  wood from a  of staking out a section of land and identifying

will lead you to the **GOAL**

and classifying **CREATURES** in that environment. A *magnifying* glass, string, rulers, *tongue depressors* will also help you to stake your claim. Indoors, explain to students that they will be taking a hike to stake a claim of land. Have each child take 4 tongue depressors and estimate the size of his square yard (meter) of land. Then have him measure his estimate with a yardstick (meter stick made from scrap lumber on page 38). Ask what kinds of things you might expect to see in a square yard (meter) of land outdoors. Will you need any special equipment? Go for a hike outdoors. Have each child actually stake out his own square yard (meter) of land and write down what he sees using the mini sketch pad found on page 69. Encourage children to move slowly and observe carefully—belly button exploring. Do this activity at least four times per year and note the changes in your claim during different seasons. Your children may write poems such as that written by Kenneth Bierly below.

A BLADE OF GRASS

A blade of grass is nothing
until you look at it up close.
It's big then — the size of a finger
or a person standing far away.
You can see its veins, and its
bumpiness.
Up close, a blade of grass
becomes somebody,
something important.
Something to be noticed
and admired.
Have you ever seen a kid up close?

by Kenneth Bierly

Stake Your Claim

Some wintergreen Life Savers from a  will lead you to the

GOAL of investigating the properties of CHEMICALS, how light travels and other mysterious things. This is a good culminating activity after a night hike outside or can be easily done in the classroom after a nature hike. Make classroom as dark as possible. Give each member of the class a wintergreen Life Saver and ask each one in turn to chew the Life Saver with his mouth open as wide as possible while others observe carefully and make mental notes. The resulting mysterious sparks are fun to observe. Can you find out what causes the sparks? No one seems to know. Do they carry an electrical charge? Write about your findings in your science log. This activity could be extended to an investigation into what causes a firefly to light up. NOTE: Allow at least 10 minutes for youngsters' eyes to become night adjusted in the darkened room before doing the activity.

Light Up Your Life

POST NATURE HIKE ACTIVITY CARDS

After sharing the results from your Nature Hike and Nature Hike Treasure Hunt, you may want to extend the activities further by doing these Post Nature Hike Activities. You may want to put these on activity cards to get the study off to a fast start.

Card 1
Classify pine needles by number of needles in a packet, length of needles, shape of needles, etc. Try needles from other coniferous trees. Make a record of your data in your science log.

Card 2
Make a leaf chart using poster board and clear Con-Tact paper for use with your friends. Identify and label leaves properly. This will make an excellent reference chart.

Card 3
Make a leaf creature. Glue a leaf to drawing paper. Then add features to make a creature. Cover with wax paper, add crayon, and press with iron.

Card 4
Find the surface area of a number of leaves you collected as found on page 92. You may use a geoboard, string, graph paper, etc. Record your data using both customary and metric measurements.

Card 5
Do some bark rubbings from the different kinds of bark that was collected. Do you see any unique features in the bark? Make a collection of your rubbings to display in the classroom.

Card 6
Study and draw all the different kinds of twigs that were collected. Note the patterns of leaves growing from the twigs. Are the leaves arranged in whorl, alternate or opposite patterns? Record your findings in your science log.

Card 7
Using customary and metric measurements, find the length, width and circumference of a catalpa leaf or seed pod. Measure the actual seed. Weigh the seeds. Grow them. Chart your results over a period of time.

Card 8
Collect a green leaf from a sassafras tree. Crush and then smell the stem of the leaf. Paint a picture of that smell.

Card 9
Compare the weights of a downed leaf and a living leaf on a tree. Do this for a number of trees. Record your data both numerically and graphically using customary and metric measurements.

Card 10
Classify and identify all leaves that were collected. Consider size, shape, color, venation patterns, etc. Record your findings in your science log.

Card 11
Classify all the different seeds that were collected in as many different ways as possible. You may want to consider size, shape, how seeds travel, etc. Make a record of your findings.

Card 12
Make leaf rubbings from a variety of leaves. Place underside of leaf up. Lay piece of paper over leaf and rub gently with side of crayon. Develop a collection of leaf rubbings to share with the class.

Extend your nature hike further and do the following classroom activities.

A clear glass  from a  will

an ECOSYSTEM and

You will also need some *small pebbles*, *charcoal*, *sand*, *soil*, and *plants* like ferns and mosses.

Mosses, small ferns, lichens, liverworts, and tiny Virginia Creepers make interesting plants for this type of terrarium. A small toad or salamander may be added. Find out what foods they will need in order to survive. Keep a record of your observations in your science notebook.

lead you to the  of developing an understanding of

a balanced

TERRARIUM

For these terraria, mix 3 parts of clean sand to one part potting soil. Spread this mixture several inches (5 cm) thick over the base layer of gravel. Sink a dish full of water in one corner to provide water for the desert animals. Use pincushion cactus, an opunita, fishhook cactus, and night-blooming cereus as basic plants. Water the surface around plants once a week.

Add a desert tortoise, snake, or a horned lizard for animal life. They will feed on the succulents that are growing and on bits of fruit and insects.

For the bottom layer use aquarium gravel. If you use sand, make sure it is rinsed clean and has settled to the bottom before adding the animals. Beach sand is too fine to use and it will not permit plant roots to grow well. Pond water can be used. If you use tap water, be sure that it has been allowed to air out 24-48 hours before placing in the terrarium. Pond plants can be collected in plastic bags or purchased from a pet store. Cabomba, Vallisneria, Anacharis, or Elodea are good pond plants to use.

You can use guppies, snails, tadpoles, newts, crayfish, and water insects (be sure not to get mosquito larvae). These will add interest to a pond terrarium.
Be sure to research the types of food needed by each of these animals. Keep accurate records of your observations on changes occurring in your pond terrarium.

A bog is a pond on its way to becoming a woodland or field. The soil of a bog is quite moist. Any surface water is usually shallow; not more than a few inches (centimeters) deep. In a bog, the pond begins to fill with soil, decaying plants and animals, and the water level begins to sink below the soil. The plant and animal life making up the community begins to change and plants and animals better suited to the new environment appear.

Bog Terrarium

To build, first put a layer of gravel; then a thin layer of sand and soil mixture. Next, mix two parts sphagnum moss with one part humus and make a layer. Slope surface to get a low spot in one corner. Add water to level.

*Plants found growing in swamps or in very damp places (where water stands) will do well in this type of terrarium. Small salamanders, frogs, and turtles can live in a bog terrarium.

*such as Venus's-flytrap and bladderwort plants

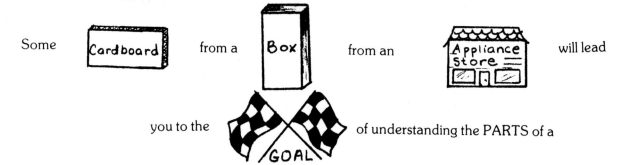

Some Cardboard from a Box from an Appliance Store will lead

you to the GOAL of understanding the PARTS of a

BIRD and their FUNCTIONS. You will also need some *magnetic tape* or *Velcro.* Draw large bird on cardboard (use bird below and place under opaque projector to project image onto cardboard). Print parts of bird on separate pieces of cardboard. Glue bits of Velcro or magnetic tape to reverse side of cards and onto bird at proper locations. Children then match the cards with those parts of the bird's body and relate functions of those parts. This is especially useful for very young children.

Bill

Throat

Breast

Leg

Foot

Wing

Tail

Back

Head

Eye

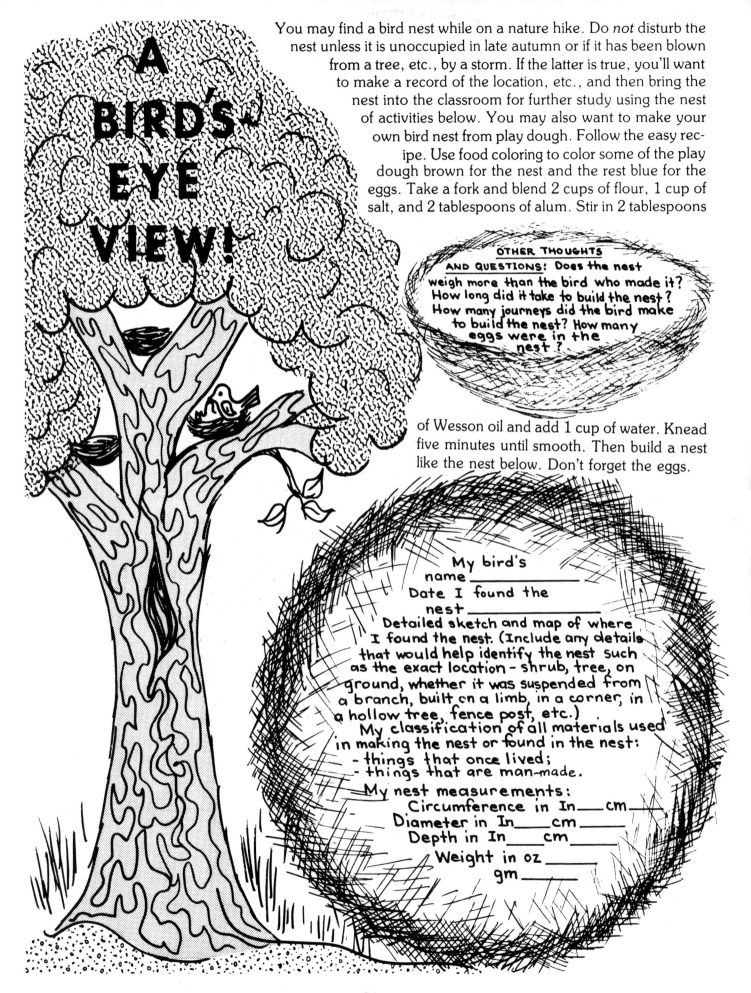

A BIRD'S-EYE VIEW!

You may find a bird nest while on a nature hike. Do *not* disturb the nest unless it is unoccupied in late autumn or if it has been blown from a tree, etc., by a storm. If the latter is true, you'll want to make a record of the location, etc., and then bring the nest into the classroom for further study using the nest of activities below. You may also want to make your own bird nest from play dough. Follow the easy recipe. Use food coloring to color some of the play dough brown for the nest and the rest blue for the eggs. Take a fork and blend 2 cups of flour, 1 cup of salt, and 2 tablespoons of alum. Stir in 2 tablespoons

OTHER THOUGHTS AND QUESTIONS: Does the nest weigh more than the bird who made it? How long did it take to build the nest? How many journeys did the bird make to build the nest? How many eggs were in the nest?

of Wesson oil and add 1 cup of water. Knead five minutes until smooth. Then build a nest like the nest below. Don't forget the eggs.

My bird's name _____

Date I found the nest _____

Detailed sketch and map of where I found the nest. (Include any details that would help identify the nest such as the exact location - shrub, tree, on ground, whether it was suspended from a branch, built on a limb, in a corner, in a hollow tree, fence post, etc.)

My classification of all materials used in making the nest or found in the nest:
- things that once lived;
- things that are man-made.

My nest measurements:
Circumference in In____cm____
Diameter in In____cm____
Depth in In____cm____
Weight in oz_____
gm_____

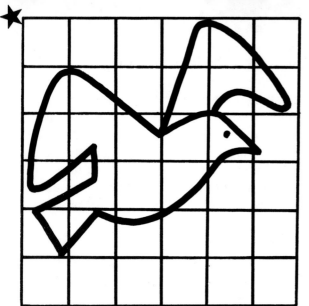

Growing Gull

Kids need to develop the skill of sketching animals, etc., according to scale in science. Use the gull at the left to increase the size of the gull below. How many times larger will the gull be? Read *Jonathan Livingston Seagull* and make a science report to the class on how Jonathan relates to science and life.

An egg  from HOME can lead you to the  GOAL of

finding out about the LIFE CYCLE of a CHICKEN. Children have often asked me the questons below. Use the questions as a springboard to get your study underway. Then have the children bring in chicken bones and put chicken skeletons together. Be sure to strip off all meat, boil, then soak in hydrogen peroxide to make bones white. Allow time to dry thoroughly. Glue on cardboard or hold bones together with the stiff wire.

From Egg to Chick to Chicken

1. Where do you get eggs for hatching? **2.** How can you tell whether an egg is fertile or not? **3.** Is the egg alive? **4.** How does it (embryo) grow bigger? **5.** Why is it in a sac? **6.** Why does the egg have an air sac? **7.** Why do you put water in the incubator? **8.** Why do you have to turn the eggs? **9.** Why do we have to keep the temperature so high? **10.** How do chickens mate? **11.** Why are the chicken's eyes so big? **12.** What is the white spot on its beak? **13.** Why does it have goose bumps? **14.** Why is it peeping? **15.** Is it a boy or a girl? **16.** How does the chick inside the egg know how to eat? **17.** Can we eat fertilized eggs? **18.** What's that funny looking stalk (umbilical cord) for? **19.** Does the chick come out of the egg fast or slow? **20.** How come they peck in a circle? **21.** How come they peck for a-while, stop, and start up again? **22.** Why are we making another box to put the baby chicks in? **23.** What do baby chicks eat once they're out of the egg? **24.** Do we have to crack open the eggs? **25.** What's candling?

Some from  will lead you to the

of first making a CARVING BLOCK and then carving animal characters. You will need two cups (480 mL) of *sawdust, dry coffee grounds* or ½ cup (120 mL) of *kitty litter*, two cups (480 mL) *plaster of Paris* and two tablespoons (30 mL) of *white Elmer's glue*. Add water to make a thick but pourable batter. Pour into mold like a paper cup, milk carton, etc. Hardens in a day. Then carve your favorite science creature using a scissors, a wooden stick, or plastic knife. Display your creature. Make a sketch of your creature and enter it in your science log.

You will want to extend this activity into making casts for animal tracks and fossils found on page 176. You may also want to take some detergent soap flakes and add water to make a pourable batter. Pour into tracks. Or, make your favorite science creature out of this soapy mixture. Then study soap carving. Happy carving.

Some flowers from a  will lead you to the

of understanding the PARTS OF A FLOWER and their functions. You will also need a *magnifying glass, glue,* and a *sketch* like the one below.

FLOWER POWER!

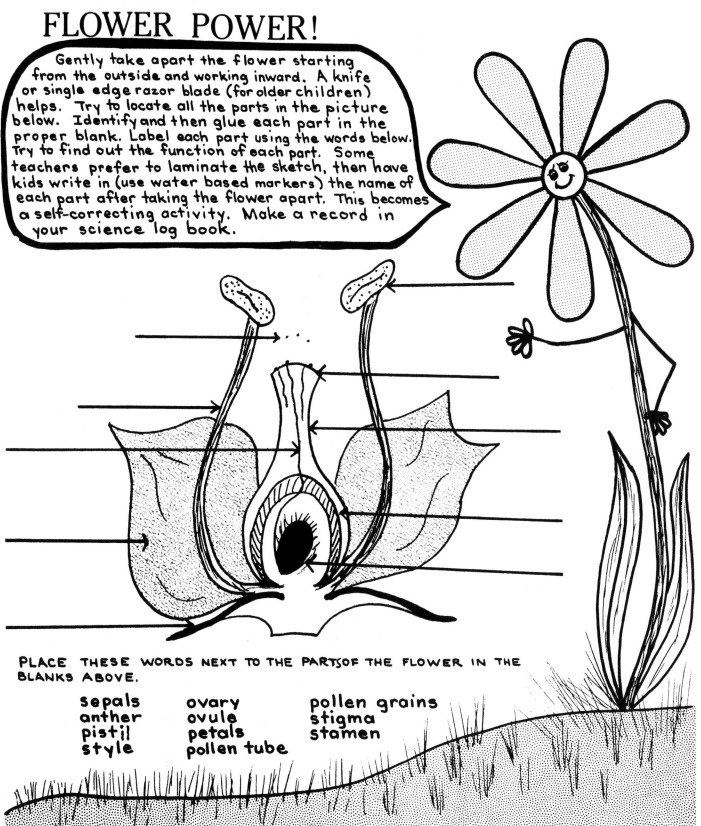

Gently take apart the flower starting from the outside and working inward. A knife or single edge razor blade (for older children) helps. Try to locate all the parts in the picture below. Identify and then glue each part in the proper blank. Label each part using the words below. Try to find out the function of each part. Some teachers prefer to laminate the sketch, then have kids write in (use water based markers) the name of each part after taking the flower apart. This becomes a self-correcting activity. Make a record in your science log book.

PLACE THESE WORDS NEXT TO THE PARTS OF THE FLOWER IN THE BLANKS ABOVE.

sepals	ovary	pollen grains
anther	ovule	stigma
pistil	petals	stamen
style	pollen tube	

Some lima beans from  will lead you to the

of understanding PLANT GROWTH. You will also need some *water, milk carton containers,* a *magnifying glass* and some *soil.*

SPROUTING BEANS

Soak lima beans in water overnight. Carefully remove the outer covering from a few beans and find out what is inside the bean seed. Make a sketch. Next, plant remaining seeds in milk carton containers about ¼" (1 cm) into the soil. Water seeds daily. Observe growth. Make a photograph, picture, or chart of each day's growth (see page 38). Record your findings on My Plant Growth Record found on opposite page. Then make a hanging bean plant milk carton holder and hang from ceiling of your classroom. NOTE: A 6-pack of soft drink containers including plastic rings make excellent plant holders and places for plants and flowers to grow on.

GROUND
feet
feet

MY PLANT GROWTH RECORD

DAY ONE	DAY TWO	DAY THREE	DAY FOUR	DAY FIVE	DAY SIX	DAY SEVEN
DAY EIGHT	DAY NINE	DAY TEN	DAY ELEVEN	DAY TWELVE	DAY THIRTEEN	DAY FOURTEEN

Some  will lead you to understanding changes of state and using your FIVE SENSES

You will need *popcorn, vegetable oil, hot plate,* and a *pan* or *popcorn popper.* Use the activity sheet on the opposite page to lead you into some interesting discoveries. NOTE: This activity is a good one to use as a culminating activity for a unit on the five senses as all five senses are used during the activity. You may also want to use this recipe and make your own butter. Then, weigh the butter and add to popcorn. Allow children to shake mixture while you read a story to them. One half pint of Half and Half, a pinch of salt and food coloring will make butter. Add some Knox gelatin, honey, strawberry or grape jelly or instant pudding for flavoring.

After counting, put popcorn seeds into a container.

Have the class estimate the number of seeds.

My Choice

My Choice

POP OFF WITH POPCORN

Write a report on the history of popcorn. Do some research. Where does popcorn come from? Why are some kernels white and some yellow?

Plant a popcorn seed. Record date planted, how often watered, height after it begins to grow. Draw the popcorn plant.

Find out what a hybrid is. Chat with a farmer about how one hair on a corncob fertilizes one kernel and why there are always an even number of kernels around a cob.

Color some popped popcorn and string these for a holiday season.

Cut a seed of popcorn in half. Then try to pop it. Find out what happens.

Find out the history of Indian corn. What is the difference between sweet corn and field corn?

Write a story about how it would feel to be a grain of popcorn that gets popped. What would you say if you could talk?

Design your own popcorn experiment and perform it for the class.

88

POP OFF WITH ★

1. Draw one kernel of popcorn.

2. Later, draw a kernel of popped popcorn.

_____   _____

3. Weigh one kernel of popcorn. _____

4. Why is popcorn shaped the way it is?
_____

5. What kind of seed is popcorn? _____

6. What does popcorn seed taste like?
_____

7. If you break your seed open, describe what is inside.
_____

8. Other observations you want to make about your seed.
_____

9. Weight of total amount of popcorn before popping _____

START POPPING!

10. Starting time _____ **11.** Time completed _____

12. Total time needed for popping _____

13. Observations during popping _____
_____

14. Weight of popcorn after popping _____

15. Does popcorn weigh more or less than unpopped corn? _____
Why? _____

16. Observe how many seeds did not pop compared to how many that did pop. What is the ratio? _____

17. Why did some seeds not pop? _____

18. Measure the amount of salt added to popcorn to make it tasty. Study the effects of salt on the human body.

19. Study the amount of calories found in buttered and nonbuttered popcorn. Does margarine make a difference? Write a story on what you find out.

POPCORN

 Some leaves from the school yard will lead you to the  GOAL

of developing an understanding of LEAVES and TREES. Here are some tips and possible activities. Remember to pick only those leaves that you really need. Get the entire leaf if you can. Do not tear off branches. Leave the environment as you found it.

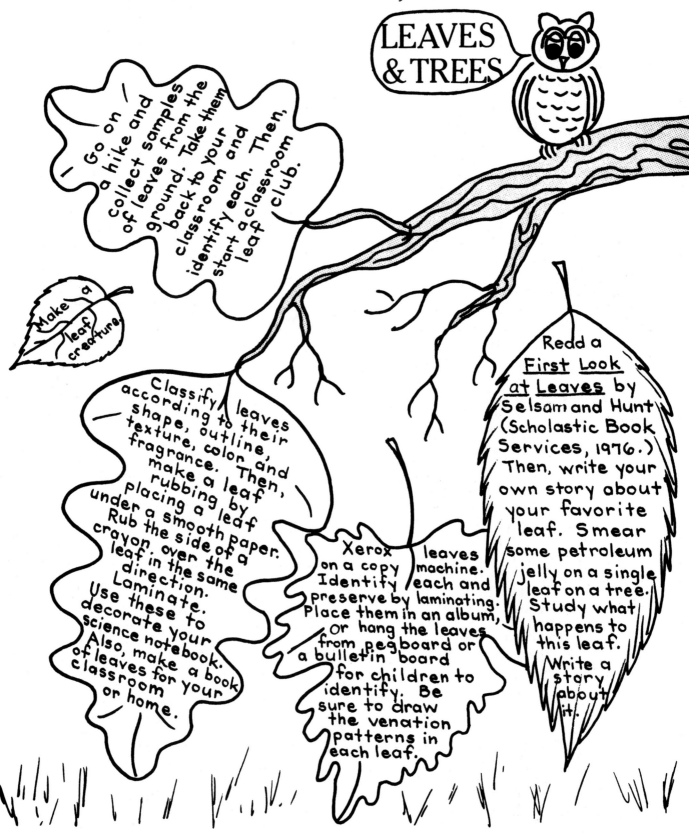

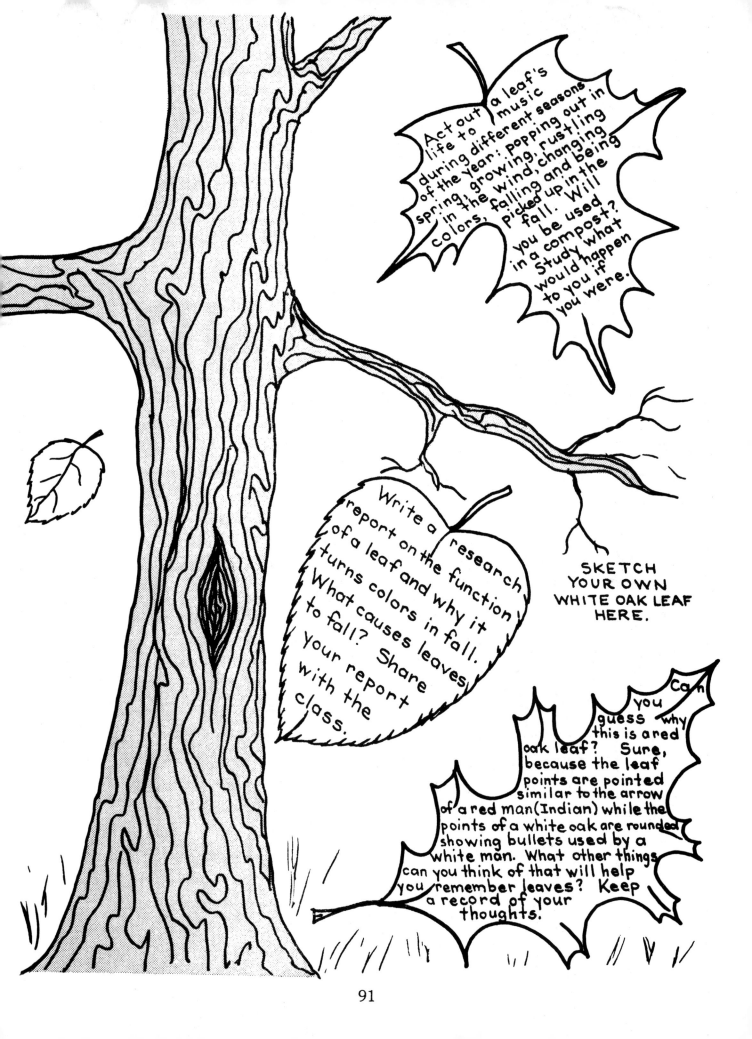

Act out a leaf's life to music during different seasons of the year; popping out in spring, growing, rustling in the wind, changing colors, falling and being picked up in the fall. Will you be used in a compost? Study what would happen to you if you were.

Write a research report on the function of a leaf and why it turns colors in fall. What causes leaves to fall? Share your report with the class.

SKETCH YOUR OWN WHITE OAK LEAF HERE.

Can you guess why this is a red oak leaf? Sure, because the leaf points are pointed similar to the arrow of a red man(Indian) while the points of a white oak are rounded showing bullets used by a white man. What other things can you think of that will help you remember leaves? Keep a record of your thoughts.

91

Kids need to be able to measure objects and quantities in science using one, two and three dimensions. Inch or centimeter graph paper is very helpful when measuring the surface area of an irregularly shaped object like a leaf. Merely trace around leaf onto grid paper. Find the number of whole squares within the leaf and color them. Next, find the number of fractional squares within the lines and color a different color. These partial squares can be added together to form full squares. Approximate. The total area, therefore, is approximated by adding the total number of squares from each of two colors together. How many square inches (centimeters) of surface area is contained in this leaf? If your answer is close to the age that Albert Einstein was when he discovered $E = MC^2$, you are right. Also, can you find out what type of tree this leaf came from? Now, find your own leaf and use the graph paper on pages 244-247 and find out the surface area of your leaf.

A cross section  of a downed tree can lead you to the **GOAL**

of understanding the HISTORY OF A TREE. You'll need *keen eyes* for observation and a *pen*.

Section a Tree

Carefully observe a log or downed tree. Identify the heartwood, sapwood, outer bark, and the four types of tissue including the cork, xylem, phloem and cambium. Look for scars that might indicate insect, fire, or lightning damage. Identify cracks. Observe inward turning of rings which indicates a branch may have grown at that point. Count the rings and find the age of your tree. Measure the distance between the rings. What does this tell you about the history of your tree? Record your findings in your log book.

Hoop a tree below. Obtain an *embroidery hoop, small pencil* and *pop bottle*. Place hoop on pop bottle. Balance pencil on hoop as below. Strike outside of hoop with fingers in sweeping hand motion. What happens?

Hoop - A - La

Then, do same but strike inside hoop. Why does the pencil fall into the pop bottle? What can you say about the characteristics of wood? Does gravity affect the pencil? Record your findings in your science log.

MAKE PAPER

Your knowledge of TREES will lead you to MAKING PAPER which in turn will lead you to TESTING CONSUMER PRODUCTS. Follow this sample sequence of activities. You will need some old *newspapers, water, powdered detergent, eggbeater, sponge, window screen,* or *netted orange bag, iron,* and *paper towels.*

FIRST: MAKE PAPER

Tear newspaper into bits and add to dishpan filled with lukewarm to hot water. Add a pinch of detergent. Beat mixture with eggbeater or blender into slurry. Scoop slurry out of pan with window screen or netted orange bag.

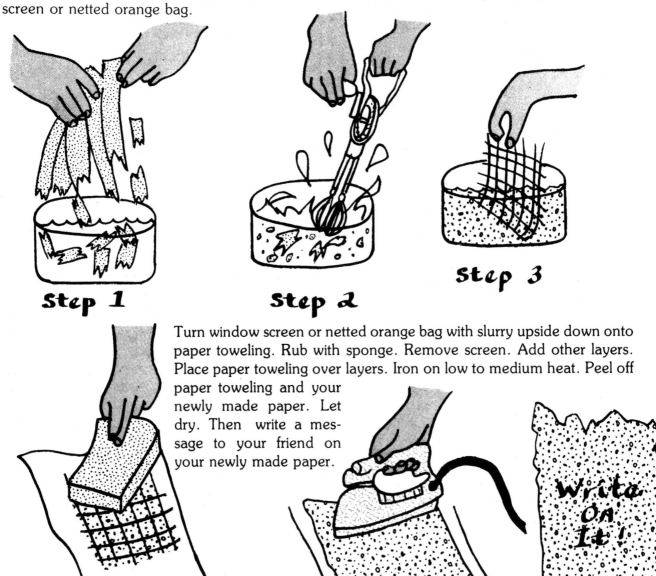

Step 1

Step 2

Step 3

Turn window screen or netted orange bag with slurry upside down onto paper toweling. Rub with sponge. Remove screen. Add other layers. Place paper toweling over layers. Iron on low to medium heat. Peel off paper toweling and your newly made paper. Let dry. Then write a message to your friend on your newly made paper.

Step 4

Step 5

Step 6

Write On It!

SECOND: TEST STRENGTH OF NEWSPAPER

Test the strength of newspaper by finding out how many books a stretched out piece of newspaper will hold. Wet newspaper and allow to dry overnight. Test strength again. Keep a record of how the strength of your newspaper is affected by soaking the newspaper in water.

CONSUMER'S REPORT

THIRD, do these activity cards and complete the chart (on opposite side) of activities. Work on your own *Consumer Reports*.

CARD ONE

Activity

Conduct a survey of the students in the class on which of the five brands of paper toweling are normally used in their homes.

Brand Name	Number	Brand Name	Number
A	_____	D	_____
B	_____	E	_____
C	_____		

Represent the results of your survey on a bar graph.

CARD TWO

Activity

Select two of the five brands of paper toweling and find their prices in five different stores. Based upon the best buy, find the percent of the cost that is saved by purchasing each brand at the lowest price rather than the highest price.

CARD THREE

Activity

Make a line graph that will show the amount of water absorbed by each of the five brand name paper towels versus the length of time (one minute) for each test.

CARD FOUR

Activity

Develop a television commercial that would persuade others to purchase your brand of paper toweling. Investigate different types of advertising and use one type in your commercial.

CARD FIVE

Activity

Determine the cost of a ream of paper. Then, determine the cost per sheet found in the ream. Weigh 1, 5, 10 sheets and the ream of paper. Based on your findings predict the weight of 150 sheets. Show your results in the form of a graph. What can you conclude about the relationship between the number of sheets of paper and their respective weights?

MY CONSUMER'S REPORT CHART

	Brand E	Brand D	Brand C	Brand B	Brand A	
						PRICE
						SALE PRICE
						SOLID COLOR PRINTED DESIGN or WHITE
						METRIC MEASUREMENTS ON LABEL (YES or NO)
						ROLL LENGTH in FEET (METERS)
						WEIGHT w/WRAPPER in OZ (GMS)
						WEIGHT w/o WRAPPER in OZ (GMS)
						SURFACE AREA 1 SHEET in SQ. IN. (CM^2)
						SURFACE AREA ROLL in SQ. IN. (CM^2)
						ML of H_2O ABSORBED by 1 SHEET
						TIME ABSORPTION 1 SHEET
						THICKNESS: 1 SHEET
						TEAR TEST
						BURN TEST
						SCRUB TEST
						DROP WEIGHT TEST
						OVERALL BEST BRAND RANKING

6 PHYSICAL SCIENCE ACTIVITIES

 from a **HARDWARE** store will lead you to the

GOAL

of developing a feeling for SURFACE TENSION. You will need a tube of *Duco Cement*, some *oil*, and a *pan, tray,* or *clear dish* filled with water.

Drop one drop of Duco Cement into a container of tap water. Carefully observe the movements of your creature. List them. Why does this happen? Find out how long it will swim and dance. Add other drops. How do they act together? Add one drop of soap to the solution. What happens? Change water. Place clear dish on overhead projector. Add water. Add a ring of Duco Cement to the dish. Study its movements. Place several drops of oil inside the ring to simulate an oil slick. Note colors. What happens to the oil? Add food coloring. Paint a picture of what you see. Then, choose a partner and act out what two drops of Duco Cement do in the water. What happens to you and your friend if one drop of soapy water is added to the water? Write a story of your experiences.

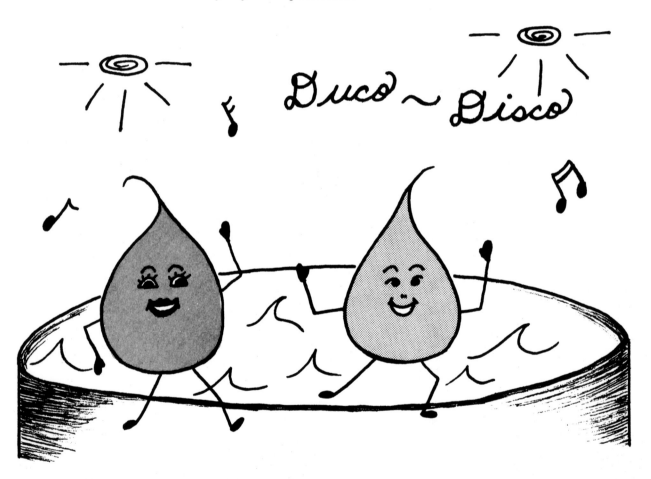

A plastic 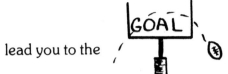 fruit holder from a local  will

lead you to the of understanding SURFACE TENSION. You will also

need a *glass container of water, paper toweling, liquid soap* and *salt*. Place fruit holder in container of water. Observe carefully what happens. Place on overhead projector. Count the number of squares in the bottom of the fruit holder. Determine its surface area. Mark off a strip of paper toweling in ½ inch (1 cm) marks. Hold a strip of paper toweling vertically in holder so it touches water. Determine how many inches (cm) that the water rises up the paper toweling before the fruit basket sinks. How long in seconds does it take for the basket to sink? Try to find other ways to get the basket to sink by adding several drops of liquid soap. Try same in salt water. Record your results in your science log. Use your fruit basket for a rock collection, seashell collection or in sinking and floating experiments found on page 110.

Fruitful Tension

A penny from HOME will lead you to the GOAL of developing a feeling for SURFACE TENSION and for CONTROLLING VARIABLES. You will need some *pennies, medicine cups, soapy water, eyedroppers, water, plenty of paper towels,* and *Mission tape.*

Play *Mission Impossible* theme song dubbing in the following mission: "Your mission, should you decide to accept it, is to predict and then find out how many drops of regular water you can fit on the head side of a penny. This tape will self-destruct in five seconds. Good luck in your mission!" (Some teachers have used dry ice to simulate the actual destruction of the tape and tape recorder.)

Have student record data on the Mission Impossible Student Record Sheet found on the next page. Then complete a total class Mission Impossible Record Sheet as a total class project. Be sure to keep a record of the variables that affect your ability to put drops of water on your penny. Then try nickels, dimes, and quarters.

P.S. Find out how many mL of water you can put on the penny. There are usually 25 drops of water in one mL, but this often depends upon the size of the bore in the eyedropper.

MISSION IMPOSSIBLE STUDENT RECORD SHEET

Name _____

TRIAL NUMBER	REGULAR WATER HEADS	REGULAR WATER TAILS	REGULAR WATER EDGE	SOAPY WATER HEADS	SOAPY WATER TAILS	SOAPY WATER EDGE	MY VARIABLES	DRAWINGS and WORDS of THOUGHTS and FEELINGS
ONE								
TWO								
THREE								
FOUR								
FIVE								
AVERAGE								

MISSION IMPOSSIBLE TOTAL CLASS RECORD SHEET

NAME								
TOTAL								
AVERAGE								

101

Some  medicine cups from a local  will lead you to the of developing a feeling for SURFACE TENSION. You will also

need an *eyedropper, paper clips*, and some *regular* and *soapy water*. First, estimate the number of drops of regular water needed to fill a medicine cup and then do it. Find out if you can fit more drops of regular or soapy water in the medicine cup. Which heaps highest, regular water or soapy water? Draw a picture. Keep a record of the variables that influence the number of drops that you can fit into the medicine cup. Try floating a paper clip on top of the water. Next, find out how many cubic centimeters of water are in the cup. How many milliliters? How many drops equal one cubic centimeter or milliliter? Record your findings in your science log. NOTE: For younger children the task of counting each drop is difficult, so have them fill the cup level with water before starting to drop drops into the cup. A ruler scraped across the top of the cup will make the water level with the cup.

Some Possible Variables
- Size of drop of water
- Size of hole in dropper
- Amount of water in the dropper

The Heap

SOAP

 from a will lead you to the  of

developing a feeling for BUOYANCY and GASES. You'll need some *baking soda, water,* and *vinegar* in addition to *raisins.* Put some baking soda into a container of water and observe carefully for several minutes. Drop six raisins into the container. Observe. Gradually add vinegar. Observe carefully for at least five minutes. Can you explain why the raisins go up and down? Count the number of times each raisin goes up and down in five minutes. Make a record of your results. Study the differenes. Then set up two containers and add noncoated and chocolate-coated raisins. You may want to extend this activity by dropping *Life Savers* or *sugarless* and *nonsugarless gum* into the container. Test at least two different brands. Record all results in your science log. What do you feel causes the raisins, Life Savers and bits of gum to go up and down? Does $C_{12}H_{22}O_{11}$ give you a clue? Make a vocabulary chart that describes these interesting movements. Do the Life Savers remind you of an aquifer? How about geothermal energy? The list is seemingly endless. Record your list in your science log.

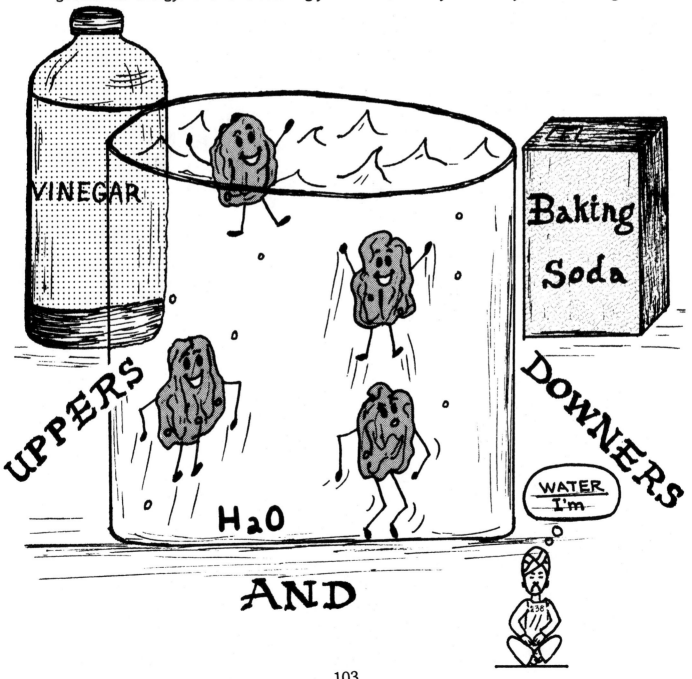

A clear plastic straw from a Restaurant or fast food place will lead you to the GOAL of understanding DENSITY. You will also need *five water glasses*, *salt*, *food coloring*, *clay* or *bits of styrofoam*, *water* and *soda pop*.

LOFTY

one one

1238

237

LAYERS

Fill glasses with water and add salt and food coloring as follows:

Glass #	Amount of Salt	Color of Food Coloring	
1	.5 teaspoon	Blue	*(Teacher Hint:* These are
2	1 teaspoon	Green	in alphabetical order so
3	1.5 teaspoons	Red	you can remember the
4	2 teaspoons	Yellow	order of layering.)

Dip straw ½″ (1 cm) into solution number one. Lift off finger on end of straw; then place finger back on. Lift straw out of solution one and dip into solution two. Repeat. Wait 5 seconds. Do the two solutions layer or mix? If so, why? Then use the activity cards on the following page. These cards can be laminated and reused over and over again using a grease pencil. Remember, always record your prediction (guess) first, then try out and record, then circle whether you were correct or incorrect. By keeping accurate records of your results, you can predict (guess) how all four solutions layer in the straw. Add a piece of clay or styrofoam to keep layers intact. Next, find out where *soda pop* layers with the other 4 solutions. Then try other solutions like alcohol, oil, etc., and record the greatest number of solutions you can layer in your Guinness Book of Science Records found on page 49. Our record is 15 different solutions layered in a long piece of clear stiff plastic tubing. Can you top that?

LOFTY LAYERS PREDICTION SHEET

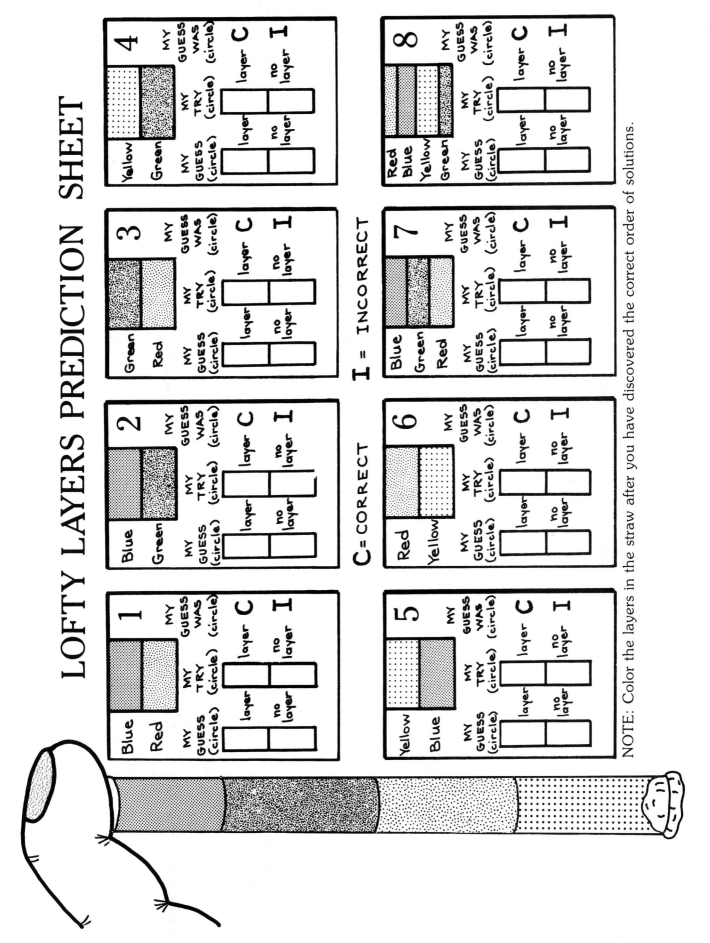

1
Blue
Red
MY GUESS WAS (circle)   C   I
MY TRY (circle)   layer   no layer
MY GUESS (circle)   layer   no layer

2
Blue
Green
MY GUESS WAS (circle)   C   I
MY TRY (circle)   layer   no layer
MY GUESS (circle)   layer   no layer

3
Green
Red
MY GUESS WAS (circle)   C   I
MY TRY (circle)   layer   no layer
MY GUESS (circle)   layer   no layer

4
Yellow
Green
MY GUESS WAS (circle)   C   I
MY TRY (circle)   layer   no layer
MY GUESS (circle)   layer   no layer

5
Yellow
Blue
MY GUESS WAS (circle)   C   I
MY TRY (circle)   layer   no layer
MY GUESS (circle)   layer   no layer

6
Red
Yellow
MY GUESS WAS (circle)   C   I
MY TRY (circle)   layer   no layer
MY GUESS (circle)   layer   no layer

7
Blue
Green
Red
MY GUESS WAS (circle)   C   I
MY TRY (circle)   layer   no layer
MY GUESS (circle)   layer   no layer

8
Red
Blue
Yellow
Green
MY GUESS WAS (circle)   C   I
MY TRY (circle)   layer   no layer
MY GUESS (circle)   layer   no layer

C = CORRECT   I = INCORRECT

NOTE: Color the layers in the straw after you have discovered the correct order of solutions.

105

Some blotter from an office supply

will lead you to the  of understanding the PHYSICAL MAKEUP of various colors

and solutions by CHROMATOGRAPHY. You will also need some *baby food jars, water, four colors of food coloring* or *dye,* a *yardstick* (meter stick) and several *desks.* Cut strips of blotter paper 36″ (90 cm) long and 2″ (5 cm) wide. Place yardstick (meter stick) between two **desks. Tape** strips of blotter paper to yardstick (meter stick) allowing them to hang freely. Mix **equal amounts** of food coloring with equal amounts of water in each of four baby food jars. **Record** the time. Insert tips of strips into baby food jars. Observe carefully and make a sketch of what happens. Then try other substances such as boiled spinach leaves, *etc.* Study how **chromatography** can help scientists learn more about the characteristics of a substance that **will help us** in our everyday lives. Sketch your results in your science log.

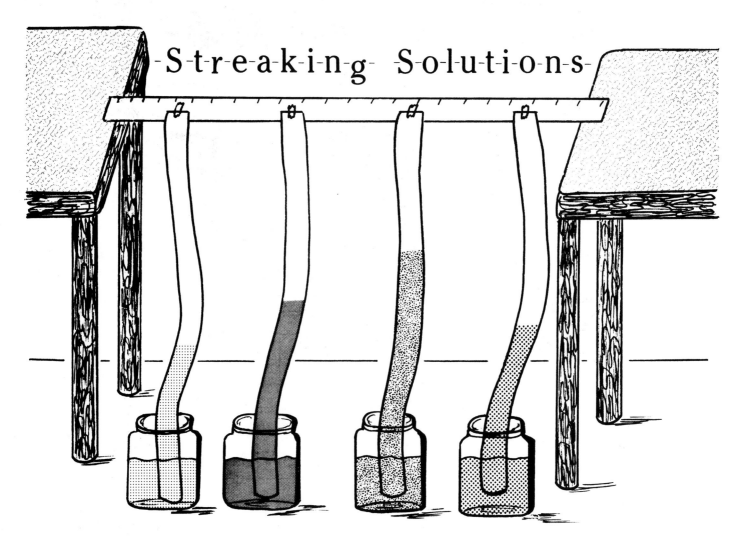

-S-t-r-e-a-k-i-n-g- -S-o-l-u-t-i-o-n-s-

A see-through bottle from  will lead you to the

 of developing a feeling for DENSITY and WAVE ACTION. You will also need some

turpentine or *vegetable oil*, *food coloring*, *water*, and pieces of *plastic* or *aluminum foil*.

Rinse plastic bottle. Fill ¾ full with water. Add drops of food coloring to water. Add some turpentine or vegetable oil to colored water. Place pieces of plastic and aluminum foil cut in the shape of an amoeba, etc., into the water. Cap bottle tightly. Tilt bottle to and fro. What happens? How does this simulate a model ocean? What can you tell about the density of the liquids in the bottle? Use bottle as a pendulum. How is this similar to an ocean? Make a record of your results.

How dense is dense?

A ball from the top of a deodorant  will help you reach the

 of understanding DENSITY. You will also need several

clear plastic or *glass containers, water, salt* and *food coloring*. Place deodorant ball in container of regular tap water. What happens? Time the rate of descent. Then slowly add salt to the solution. What happens? Why? Add food coloring. Then try other solutions, *e.g.,* alcohol, baking soda, soda pop, *etc.* What can you say about the ball's ability to sink or float? Record your findings in your science notebook.

Ball o' Fun

A squeezable  bottle from a beverage mart or  will

lead you to a  which will give you a feeling for

DISPLACEMENT. You'll need a *cap* for the soda pop bottle or liquid detergent bottle and a *medicine dropper*. Fill bottle with water. Partially fill medicine dropper with water. Place dropper in bottle. If it sinks, it contains too much water. Refill. Cap the bottle. Squeeze sides of bottle and make diver dive to the bottom and then surface again. Find a way to make the diver stay in the middle of the bottle. What would happen if you plugged the end of the diver with a piece of clay or styrofoam? Then investigate how a deep-sea diver or submarine dives and surfaces. What are "the bends"? Make a submarine and share it with the class. Record your feelings in your science log and in your Guinness Book of Science Records found on page 49.

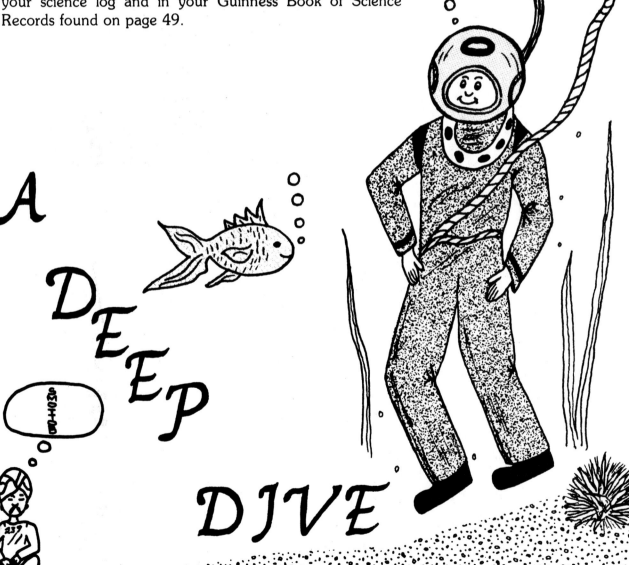

A DEEP DIVE

Some 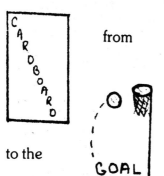 from ⬚ packages in a department store will lead you

to the ⬚ GOAL of developing a feeling for BUOYANCY of different objects.

You will also need a *marking pen* to make the following activity cards and individual pictures of the objects below. Glue picture of object onto card. Laminate. Collect actual objects. Fill container (plastic shoe boxes work well) with water. First have child guess (predict) whether the object will sink or float and circle with erasable marker on card. Then child places object in water. Circle S, F, or SF in "try out" row. Complete correct, incorrect section on card. Erase for others to use.

Some objects:

1. Marble
2. Styrofoam
3. Wood
4. Soap
5. Apple
6. Scissors
7. Pin
8. Pencil
9. Pen
10. Paper Cup
11. Eraser
12. Aluminum Foil
13. Glass Jar
14. Ruler

SINK OR FLOAT

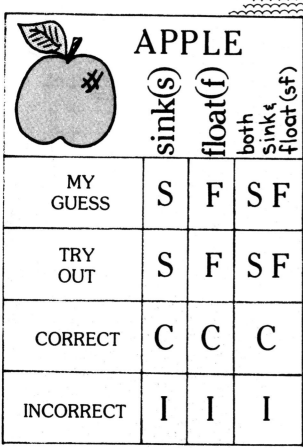

STUMPERS

1. Design a method to make styrofoam sink.
2. Make a marble float.
3. Try placing several objects in *salt water*. Do the objects float easier in salt water or regular water? Is it true that one can swim easier in salt water? Record your results in your science log.

110

Some oil-based 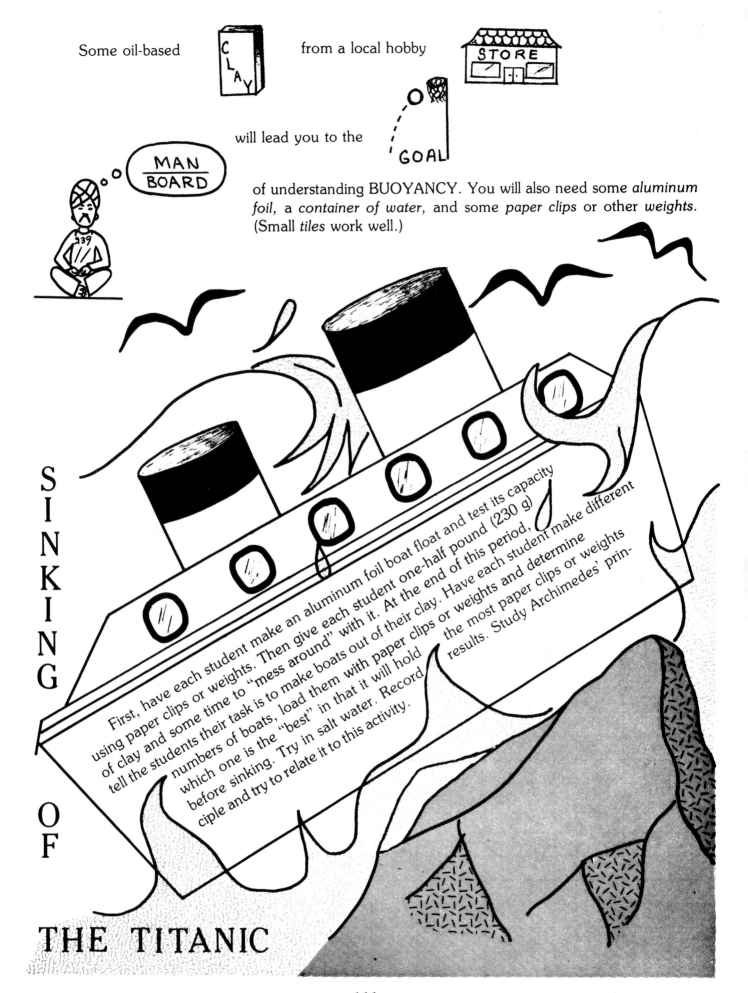 from a local hobby STORE

will lead you to the GOAL

MAN BOARD

of understanding BUOYANCY. You will also need some *aluminum foil*, a *container of water*, and some *paper clips* or other *weights*. (Small *tiles* work well.)

SINKING OF THE TITANIC

First, have each student make an aluminum foil boat float and test its capacity using paper clips or weights. Then give each student one-half pound (230 g) of clay and some time to "mess around" with it. At the end of this period, tell the students their task is to make boats out of their clay. Have each student make different numbers of boats, load them with paper clips or weights and determine which one is the "best" in that it will hold the most paper clips or weights before sinking. Try in salt water. Record results. Study Archimedes' principle and try to relate it to this activity.

A tall narrow olive **JAR** from **HOME** will lead you to the **GOAL**

of developing a feeling for GASES. You will also need some *clay, water, birthday candle, aluminum pan,* and *matches.* Place candle in bottom of pan. Hold upright with clay. Pour water into pan. Light candle. Place olive jar upside down over candle. Watch carefully what happens. Why does the water rise up the jar? Mark the level of water in the jar with a rubber band. Redo the experiment.

Does the water rise as far up the jar on this trial? Keep an accurate record of your observations in your science log. Then write a story about Robert Boyle and his famed "Boyle's Law."

what

a

P.S. Clear plastic graduated cylinders from a hospital (*see* page 45) also work well for this activity because children can read the actual displacement of liquid in mL after each trial.

gas

A plastic syringe from a  will lead you to the

of understanding DISPLACEMENT. You will also need *rubber* or *plastic tubing, water,* a *pan,* a *glass tumbler, index card,* and some *food coloring.* Fill glass tumbler and pan with water and add food coloring. Stir. Place index card over glass tumbler. Invert and place glass tumbler in pan of water. Remove index card. Using syringe and rubber tubing, can you find a way to remove all the water from the glass tumbler *without* lifting the tumbler above the level of the water in the pan? Once this is accomplished, can you find a way to put all the water back into the glass tumbler without lifting the tumbler above the level of the water inside the pan? Now, take a really-big Deep Dive on page 109 and find out what happens. Record your feelings in your science log. See page 46 for further extending activities.

Fill & Refill!

A thoroughly rinsed DITTO FLUID can from  SCHOOL will help you reach the GOAL of developing a feeling for AIR PRESSURE. You also need a

cap for the can, *hot plate*, and *water*. Thoroughly rinse ditto fluid can with water. Add about 1 cm (½") of water to the can. Place can on hot plate leaving lid off the can. Heat until steam can be seen. Cap the can and remove from hot plate. Observe and record what happens. Can you explain why this is such a crushing experience? Repeat. Reheat. Place can in pan of cold water. What happens? How can this experience be related to how you feel when riding on a roller coaster or elevator? Look up some of the effects that riding a roller coaster may have on your body. Why do some amusement parks have signs saying that "You must be this tall in order to ride on this roller coaster?" Have you ridden a roller coaster? Write about your experience and this activity in your science notebook.

A CRUSHING EXPERIENCE

NOTE: Some children will want to "blow the can back up again." Do *not* use hot plate for this purpose! Rather, use a pump until the can has expanded to its original size.

A drinking glass from  will lead you to the  **GOAL**

of developing a feeling for AIR PRESSURE. You will also need *water*, a *plastic dish cover*, *index card* or *wire screen*, *liquid soap*, *pencil*, and a *toothpick*. Fill the drinking glass with water. Place index card over the mouth of the container and carefully invert the container over the sink. Think about what is happening. What happens if the glass is tilted or is only filled partially with water? Write a story in your science log on how this experience can be compared to getting catsup from a new bottle of catsup. How can you get catsup to freely flow from a new bottle of catsup? Share your ideas with your friends. Compare your results with those found in Fruitful Tension on page 99.

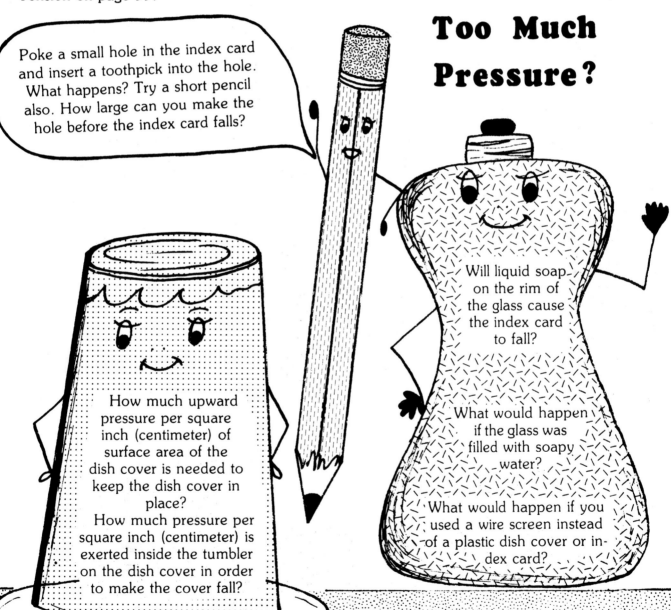

Poke a small hole in the index card and insert a toothpick into the hole. What happens? Try a short pencil also. How large can you make the hole before the index card falls?

Too Much Pressure?

How much upward pressure per square inch (centimeter) of surface area of the dish cover is needed to keep the dish cover in place?
How much pressure per square inch (centimeter) is exerted inside the tumbler on the dish cover in order to make the cover fall?

Will liquid soap on the rim of the glass cause the index card to fall?

What would happen if the glass was filled with soapy water?

What would happen if you used a wire screen instead of a plastic dish cover or index card?

Some  SALT from HOME will lead you to the GOAL of finding out

what effect a substance has on the BOILING POINT of water.

You will need *two beakers, water, a hot plate,* and *two thermometers.* Put 1 quart (liter) of water in each of the beakers. To one of the beakers, add 5 tablespoons (75 mL) of salt. Put thermometers in beakers, place on hot plate and begin heating. Record results. Does salt affect the boiling point of water? How? Try again with other substances. Are results the same? Record your results in your science log. Extend your study to find out what effect altitude has on the boiling point of water. Will water boil faster while on top of a mountain or in Death Valley? Does it take longer and thus use more energy to boil water in higher or lower elevations? Record your results in the form of a chart and share with the class.

BOILING POINT

Some 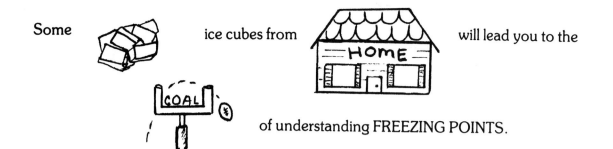 ice cubes from will lead you to the of understanding FREEZING POINTS.

You will also need a *beaker, thermometer, salt, grid paper,* and a *hot plate*. Put ice cubes in a beaker. Place the thermometer in with the ice. Prepare graph to show temperature changes in comparison to time. Record the results for 5-minute intervals. How long does it take before the temperature makes a steady rise? When did the temperature stop rising? Then try the experiment again, only this time add various amounts of salt to the ice. Record the results. What effect does salt have on the freezing point? Investigate why salt is placed on roads in winter. What can be said about the freezing point of the ice on roads when salt is added to the ice? Ask a member of your city street crew and record your results in your science log.

117

An **Alka-Seltzer** tablet from **HOME** can lead you to the **GOAL** of

developing a feeling for PROPERTIES in a SUBSTANCE. You will also need a *hand lens, clear glass* or *plastic tumbler*, and some *litmus paper* if you have some handy. Fill clear glass or plastic tumbler with water. Drop in tablet. What do you observe? Look again carefully with your hand lens. Record what you see. Take litmus paper and find out if Alka-Seltzer is acid, base, or neutral. Record your findings in your science log. Extend this activity further by finding out the proper pH level for an aquarium and soil. Test acid content of various shampoos and fruit juices. Find out about "acid rain" due to pollution. Record your results in your science log.

The Acid Test

A 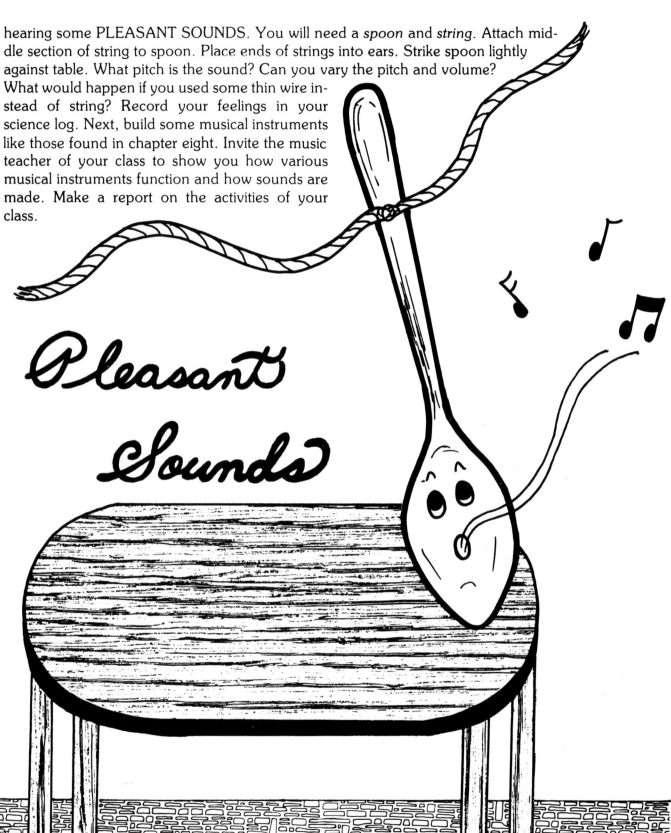 from your HOME can bring you to the GOAL of hearing some PLEASANT SOUNDS. You will need a *spoon* and *string*. Attach middle section of string to spoon. Place ends of strings into ears. Strike spoon lightly against table. What pitch is the sound? Can you vary the pitch and volume? What would happen if you used some thin wire instead of string? Record your feelings in your science log. Next, build some musical instruments like those found in chapter eight. Invite the music teacher of your class to show you how various musical instruments function and how sounds are made. Make a report on the activities of your class.

Pleasant Sounds

Forks from  will lead you to the  of

developing a feeling for CENTER OF GRAVITY. You will need *two forks, two corks,* a *penny, needle,* and a *bottle* of some type. Insert needle into top of cork and insert into bottle. Push penny into second cord. Add forks. Can you figure out a way to balance the penny on the tip of the needle? Tape note cards to forks. Turn on electric fan and have a revolving penny on the tip of the needle. How many revolutions will it make before it falls from the penny? Can you compare this to an anemometer? Construct a wind tunnel. Record your findings in your science log including a description of why you can balance the penny on the tip of a needle.

PENNY
NEEDLEPOINT

LEVEL

120

A 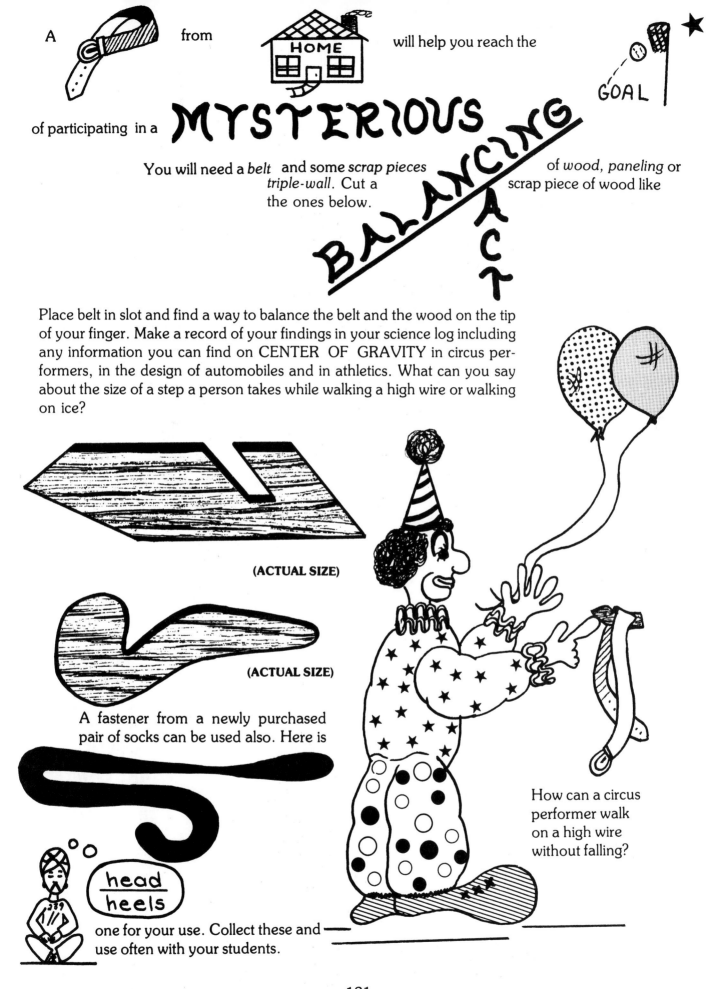 from HOME will help you reach the

of participating in a **MYSTERIOUS**

BALANCING ACT

GOAL ★

You will need a *belt* and some *scrap pieces* of *wood, paneling* or *triple-wall*. Cut a scrap piece of wood like the ones below.

Place belt in slot and find a way to balance the belt and the wood on the tip of your finger. Make a record of your findings in your science log including any information you can find on CENTER OF GRAVITY in circus performers, in the design of automobiles and in athletics. What can you say about the size of a step a person takes while walking a high wire or walking on ice?

(ACTUAL SIZE)

(ACTUAL SIZE)

A fastener from a newly purchased pair of socks can be used also. Here is

head
heels

one for your use. Collect these and use often with your students.

How can a circus performer walk on a high wire without falling?

A  from HOME will lead you to the  GOAL of developing a feeling for how

CONCAVE and CONVEX LENSES work. You will need a *metal spoon* to start your activity.

Look at your image in a spoon. What does it look like? Make a sketch. Can you improve your image by turning the spoon over? Carefully observe your spoon for its mysterious qualities. Can you do the same with mirrors? Make some sketches in your science notebook.

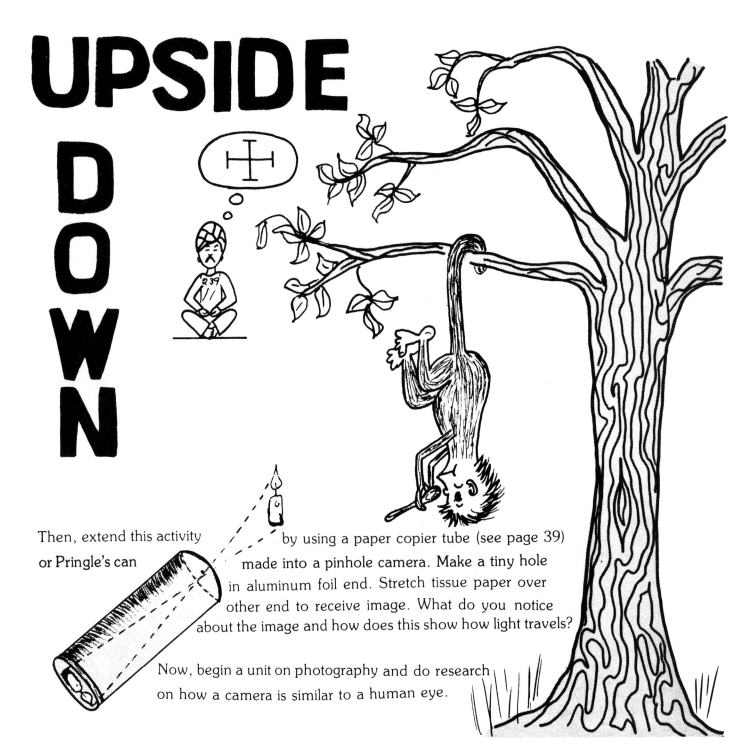

UPSIDE DOWN

Then, extend this activity

or Pringle's can by using a paper copier tube (see page 39) made into a pinhole camera. Make a tiny hole in aluminum foil end. Stretch tissue paper over other end to receive image. What do you notice about the image and how does this show how light travels?

Now, begin a unit on photography and do research on how a camera is similar to a human eye.

Some  string or fish line and some weights from will lead you to

the COAL of understanding how a PENDULUM works. You will also need several *desks*, a *clock*, or *stopwatch*, and a *ruler* or *meter stick*. Set up pendulum between desks and swing different objects. Observe the movements carefully. Then complete the table below by making pendulums with strings of the various lengths and by using two different weights, Wt. #1 and Wt. #2.

STRING LENGTH	4″ (10 cm)	8″ (20 cm)	12″ (30 cm)	16″ (40 cm)	20″ (50 cm)	24″ (60 cm)	28″ (70 cm)	32″ (80 cm)	36″ (90 cm)	40″ (100 cm)
Swings Per Minute (#1)										
Swings Per Minute (#2)										

What seems to be the effect of varying the weight on the number of swings of a pendulum?

What seems to be the effect of varying the length of the string on the number of swings of the pendulum?

Using the numbers above, compute the number of seconds per swing for each length pendulum.

STRING LENGTH	4″ (10 cm)	8″ (20 cm)	12″ (30 cm)	16″ (40 cm)	20″ (50 cm)	24″ (60 cm)	28″ (70 cm)	32″ (80 cm)	36″ (90 cm)	40″ (100 cm)
Seconds Per Swing										

Locate points on the graph below showing the points from the table above. Sketch the smooth curve through the points.

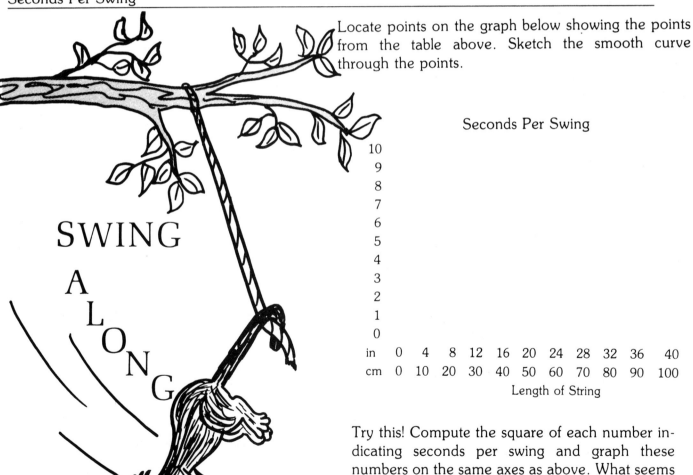

SWING A LONG

bong!

Seconds Per Swing

Try this! Compute the square of each number indicating seconds per swing and graph these numbers on the same axes as above. What seems to be true of *this* graph?

Now try various diameters of string! Make a record in your science log book.

123

A burned out light bulb from will lead you to the of understanding how ELECTRICITY FLOWS through a bulb. You'll also need some *paper bags, balance,* and some *papier-maché material* if you want to make maracas from the light bulbs to use in the study of SOUND WAVES and MUSIC (*see page 119*). Closely examine the burned out light bulb. Light up your knowledge by answering these questions.

—LIGHT—UP AND

What is the average hours of life-span of the bulb?

_____

Is the bulb clear or frosted? _____
Wattage of bulb? _____
Voltage of bulb? _____
Number of threads in base of bulb? _____
Location where bulb was made? _____
A sketch of what is or what I think is inside the bulb.

_____

What is the function of the piece of solder on the side of the bulb? _____
Weight of bulb before breaking?_____
ozs.   gms.

Take bulb and place in paper sack. Rap paper sack over solid surface to break bulb. *Caution:* Remove inside light bulb from sack. Draw a picture of what this looks like. Weigh this part. Weigh glass. Make a large chart showing how electricity travels through the bulb. To make maracas: Dip paper toweling into **papier-maché** mixture. Wrap around bulb. Let it semidry. Break glass with hammer. Allow to dry fully. Paint. Use maracas in the study of sound. Then have children hold hands and do activity on page 53. *Simulate* electrical circuit with each child being a conductor and test how long it takes an electron (squeeze of hand) to travel around circle.

DO: Have child stand in this position and trace the path of electricity through the person's body. *Caution:* Never allow the body to become a path for the actual electricity.

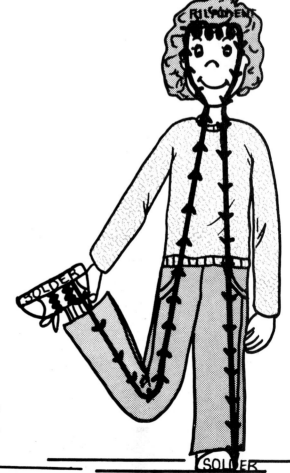

A watchful 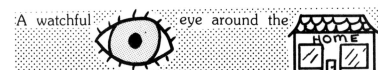 eye around the 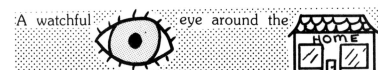 or school will lead you to the

of CONSERVING ENERGY. Here are some activities that will help you in your study of energy consumption and conservation.

TURN ON TO THESE ENERGY ACTIVITIES

Make a comprehensive study of how much electricity is used in your home and school in one month. Learn to read the electric meters and find out the number of kilo-

watt-hours consumed. Have your friends do the same and find out which family can reduce electrical consumption the most in one month. Graph your results. Have other classes in your school do the same study and share the results with each other. Which class can conserve the most energy?

Do a study of how much gas is used in your home or school in three months. Learn to read the gas meters and find out the number of cubic feet consumed. Have your friends do the same and find out which family can reduce gas consumption the most during the time span. Graph your results. Have classes in your school do the same study and share the results with each other.

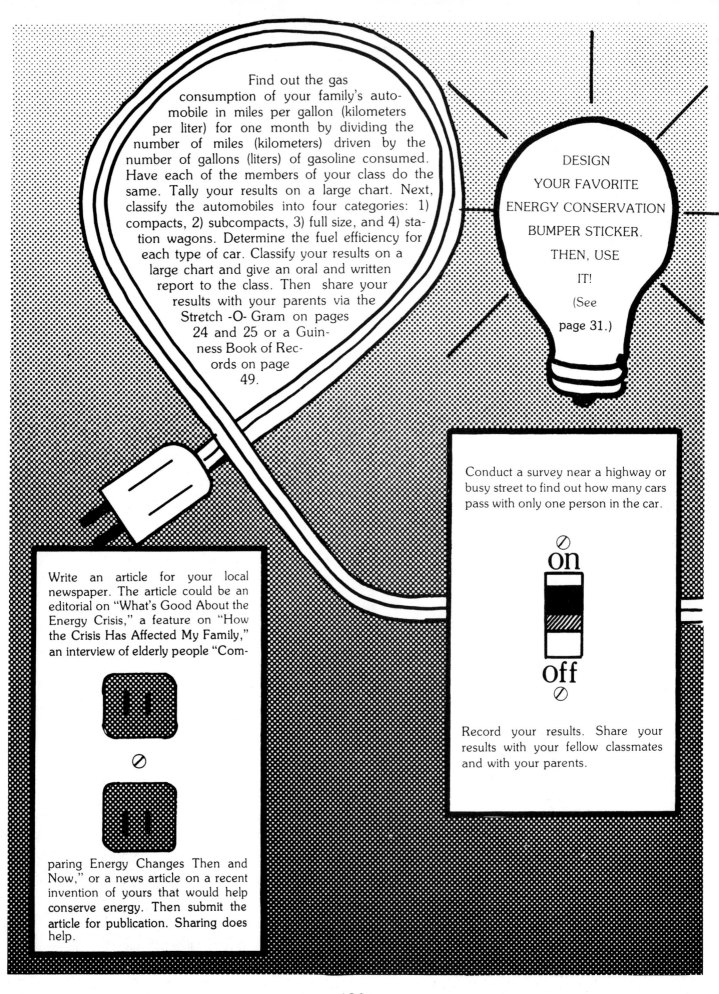

Find out the gas consumption of your family's automobile in miles per gallon (kilometers per liter) for one month by dividing the number of miles (kilometers) driven by the number of gallons (liters) of gasoline consumed. Have each of the members of your class do the same. Tally your results on a large chart. Next, classify the automobiles into four categories: 1) compacts, 2) subcompacts, 3) full size, and 4) station wagons. Determine the fuel efficiency for each type of car. Classify your results on a large chart and give an oral and written report to the class. Then share your results with your parents via the Stretch -O- Gram on pages 24 and 25 or a Guinness Book of Records on page 49.

DESIGN YOUR FAVORITE ENERGY CONSERVATION BUMPER STICKER. THEN, USE IT! (See page 31.)

Conduct a survey near a highway or busy street to find out how many cars pass with only one person in the car.

on

off

Record your results. Share your results with your fellow classmates and with your parents.

Write an article for your local newspaper. The article could be an editorial on "What's Good About the Energy Crisis," a feature on "How the Crisis Has Affected My Family," an interview of elderly people "Comparing Energy Changes Then and Now," or a news article on a recent invention of yours that would help conserve energy. Then submit the article for publication. Sharing does help.

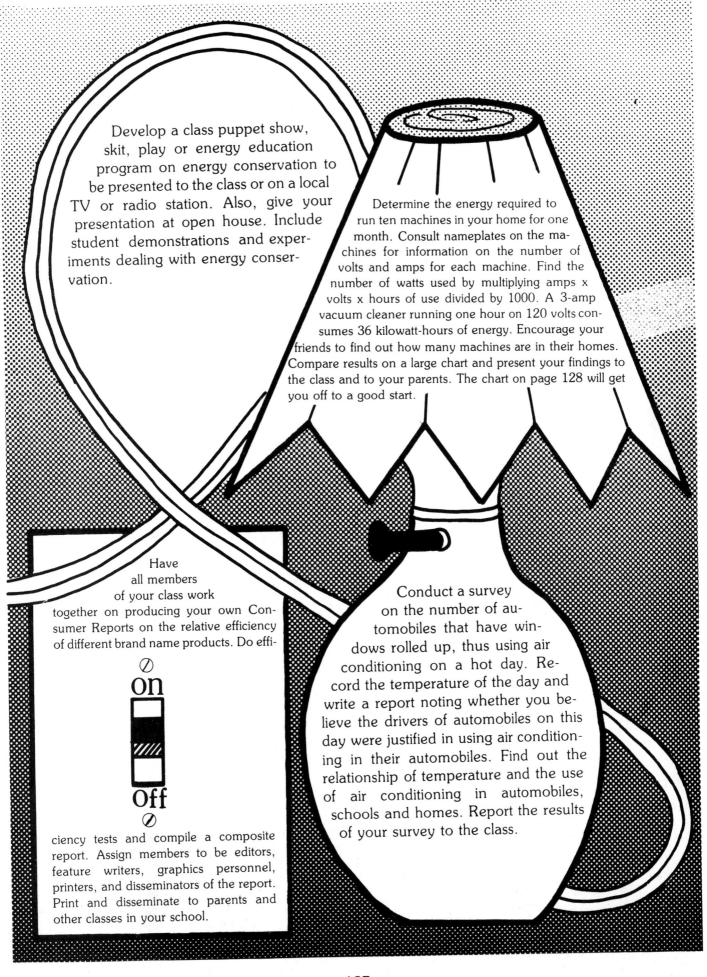

Develop a class puppet show, skit, play or energy education program on energy conservation to be presented to the class or on a local TV or radio station. Also, give your presentation at open house. Include student demonstrations and experiments dealing with energy conservation.

Determine the energy required to run ten machines in your home for one month. Consult nameplates on the machines for information on the number of volts and amps for each machine. Find the number of watts used by multiplying amps x volts x hours of use divided by 1000. A 3-amp vacuum cleaner running one hour on 120 volts consumes 36 kilowatt-hours of energy. Encourage your friends to find out how many machines are in their homes. Compare results on a large chart and present your findings to the class and to your parents. The chart on page 128 will get you off to a good start.

Have all members of your class work together on producing your own Consumer Reports on the relative efficiency of different brand name products. Do efficiency tests and compile a composite report. Assign members to be editors, feature writers, graphics personnel, printers, and disseminators of the report. Print and disseminate to parents and other classes in your school.

on

Off

Conduct a survey on the number of automobiles that have windows rolled up, thus using air conditioning on a hot day. Record the temperature of the day and write a report noting whether you believe the drivers of automobiles on this day were justified in using air conditioning in their automobiles. Find out the relationship of temperature and the use of air conditioning in automobiles, schools and homes. Report the results of your survey to the class.

Energy Crunch

Amps x Volts   x # of Hours ÷ 1000 =   Kilowatt-Hours

Total amounts of electrical energy consumed in kilowatts can be found by multiplying the current in amperes by the voltage in volts by the time in hours and dividing by 1000. Thus, a 3-amp vacuum cleaner running one hour on 120 volts consumes .36 kilowatt-hours of energy. Investigate the amount of total energy used by appliances in your house and school and complete the chart below. The first one is done for you. Then contact your local power company; find out the current rate per kilowatt-hour and calculate your monthly bill.

APPLIANCE	AMPERES (AMPS)	VOLTAGE (VOLTS)	TIME (HOURS)	TOTAL WATTS	TOTAL KILOWATT HOURS	PRICE PER KWH	TOTAL BILL
Vacuum Cleaner		120					
Sabre Saw		120					
Electric Frying Pan		120					
Blender		120					
Toaster		120					
Television		120					
Iron		120					
Clothes Dryer		120					
Elec. Popcorn Popper		120					

MY VERY OWN ENERGY CONTRACT

I, _____, hereby agree to sign this contract which represents an official
  Print Name

and legal document and to fulfill at least _____ of the prescribed activities below or those
                                             Number

suggested by my teacher on pages 124-128, in an effort to reduce energy consumption. By
doing these activities, I am charged with the responsibility to enter and proceed without hesitation into, and live in, a world that uses less energy. I am also hereby empowered with the
responsibility of encouraging the spread of energy conservation measures by lending my hands
in sharing energy conservation thoughts/ideas and hands-on activities with others throughout
the world.

_____   _____
Date   Signed by Student

_____   _____
Date   Signed by Teacher

_____   _____
Date   Signed by Witness

R|E|A|D

SOME SAMPLE ENERGY ACTIVITIES

	Date Started	Date Completed

I will:
* Contribute interesting articles and pictures about the energy crisis
  to a class bulletin board.
* Develop a list of ways that I plan to conserve energy in my home
  and school. I will staple my list to this contract and keep in my
  science folder.
* Design a poster that will encourage people to conserve energy. I
  will then display my poster in my home, school, and classroom.
* Discover a new possible source of energy similar to Duco Disco on
  page 98 or Going Further on page 66. I will identify my new
  source, the machinery used to collect and refine it, draw a picture
  of what it looks like, and make an ad to show why my product will
  help conserve energy.
* Write a letter to the President, my senator, representatives, governor and mayor expressing my concern about the energy crisis and
  offering some suggestions on what the world, nation, state, community, and individuals can do. I will also tell my representatives
  what my class is doing to help out.
* Collect aluminum cans, glass and paper for recycling.

* Test the quality of products such as those found on page 95, become more
  consumer aware and develop my own Consumer Reports as found on page 49.
* Other possible activities:

  1. _____

  2. _____

129

Some magnets  and electrical  discarded by electrical utilities

will lead you to the 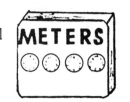 of understanding LINES OF FORCE in a

magnet. You will also need some *iron filings* (can be obtained free from a machine shop), a *piece of glass* and an *overhead projector*. Place magnets on overhead projector. Lay glass over magnets. Sprinkle iron filings onto glass using an old saltshaker for filings. What do you *see*? Draw a picture of what you see. Then switch position of magnets in different ways. Make a drawing of what you see. How will these lines of force help your motor run on the next page? You also can see how lines of force pick up filings by attaching an uninsulated wire to a dry cell and dipping the wire into the filings. How is this action similar to that of a crane in a junkyard? TIP: Be sure to save the dials on your meters as they can be used to study place value in mathematics and help you read your electric meter found in your home for activities on pages 124-129.

METER MAGNET

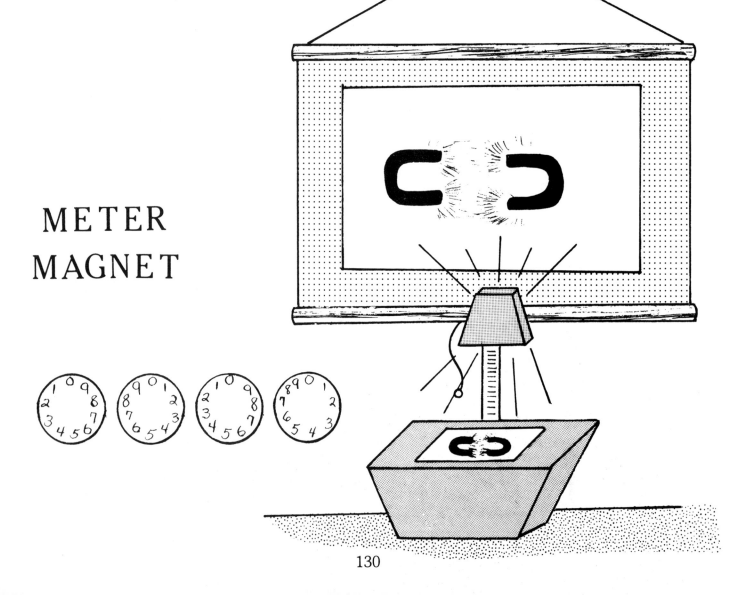

The magnets  that you used in METER MAGNET will lead you to the

of understanding how a MOTOR is made and how it works.

You will need a *piece of triple-wall cardboard* or *wood, thumbtacks,* some *wire,* and a *dry cell.* A motor is one magnet spinning inside another magnet. You found out in Meter Magic that anytime you have an electrical current you have a magnetic field. You will need to set up fields in your motor. Gouge out hole in triple-wall or wood and set magnet in hole. Make two support wires like this and attach to triple-wall or wood with thumbtacks.

Next, make a coil of wire like this.

Place coil of wire in supports. Hook up dry cell to supports. Hold magnet on top of coil. What happens? Why? Turn magnet 90°, 180°. What happens? Compare your motor to a real motor. Write about your findings in your science log. Add a color wheel to the ends of the coil. Can you make white light?

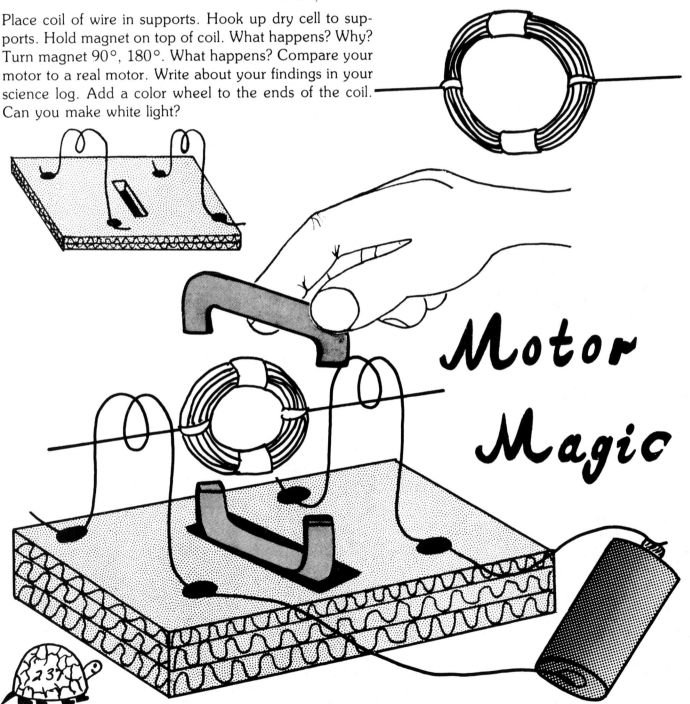

Motor Magic

Some paraffin   from a  will lead you to the

of understanding LIQUIDS and SOLIDS and may even lead you

into caves or to the depths of outer space. You will also need some *small aluminum pans, hot plate, pan of boiling water, kitchen kettle, tongs,* and *food coloring.* Melt wax in aluminum pan over pan of boiling water on hot plate. When all wax is melted, hold pan with tongs and plunge into cold water in kettle. What happens? Why? What shapes can you identify? Now, add food coloring to melted wax. Record your feelings in your science log and get ready for some exciting earth and space science activities to follow.

Changing Shapes

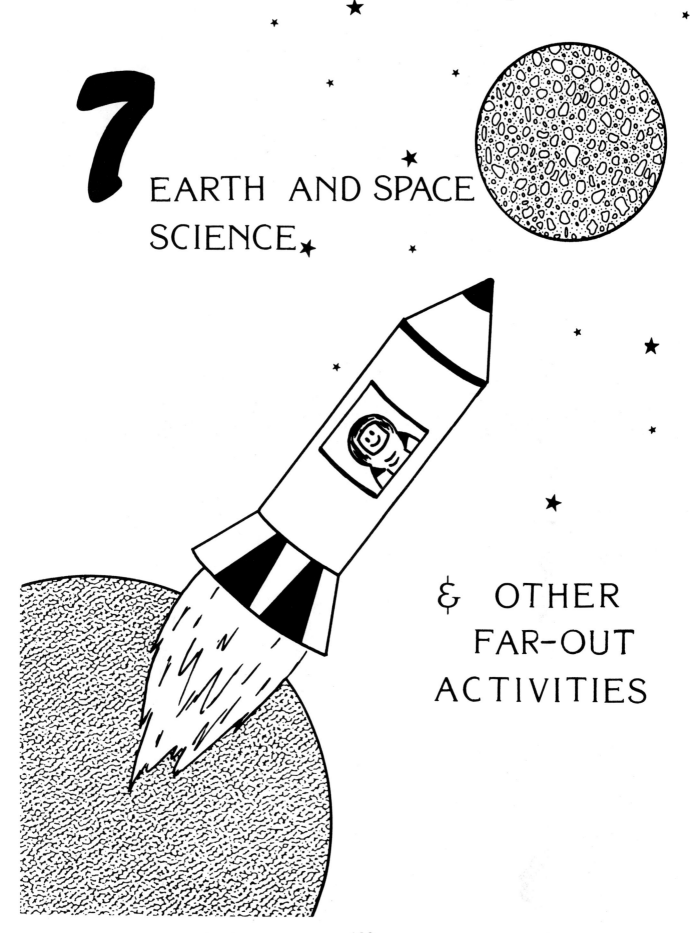

7

EARTH AND SPACE SCIENCE

& OTHER FAR-OUT ACTIVITIES

WEATHER WATCH

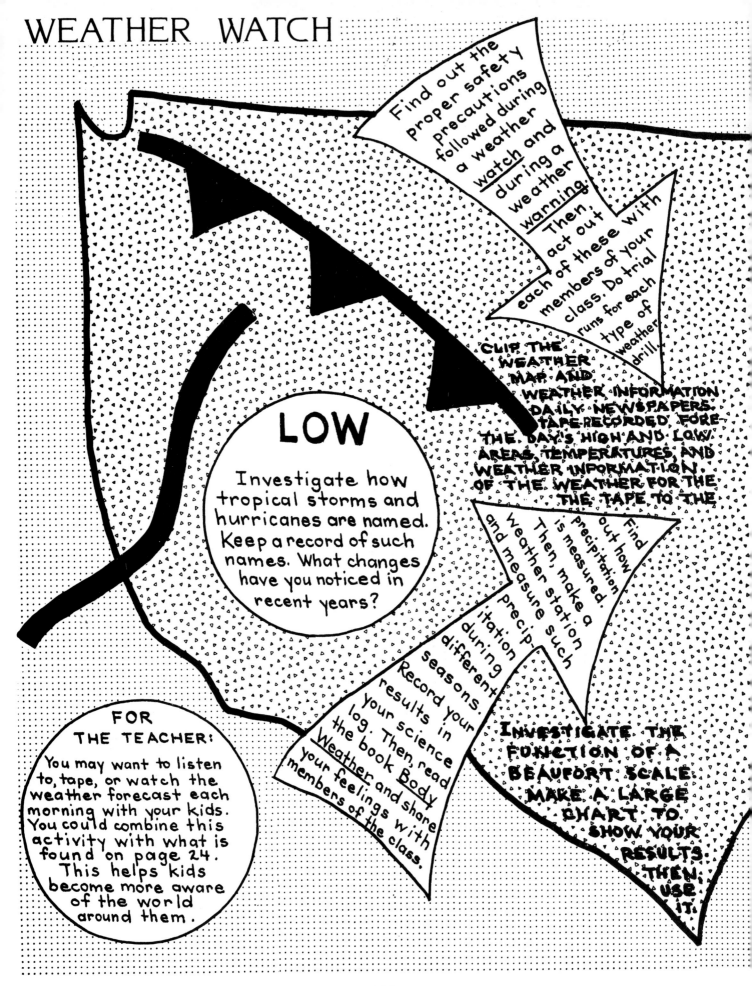

Find out the proper safety precautions followed during a weather watch and during a weather warning. Then, act out each of these with members of your class. Do trial runs for each type of weather drill.

CLIP THE WEATHER MAP AND WEATHER INFORMATION DAILY NEWSPAPERS. TAPE-RECORDED FORE- THE DAY'S HIGH AND LOW AREAS, TEMPERATURES, AND WEATHER INFORMATION OF THE WEATHER FOR THE THE TAPE TO THE

LOW

Investigate how tropical storms and hurricanes are named. Keep a record of such names. What changes have you noticed in recent years?

Find out how precipitation is measured. Then, make a weather station and measure such precipitation during different seasons. Record your results in your science log. Then, read the book *Weather* and share your feelings with members of the class.

INVESTIGATE THE FUNCTION OF A BEAUFORT SCALE. MAKE A LARGE CHART TO SHOW YOUR RESULTS. THEN, USE IT.

FOR THE TEACHER:

You may want to listen to, tape, or watch the weather forecast each morning with your kids. You could combine this activity with what is found on page 24. This helps kids become more aware of the world around them.

Investigate how satellites are used in predicting the weather. Report your results to the class.

Find a quiet spot where you will be alone and undisturbed for ten minutes. Close your eyes and become the rising air, a cold front or a tornado. Feel what these features would be like. Write a description of your experience and share it with members of your class.

LOW
Investigate steps you should take when a storm threatens your electric service. Simulate a radio alert, procedures followed for water and food storage, and living without electricity.

FROM MAKE A CAST OF PRESSURE RELATED MAKE YOUR PREDICTION NEXT TWO DAYS AND PLAY CLASS. THEN, FIND OUT HOW ACCURATE YOU WERE.

PAINT OR DRAW THE BASIC CLOUD TYPES AND NOTE WHAT KINDS OF WEATHER ARE RELATED TO EACH. NOTE APPROPRIATE SYMBOLS FOR EACH TYPE OF CLOUD.

Investigate how a hot air balloon works. Make one. Try it out.

Design a place mat that features all the weather terms and symbols. Then, have a meal and use your place mat.

Build a nephoscope and study its use in predicting the weather.

Investigate how clouds are formed. Then make your own cloud in a large jar and share your findings with members of your class.

HIGH
Do research to dispel such myths as "lightning does not strike the same place twice," and "an enclosed automobile is the safest place to be during a lightning and rainstorm." Study the relationship of steel belted tires to lightning in the latter case.

★ MY DAILY WEATHER RECORD

Use this handy daily weather record to record weather happenings for at least one month. You'll need four of these to finish your task.

WEEK NUMBER _____   NAME _____

Today's Date							
DAY OF WEEK	MONDAY	TUESDAY	WEDNESDAY	THURSDAY	FRIDAY	SATURDAY	SUNDAY
Time of Day							
Temperature: °F (°C)							
Wind Direction							
Wind Speed: mph (km/hr)							
Cloud Type							
Cloud Cover							
Precipitation: In (cm)							
Barometric Pressure: In (cm)							
Relative Humidity							
Dew Point: °F (°C)							
Air Pollution Index							
Air Pollution Range							
Major Air Pollutant							
Other							

MY FEELINGS:

_____

_____

_____

_____

A  from  will lead you to the

of developing a feeling for the WATER CYCLE. You also need a *cookie sheet, ice cubes, water, hot plate,* and *two chairs* or similar support.

Set up materials so they look like those below. Then, heat the water in the teakettle and closely observe what happens. How long does it take before you see something coming from the teakettle? Investigate the differences between steam and water vapor. What happens on the bottom of the cookie sheet? The three stages of the water cycle are:

1. _____
2. _____
3. _____

Study the relationship between the water cycle and the weather. Record your results in your science log.

P.S. How does a cold jar of lemonade on a hot summer day described in the preface relate to the water cycle?

*ACTIVITIES with TEMPERATURE

At which temperature does the following occur?

Drawing	Description	°F Temperature °C		
	SUNNY DAY			
	BAKING A CAKE			
	BODY Temperature			
	WATER BOILS			
	COLD WINTER DAY			
	WATER FREEZES			

138

Shady Deal

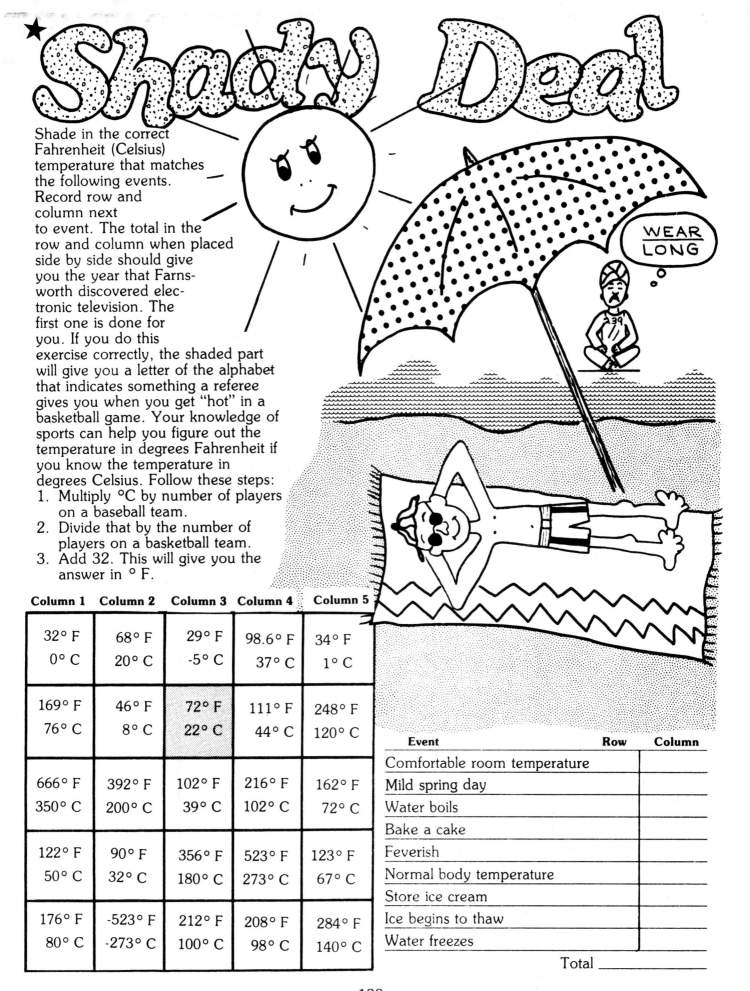

Shade in the correct Fahrenheit (Celsius) temperature that matches the following events. Record row and column next to event. The total in the row and column when placed side by side should give you the year that Farnsworth discovered electronic television. The first one is done for you. If you do this exercise correctly, the shaded part will give you a letter of the alphabet that indicates something a referee gives you when you get "hot" in a basketball game. Your knowledge of sports can help you figure out the temperature in degrees Fahrenheit if you know the temperature in degrees Celsius. Follow these steps:

1. Multiply °C by number of players on a baseball team.
2. Divide that by the number of players on a basketball team.
3. Add 32. This will give you the answer in ° F.

Column 1	Column 2	Column 3	Column 4	Column 5
32° F 0° C	68° F 20° C	29° F -5° C	98.6° F 37° C	34° F 1° C
169° F 76° C	46° F 8° C	72° F 22° C	111° F 44° C	248° F 120° C
666° F 350° C	392° F 200° C	102° F 39° C	216° F 102° C	162° F 72° C
122° F 50° C	90° F 32° C	356° F 180° C	523° F 273° C	123° F 67° C
176° F 80° C	-523° F -273° C	212° F 100° C	208° F 98° C	284° F 140° C

Event	Row	Column
Comfortable room temperature		
Mild spring day		
Water boils		
Bake a cake		
Feverish		
Normal body temperature		
Store ice cream		
Ice begins to thaw		
Water freezes		
Total		

139

A  cricket from a local  or from outdoors will

lead you to the of estimating TEMPERATURE.

During times when the thermometer is between 64° F (12° C) and 100° F (37° C), a cricket can help children estimate temperature. To determine the number of degrees of temperature, 20 should be added to the number of times the cricket chirps in 15 seconds. Some people think this is an old wives' tale, but we've had fun with it. Why not give it a try?

Cricket Chirp

A   record player  from  or home will lead you to the

of understanding the CORIOLIS EFFECT and the WEATHER. You will also need some *black construction paper* and a *piece of chalk*. Cut disc of construction paper about the size of turntable disc. Punch hole in center. Place on turntable. Turn on low speed. Have child try to make a straight line across construction paper disc while turntable is spinning. What happens? Notice the direction of the curve in the Northern Hemisphere. Right or left? Study how this affects our weather. Then carefully observe what direction, clockwise or counter clockwise, water spins when running down a sink. Will the direction be the same in the Southern Hemisphere? Write a pen pal in the Southern Hemisphere to verify your results (see NOTES page 237 for addresses). Share your results with the class on whether the direction of spin of water down a sink is a tall tale for people who live in the Northern or Southern Hemisphere or both.

SPECIAL EFFECTS

Metal  banding from a crate found near the loading dock or a local  will lead you to the of understanding

the FLIGHT OF PROJECTILES. You will also need *two scraps of wood, nails, clay,* a *large screw,* and *protractor.* Bend banding slightly into L shape and insert "L" end between two pieces of wood. Glue and nail wood together. Insert large screw into wood. Glue protractor vertically on side of catapult slightly toward front. Place ball of clay at tip of banding. Bend and release. Note how far ball of clay travels at each 10° mark. Make a record of your findings using the chart below. Graph your results. Then study how ancient warriors used the catapult. How does modern day weaponry differ? Make a record in your science log.

DISTANCE:		TRIAL 1		TRIAL 2		TRIAL 3		TRIAL 4	
		IN	CM	IN	CM	IN	CM	IN	CM
NUMBER of DEGREES	10°								
	20°								
	30°								
	40°								
	50°								
	60°								
	70°								
	80°								
	90°								
	100°								
	110°								
	120°								

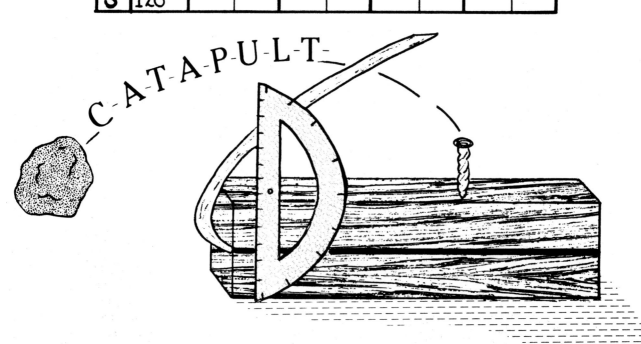

C-A-T-A-P-U-L-T

"BUT TEACHER: HOW, WHY, WHAT ?"

KIDS' QUESTIONS

These questions represent a few of the many questions youngsters of all ages have asked me while studying astronomy. How would you answer their questions? Better yet, what activities and materials could you provide youngsters with to help them answer their own questions? Give it a try. This will lead to even more questions.

Why do stars twinkle?

How does an astrolabe work? Can we make one?

What is an eclipse?

How is this space shuttle thing going in Alaska to work? Why don't people have sunlight during the winter?

What causes the northern lights?

Who are Leo, Venus, Aquarius and all those guys?

Why is the sun red sometimes?

Can I see Venus tonight?

What are sunspots and how are they caused?

Where do astronauts go to the bathroom while they're in space?

Why do I see only parts of the moon sometimes and other times I see all of it?

What's a sundial and how does it work? Can we make one?

What are black holes?

Who is Roy G. Biv?

Why do astronauts float around in their cabins?

What's a meteor?

What's an "analemma?"

Is there life in outer space?

How come some people think there are UFO's flying around?

What are sunspots?

What's the Big Dipper?

What causes a rainbow?

Why does the sun sometimes look really big and then really small?

What's the best way I can find the North Star?

143

LOOK TO

Read the *Farmer's Almanac* for current astronomy information. Make a report to the class on your findings.

Keep your horoscope for several months. Is it accurate? Find out all the signs of members of your class.

Investigate the significance of Stonehenge and relate it to your sundial found on page 154.

Clip and study the horoscope section of your local newspaper. What is your sign? Are horoscopes accurate in predicting events?

Study black holes, white dwarfs, red giants, quasars, and neutron stars. What's unique about each of these? Record your findings in your science log.

Build a model solar system to scale. Pages 148-9 will help you with this task.

Construct an eclipse board to show the relative positions of the sun, earth, and moon at the times of a solar and lunar eclipse. Repeat for times of new moon, first quarter, last quarter, and full moon phases of the moon.

THE SKY

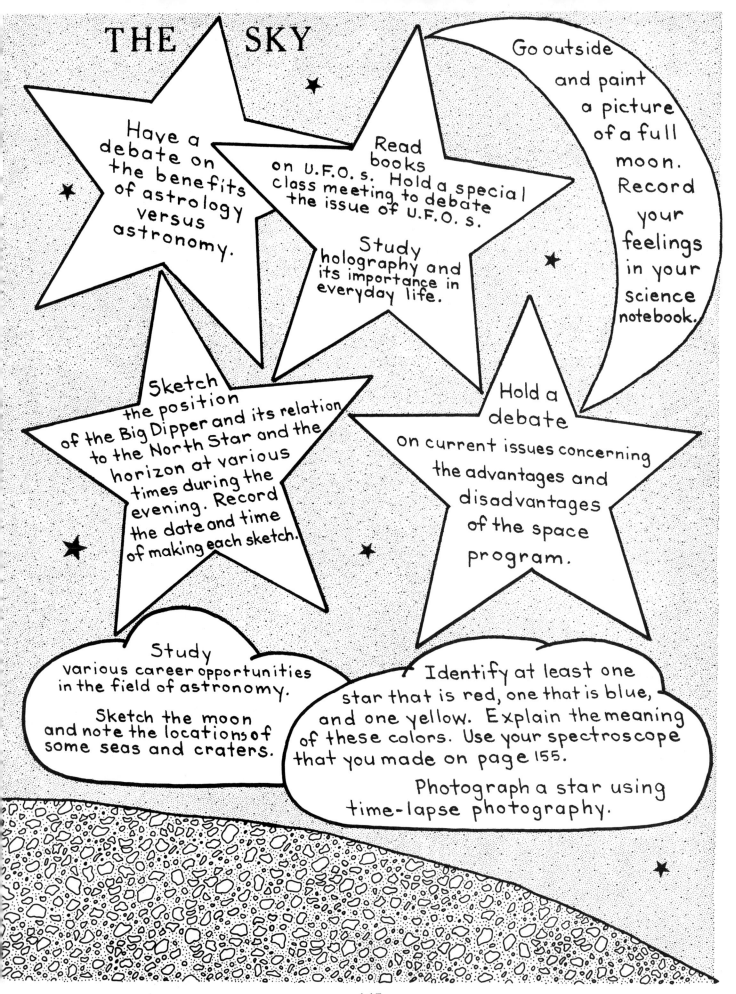

Have a debate on the benefits of astrology versus astronomy.

Read books on U.F.O.s. Hold a special class meeting to debate the issue of U.F.O.s.

Study holography and its importance in everyday life.

Go outside and paint a picture of a full moon. Record your feelings in your science notebook.

Sketch the position of the Big Dipper and its relation to the North Star and the horizon at various times during the evening. Record the date and time of making each sketch.

Hold a debate on current issues concerning the advantages and disadvantages of the space program.

Study various career opportunities in the field of astronomy.

Sketch the moon and note the locations of some seas and craters.

Identify at least one star that is red, one that is blue, and one yellow. Explain the meaning of these colors. Use your spectroscope that you made on page 155.

Photograph a star using time-lapse photography.

Some polyethylene plastic film from a  will lead you to

the  of understanding the depths of SPACE. Obtain two 6

mil 10′ × 25′ (3 m × 8 m) *sheets of Visqueen plastic* or *polyethylene film* from a building supplier. Fold the plastic sheets in half and tape edges with clear tape. Cut a 24″ (60 cm) slit at the fold for an entrance. Make a 24″ (60 cm) square hole in one end and attach an additional piece of plastic to feed the flow of air from a 3-speed electric fan into the bubble. Tape plastic to fan and inflate bubble. Enter bubble and project celestial bodies onto walls and ceiling of planetarium using flashlights (see page 152) or slide projectors. Observe from inside and outside of bubble. Make large sketches of what you see. Then add cardboard fins to the outside of bubble to make a spaceship. Take an imaginary trip to outer space like that of *Pioneer 10* and *11* on page 179 or *Voyager* on page 182. Play your favorite space music to accompany you on your journey. Record your feelings in your science log especially if you encounter any black holes.

SPACE BUBBLE:
A FAR-OUT PLACE

Some  construction paper or tagboard from  will lead you

to the of making a SOLAR MOBILE that balances. You will also need some *pieces of*

doweling, tree branch, or *broom handle, markers, paper punch, string,* and *scissors.* Cut out each planet according to approximate diameter found on page 149 although each piece may be many times larger. Label and laminate. Punch hole in each and hang in order of planets from doweling. Can you make all planets balance and function as a moveable solar system? Share your model with the class. What would happen if you turned on an electric fan to spin your planets in orbit? Would you go in orbit to other planets? What would you weigh? Here's a chart that will help you with your task.

SOLAR   MOBILE

Interplanetary Weight Chart

IF YOUR EARTH WEIGHT IS –	You Would Weigh on — (to the nearest pound) (Divide by 2.2 for Kilograms)				
	MOON	SUN	VENUS	MARS	JUPITER
50 lb.	8	1395	43	19	132
60 lb.	10	1673	51	23	159
70 lb.	11	1952	60	27	185
80 lb.	13	2231	68	30	211
90 lb.	14	2510	77	34	238
100 lb.	16	2789	85	38	264
110 lb.	18	3068	94	42	290
120 lb.	19	3347	102	46	317
130 lb.	21	3626	111	49	343
140 lb.	22	3905	119	53	370
150 lb.	23	4184	128	57	396
160 lb.	25	4462	136	61	422

Some construction , tagboard or cardboard from  will

lead you to the of making a MODEL SOLAR SYSTEM to scale that shows the

approximate SIZE and DISTANCE of planets compared to the size of the sun and distance from the sun. You will also need some *rulers, scissors, string, pencils, paper punch,* and *wire* long enough to reach across the room. Cut out a circle of tagboard for each planet according to size found on the next page. Label planet. Laminate. Punch hole in each and string on wire. The sun is so large, 54″, so you may want to attach it to wall directly at end of wire. Then space out each planet according to scale based on the approximate distance of orbit from sun. Use the chart on the opposite page. NOTE: Some teachers have blown up balloons to simulate actual sizes of the planets. Others have used the solar system as a record keeping system for reading books. For example, if a child reads five books and does a creative activity with each, he moves to the planet Mercury, etc.

	SIZE (diameter)				DISTANCE of Orbit from Sun				
	IN	CM	MILES	KILOMETERS	IN	CM	MILES	KILOMETERS	AU
SUN	54	135	864,000	1,380,000					
MERCURY	$\frac{1}{6}$	0.4	3,020	5,030	2	5	31,000,000	49,600,000	0.3
VENUS	$\frac{1}{2}$	1	7,600	12,700	4	10	62,000,000	99,200,000	0.6
EARTH	$\frac{1}{2}$	1	7,918	13,197	6	15	93,000,000	148,800,000	1
MOON	$\frac{1}{8}$	0.3	2,000	3,200	6.2	15.5	93,240,000	149,184,000	1
MARS	$\frac{1}{4}$	0.5	4,180	6,970	9	22.5	140,000,000	223,200,000	1.5
JUPITER	$5\frac{1}{2}$	14	86,000	143,000	30	75	465,000,000	744,000,000	5
SATURN	$4\frac{1}{2}$	11	70,000	117,200	60	150	930,000,000	1,448,000,000	10
URANUS	4	10	30,000	50,000	120	300	1,860,000,000	2,976,000,000	20
NEPTUNE	$2\frac{1}{4}$	7	28,000	47,000	180	450	2,790,000,000	4,752,000,000	30
PLUTO	$\frac{1}{8}$	0.3	2,000	3,200	240	600	3,720,000,000	5,952,000,000	40

Some **Pizza Wheels** from a **Pizza Parlor** will lead you to the **GOAL**

of understanding vast scale distances between the planets in the SOLAR SYSTEM. You will also need some *string, tubes* or *rolls* (fish line rolls) and a *paper punch*. Obtain pizza wheels for each planet and label with name of planet. Attach length of string to each planet (see below). Identify two students per planet. Attach roll of string to each planet. Students walk off appropriate distance unraveling string to show model solar system. Then continue your study by doing Scientific Notation on page 151. "Pluto, where are you?" "Inside the orbit of Neptune until the year 1999."

150

• GOAL

science X-PERT using SCIENTIFIC NOTATION. This will help you discover vast distances between the PLANETS and the SUN in our solar system. A number is expressed in scientific notation if it is a product of a number between 1 and 10 and a power of 10. For example, 176830 is written as 1.7683×10^5. Scientific notation is used to express very large and small numbers. The first one is already done for you below.

Complete the chart below changing measurements by using scientific notation.

SCIENTIFIC NOTATION

PLANET	Distance of Orbit From Sun in Miles	Distance of Orbit From Sun in Kilometers	Astronomical Units 1 Au = 93,000,000 Miles	Scientific Notation of Orbit in Miles	Scientific Notation of Orbit in Kilometers	Approximate Diameter of Planet in Miles	Approximate Diameter of Planet in Kilometers	Scientific Notation of Diameter of Planet in Miles	Scientific Notation of Diameter of Planet in Kilometers
MERCURY	31,000,000	49,600,000	.3	3.1×10^7	4.96×10^7	3,000	5,000	3×10^3	5×10^3
VENUS	62,000,000	99,200,000	.6			7,600	12,700		
EARTH	93,000,000	148,000,000	1.0			8,000	13,000		
MARS	140,000,000	223,200,000	1.5			4,200	7,700		
JUPITER	465,000,000	744,000,000	5			86,000	143,000		
SATURN	930,000,000	1,448,000,000	10			70,000	117,000		
URANUS	1,860,000,000	2,976,000,000	20			30,000	50,000		
NEPTUNE	2,790,000,000	4,752,000,000	30			28,000	47,000		
PLUTO	3,720,000,000	5,952,000,000	40			8,000	13,000		

A thick cardboard tube from a  will lead you to the

of identifying the CONSTELLATIONS. You will also need a *flashlight, black construction paper, compass* or *pins* and some *flat black paint.*

Using a pin point of a compass or different sized nails for various magnitudes, punch out constellation on black construction paper. Place over end of tube. Paint inside of tube black. Insert flashlight into other end of tube and project constellation onto a dark surface. Learn as many constellations as possible. Make constellation cards/booklets and share it with members of the class. TIP: A Pringle's can with the constellation on one end and a black paper with a small hole mounted on the other end to look through also works well for this activity. Make a record of what you see.

TUBE CONSTELLATIONS

Thick opaque plastic can be purchased from various outlets for use in constellation study. Punch constellations using a pin or different sized nails and place on overhead to project night sky on a screen in the classroom.

Some  from an

will lead you to understanding SEASONAL CHANGES caused by the angle of the sun's rays.

You will also need some *grid paper, glue, flashlight,* and *astrolabe* (see page 157). Bend a piece of cardboard to make a square tube 1″ (2.5 cm²) in cross section and 13″ (32 cm) in length. Secure a piece of very stiff cardboard and cut a strip 9″ (23 cm) long and 1″ (2.5 cm) wide. Paste this to one side of the tube with 6″ (25 cm) extending. Rest the end of the stiff cardboard on the table and incline the tube at an angle of about 25 degrees. Hold a flashlight at the upper end of the tube and mark off the area on the table that is covered by the light going through the tube.

Repeat experiment with tube at 15° angle and again with the tube vertically. Compare the size of the 3 lighted areas and determine the area of each. Is the amount of heat and light received from the sun greater when the rays are slanting or direct. What season would it be if the rays were direct? Record your results in your science log. TIP: Use grid paper on pages 244 and 246 to determine surface area of the sun's rays.

In the Spotlight

 from a large  box from an  will lead

you to the  of developing a feeling for TELLING TIME. You will

also need a *stick* or *piece of doweling* and some *clear Con-Tact paper*.

Glue three sheets of single-layered cardboard from the box together. Cut hole in the center and insert stick or doweling in a vertical position. Cover the base with clear Con-Tact paper. Orient sundial facing south. At 30-minute intervals go outside and mark the sun's shadow on the cardboard. Draw lines using erasable felt-tipped pens. Reuse sundial often but remember *never* to look directly at the sun for any reason. Record the results of your findings on a large chart. Then study Stonehenge.

What Time Is It?

A  **SHOE BOX** from a **SHOE STORE** will lead you to the  **GOAL** ★

of understanding the VISIBLE LIGHT SPECTRUM. You will also need some *flat black tempera paint, diffraction grating, a double-edged razor blade,* and some *tape.* The name ROY G. BIV is often used as a device to learn the colors of the spectrum: red, orange, yellow, green, blue, indigo and violet. You can learn a great deal about a celestial body by its spectra. Take a shoe box and paint the inside with flat black tempera paint to reduce reflections. Cut a 1″ (2.5 cm) square hole in the center of each end of the box. Tape diffraction grating (see page 224) inside the box covering one of the holes. Cut a 2″ (5 cm) square piece of cardboard with a ¼″ (6 mm) slit 1″ (2.5 cm) long. Cut a double-edged razor blade in half lengthwise and tape the razor blade's edges to the mounting leaving a gap of about the thickness of a note card between the blades. Tape to end of shoe box. Fasten lid to box with tape. Observe spectra of incandescent lights, fluorescent lights, street lights, neon signs, etc. Record your observations in your science log. NOTE: Tubes described on page 39 also work well for this. You may also want to try a Pringle's can for this activity.

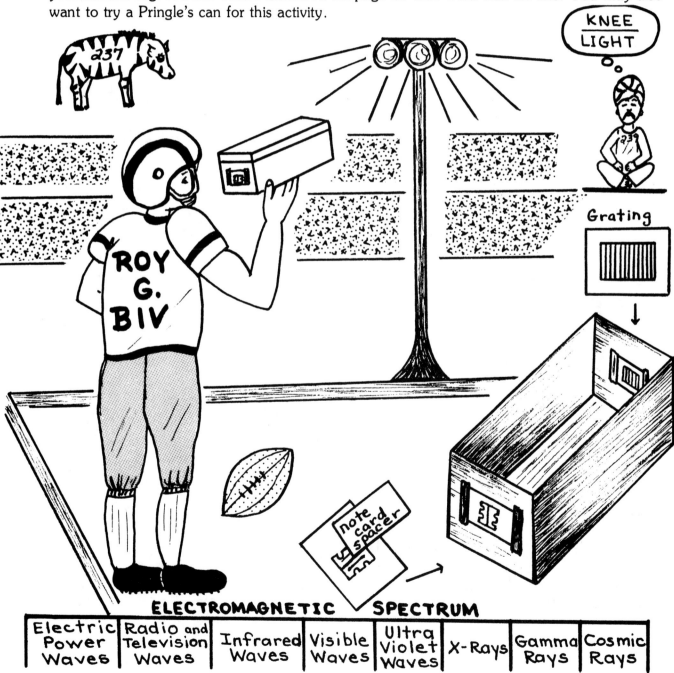

ELECTROMAGNETIC SPECTRUM

Electric Power Waves	Radio and Television Waves	Infrared Waves	Visible Waves	Ultra Violet Waves	X-Rays	Gamma Rays	Cosmic Rays

A feather  from a bird will lead you to the

of meeting ROY G. BIV and understanding the VISIBLE LIGHT SPECTRUM. Merely hold feather up to sun and look through feather. DO NOT LOOK DIRECTLY at the sun with your eyes. What do you see? Make a sketch of what you saw. Place feather under microscope and and make a sketch of what you see. Next, move with your feather. Hold feather above your head and time how long it takes it to fall to the floor. Catch the feather with your hand (back of hand also), your nose, your foot, etc. How long can you keep the feather in the air by blowing on it? Can you drop the feather, spin around, yet still catch the feather? Make a study of the different types of feathers and where they come from. Enter your findings in your science log. Make sure you find out what hackle feathers are. Then write a story using a feather. See page 81 for some real bird-watching activities.

A Feather Spectrum

SIOGUHTT

Red Orange Yellow Green Blue Indigo Violet

239

237

156

A  from  or school will lead you to the

of developing an understanding about CELESTIAL BODIES while building and then using an ASTROLABE. You will need a *piece of string*, a *nut* or *washer*, and a *straw*. Mount straw along edge of protractor or half circle of stiff cardboard. Hang piece of string with nut or washer attached, from the center of astrolabe. Mark number of degrees. Sight celestial body through straw. Press string against the astrolabe being careful not to let string stick to tape. Read the number of degrees the celestial body is above the horizon on the astrolabe. Be sure to subtract from 90° as you are using the protractor upside down. Sight the moon every evening for at least one month. Carefully make sketches noting the moon's size, shape and position. Make a large chart for each evening's moon and display in the hall of your school for others to see. (An old computer print-out sheet works well for each student to record his log of sketches and findings. See page 48.) See page 153 for related activity.

Where Are You, Moon?

Moon Walk and Talk
(teacher page)

This simulated activity will lead you and your children to the goal of increasing COMMUNICATION, improving DECISION MAKING, and learning a great deal about the moon and themselves. Give each student a copy of page 159. Read story aloud to the class. Have each individual class member rank order the importance of each item. Record ranking on page 159. Then divide the class into groups of four. Give each group one blank sheet. Tell each group to develop a procedure to rank order the importance of each item. Avoid arguing. Stress importance of group decision making. Each group must develop one and only one list. Then compare the list from each group with the list developed by NASA below. Let each individual class member and each group find out how much they agree/disagree with NASA. Write a letter to NASA telling about your results. You may also want to suggest future projects for NASA's Space Shuttle and flights to other planets and other solar systems. Then begin your study of the moon found on page 157.

WHAT NASA SAYS

Ranking	Reason for Ranking
15	Little or no use on moon
4	Supply daily food requirements
6	Useful in tying injured together, help in climbing
8	Shelter against sun's rays
13	Useful only if party landed on dark side
11	Self-propulsion devices could be made from them
12	Food, mixed with water for drinking
1	Fills respiration requirement
3	One of principal means of finding directions
9	CO_2 bottles for self-propulsion across chasms, etc.
14	Probably no magnetized poles, thus, useless
2	Replenishes loss by sweating, etc.
10	Distress call when line of sight possible
7	Oral pills of injection medicine valuable
5	Distress signal transmitter, possible communication with mother ship

Your students will suggest many interesting projects. For a list of student suggested projects already carried out, write to the address below. Anyone for Anabella?

National Aeronautics and
  Space Administration
Community Services and
  Education Branch
  (LFG-9)
Washington, D.C. 20546

OR

400 Maryland Avenue, S.W.
Washington, D.C.

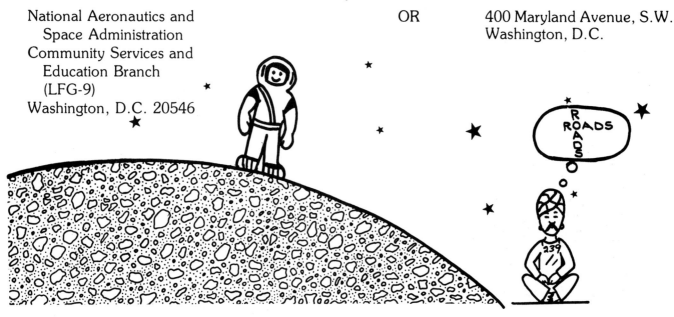

Moon Walk and Talk ★
(student page)

You are a member of the moon space crew originally scheduled to rendezvous with a mother ship on the lighted surface of the moon. Due to mechanical difficulties, however, your ship was forced to land at a spot some 200 miles (320 km) from the rendezvous point. During reentry and landing, much of the equipment aboard was damaged, and because survival depends on reaching the mother ship, the most critical items available must be chosen for the 200-mile (320 km) trip. On this sheet of paper are listed the 15 items left intact and undamaged after landing. Your task is to rank order them in terms of their importance for your crew in allowing them to reach the rendezvous point. Place the number 1 by the most important and so on through 15, the least important.

Undamaged Items	My Ranking	Group Ranking	NASA Ranking	Number Difference from NASA	
				My Difference	Group Difference
Box of matches	___	___	___	___	___
Food concentrates	___	___	___	___	___
50 feet of nylon rope	___	___	___	___	___
Parachute silk	___	___	___	___	___
Portable heating unit	___	___	___	___	___
Two 45-calibre pistols	___	___	___	___	___
One case of dehydrated milk	___	___	___	___	___
Two 100 lb. tanks of oxygen	___	___	___	___	___
Stellar map (of moon's constellations)	___	___	___	___	___
Life raft	___	___	___	___	___
Magnetic compass	___	___	___	___	___
5 gallons of water	___	___	___	___	___
Signal flares	___	___	___	___	___
First aid kit containing injection needles	___	___	___	___	___
Solar-powered FM receiver-transmitter	___	___	___	___	___
				MY TOTAL Difference from NASA	GROUP TOTAL Difference from NASA
				___	___

An  egg from  will lead you to the

of understanding VELOCITY and ACCELERATION. For your gear, you will need a *cardboard box, junk packing material* and *scraps,* and a *stopwatch* or *wristwatch* with a second hand. Flight plan: This is a simulated landing on the moon. The student is in the capsule (egg) and must design a craft (box) that will allow him to land safely on the moon. The mission is successful if the student can design a craft that can be dropped from the top of the school building and land without the egg inside breaking. Velocities of all the crafts in the class should be calculated by measuring height of school and time it takes to land. An average velocity for all crafts should also be found. Record the weight (mass) of each craft in pounds (grams or kilograms) and the acceleration in ft/per/sec (m/per/sec) in the handy chart found on the next page.

Look around for other places from which to drop your craft. How about the top of the slide or the fire escape, etc.? What would happen if the craft was dropped from the tallest building you could find? What would your success ratio be if you dropped your craft from an airplane? One teacher made a video tape of this experience. Good luck in your mission.

EGG-CELERATION

STUDENT NAME	LANDED SAFELY (YES-NO)	HEIGHT FROM WHICH CRAFT IS DROPPED in FEET (METERS)	WEIGHT OF CRAFT in POUNDS (GRAMS or KILOGRAMS)	TIME of DESCENT in SECONDS	VELOCITY in FT/SEC (M/S)	ACCELERATION in FT/SEC^2 (M/S^2)

EGG-CELERATION RECORD SHEET

This puzzle is really a piece of the moon. Observe carefully. It clearly shows craters and valleys. Your task is to take the digging apparatus on the moon rover and section this part of the moon into five equal sections of identical size and shape. Can you do it? Puzzles like this are fun and require your mind to stretch a bit. Consider all the possibilities. Making four cuts will help you unlock this puzzle. Share with your friends by studying the composition of the moon and its features. Be sure to observe carefully and find out why there are no real mares on the dark side of the moon. Compare the gravitational pull and the temperature of both the moon and the earth when they were being formed, and this will help you develop a theory as to why there are no mares on the non-earth side of the moon.

Some scrap pieces of **Cardboard** or triple-wall from a lumber yard or appliance store will lead you to the **GOAL** of understanding the PHASES of the MOON.

You'll also need some *black and white latex paint* and some *magnets* if you have them. The following phases of the moon can be made from scrap pieces of wood, cardboard or triple-wall. Make 8 equal-sized circles and one ring slightly larger than the circles. Paint white and black as shown below.

Attach magnet to back of each piece. Have children encircle the correct phase of moon using ring. Magnetic strips can also be attached to the back of each piece so pieces will adhere to metal on wall or board. Be sure to do Where Are You, Moon? found on page 157. Keep accurate records of your results in your science log or on computerized booklets on page 48. NOTE: Pizza wheels also work well for this activity.

Some rocks  from a field will lead you to the GOAL of learning about

rocks

Make some rock jewelry.

Join a local rock hound club. Have a rock hound come to speak to your class.

Read the Lapidary Journal, Rock and Gem, and Gems and Minerals for ideas.

Develop a pen pal program and exchange rocks with students from other cities, states, and countries. See page 169 for ideas.

The April 1979 issue of Lapidary Journal contains a list of over 1,000 rock clubs by city within different states in the United States.

Develop a pet rock club and show your wares.

Go to a quarry and get some rocks or dig some fossils. Then, make a collection of these for the classroom.

Do a rock sculpture.

Rocky Ideas

Take a rock hunting trip to a stream or river bank where rocks are being cut to build a road. Take your camera along and take pictures. Look in waste areas for discarded mineral material and unusual rocks for the classroom.

Visit a local rock shop. Identify rock materials that could be used in your class. Ask for samples.

Develop bulletin boards or interest centers that feature these questions:
a. Where do rocks come from?
b. What can you do with rocks?
c. How are rocks used in making things outdoors?
d. How are rocks used in things indoors?
e. What rocks are we using in our classrooms?
f. What rocks are used in making jewelry?
g. What are your favorite rock words?

Visit a natural history museum and study different eras related to rock formation.

Have children develop an interest center on rocks found at home, books about rocks, rock pictures, rock notebooks, rock music, etc.

Borrow a rock tumbler and tumble some rocks that children have found.

Integrate a study of rocks with arts and crafts by making jewelry, paperweights, mosaics, book ends, decorated rock boxes and natural rock sculptures.

STRETCH TO

HOW MOUNTAINS ARE FORMED →
HOW VOLCANOES ARE FORMED → PRECIOUS
STONES, DIAMONDS, JEWELRY → FAMOUS SCULPTURES
AND SCULPTORS → COAL MINING → CLIFF
DWELLERS → SALT → CONTOUR MAP
MAKING → EARTHQUAKES → MOON ROCKS
→ DESERTS → PETRIFIED WOOD → SHALE
OIL → ARCHEOLOGY → INDIAN
ARROWHEADS → ERRATICS → URANIUM
→ ROCK ARCHITECTURE, ETC.

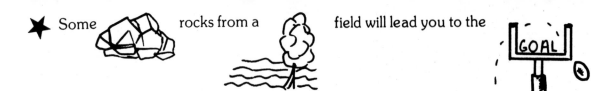

★ Some ✦ rocks from a ✦ field will lead you to the ✦ GOAL

of determining the mass, volume, and density of ROCKS. You will also need a *balance* and a *graduated cylinder* made from a bottle. Using a triple beam balance and an assortment of rock and mineral specimens, determine the mass of each specimen to the nearest tenth of a gram and record your results in the chart. Next, determine the volume of each specimen by using the water displacement method. Read the water level (at bottom of meniscus) in a graduated cylinder. Next, put a rock hanging from a string into the graduated cylinder and record the volume of displacement in cubic centimeters (milliliters). (If specimen floats, attach a sinker until specimen sinks, then record volume.) Find density (d) of each specimen by dividing the volume (v) into the mass (m). Record your results on a classroom chart or bulletin board using as many specimens as you can find. TIP: Use graduated cylinder (page 45) and the balance and weight you made on page 41 for this activity. Also, use My Rock Chart on page 172 for further investigation.

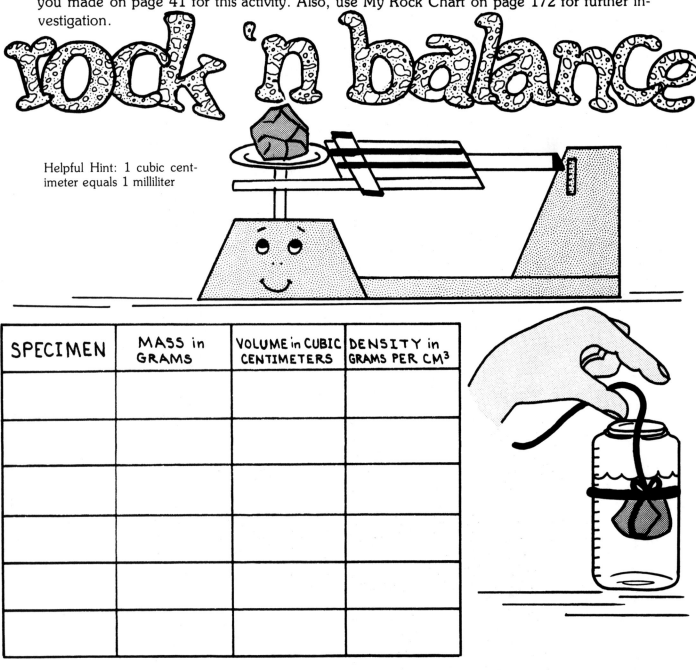

rock 'n balance

Helpful Hint: 1 cubic centimeter equals 1 milliliter

SPECIMEN	MASS in GRAMS	VOLUME in CUBIC CENTIMETERS	DENSITY in GRAMS PER CM³

Some rocks from a nearby  field will lead you to the

of CLASSIFYING ROCKS according to size. You will need some *rocks*, a *tape measure, ruler*, a *caliper* if you have one handy and some *tongue depressors*.

Each student should gather at least three rocks of different sizes. Have the class line up all their rocks in a row outdoors, from largest to smallest. Let students fill in any gaps with sizes that are missing. Have students print name on tongue depressors and stick depressor into ground by rock. Then ask them if tiny pebbles should be included. Are sand grains pieces of rock? Then label each rock according to the following and group the rocks according to size.

Boulders—More than 10″ (25 cm) across
Cobbles—2.5″ (6 cm) to 10″ (25) across
Pebbles—1/4″ (0.4 cm) to 2.5″ (6 cm) across
Granules—1/8″ (0.2 cm) to 1/4″ (0.4 cm) across
Sand—Up to 1/8″ (0.2 cm) across

TIP: See page 40, as small item organizers work well for this activity involving very small stones.

SIZING UP ROCKS

Some  from  will lead you to the  of CRYSTAL

GROWING. You will also need some *water, salt, ammonia,* a *glass* or *metal container,* and *Little Boy Bluing.*

Mix together:
1. 6 tablespoons (90 mL) of ammonia
2. 6 tablespoons (90 mL) of water
3. 6 tablespoons (90 mL) of salt
4. 6 tablespoons (90 mL) of Little Boy Bluing

crystal

Pour mixture over coal or charcoal. Add food coloring or ink. Also try adding water and sticks and perhaps a tree branch to see what happens. You may want to try using a spray bottle to spray above mixture over coal each day. Alum also works well for this activity. Record your results by making a painting of your findings.

garden

P.S. Try forming crystals using salt dissolved in water. Put a string between two containers of salt water and have crystals crawl along string. Study the designs made by crystals and the shapes of the crystals. What geometric patterns do you see? Use a stereogram book of crystals for your investigation. Record your results in your science log.

Some rocks that your students have collected will lead you to the

of developing an INTERDISCIPLINARY ROCK EXCHANGE activity with other students in your state and the United States. You will also need several large sheets of *triple-wall* or *cardboard*, a *map* of your city, a *United States map*, some *glue, string* and *thumbtacks* or *cup hooks.* Glue maps to triple-wall or cardboard. Screw in cup hooks. Hang from ceiling. Have each student bring in a small rock that he would like to exchange with a friend. Write a letter to a friend. Send rock. When friend responds, glue your friend's small rock to map where rock came from and string a string from the city of rock pal to your city. Clip correspondence to string. Conduct a study of your new rock (see page 172). Include information regarding its name, weight, location found, etc. Then send a picture of yourself and your rock activity to your new-found rock pal.

See me for some information about pen pal possibilities.

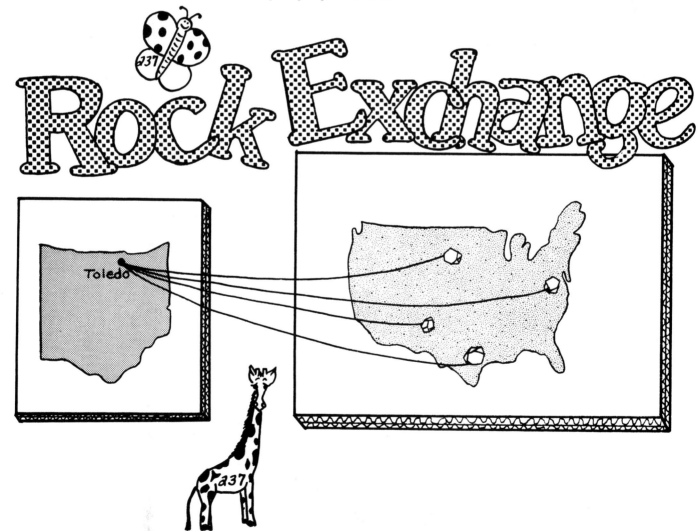

169

A long sturdy flower box [image: box] from a [image: FLOWER SHOP] will lead you to the [image: GOAL basket]

of understanding how a STREAM TABLE can be used to

study GEOLOGICAL FEATURES. You'll also need a few plastic *buckets* from restaurants, *rubber tubing, baby bottle nipple* from a hospital, *window screen, food coloring, sand,* several *cardboard boxes* and a *protractor*.

Line cardboard box with plastic. Cut hole in end of box and insert nipple. Place screen in front of nipple. Attach rubber tubing to nipple to drain water into bucket. Hook other tubing to source of running water or put into bucket of water to act as siphon. Attach protractor to box (guttering from home also works well) or gutter with plumb line to note degree of slope. Your setup may look like this:

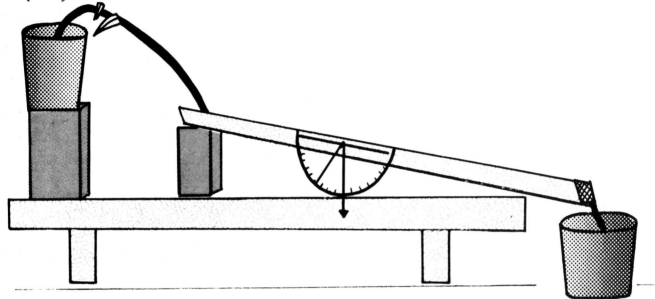

Mark off the distance in inches (cm) of the path from start to finish. Slant stream table at 3°, 6°, and 9°, etc. Time how long it takes a drop of food coloring to go down the stream. Find the average velocity in in/s (cm/s) for each trail at different slope angles. Record your data in a large chart like the one found on the next page. Then graph your results. What can be said about the relationship between slope and velocity of a stream? Now try a piece of cork or a drop of glue instead of the food coloring.

STREAM TABLE

170

STREAM TABLE RECORD SHEET

SLOPE IN DEGREES	TRIAL ONE IN SECONDS	TRIAL TWO IN SECONDS	TRIAL THREE IN SECONDS	AVERAGE TIME IN SECONDS	AVERAGE VELOCITY IN IN/S(CM/S)
3°					
6°					
9°					
12°					
15°					

VARIATIONS: Will a cork make the trip faster than a drop of food coloring? Design your own boat to be used in the stream table. What is its average velocity in in/s (cm/s)? Next, fill stream table with water and time how long it takes a fish to swim upstream. Study pollution. Empty stream table. Study geological features by using simple materials, e.g., bury an ice cube in the sand. Allow to melt. The result is a sinkhole. Here are some other features to study: *channel, valley, basin, meandering stream, oxbow lake, pond, flood plain, alluvial fans, karst, wadie, mesa, butte, erratic boulders, drumlins, eskers and kames.* Can you show contour farming? Carlsbad Caverns? Set up the Mississippi River. How many of your friends live west and east of the Mississippi River from your Rock Exchange on page 169.

MY ROCK CHART

ROCK	COLOR dry	COLOR wet	SHADE	WEIGHT	LAYERS	TEXTURE rough smooth	WRITES yes no	SHINY or DULL	CRYSTALS	VINEGAR ADDED	MOHS'* RATING	SPECIFIC GRAVITY	OTHER
A													
B													
C													
D													
E													

*MOHS' SCALE OF RELATIVE HARDNESS

MATERIAL	WHAT IT WILL DO	Rating
TALC	so soft it's used for talcum powder	1
GYPSUM	a fingernail will scratch it	2
CALCITE	a copper penny will scratch it	3
FLUORITE	a steel knife will scratch it	4
APATITE	a knife scratches if you press hard	5
FELDSPAR	will scratch a knife blade	6
QUARTZ	will scratch glass (and all previous)	7
TOPAZ	will scratch quartz (and all previous)	8
CORUNDUM	will scratch all except a diamond	9
DIAMOND	will scratch everything	10

MOHS' SCALE CHART

ROCK	Finger Nail	Penny	Nail	Knife	Glass	Tile	Color	Other
A								
B								
C								
D								
E								

172

Some 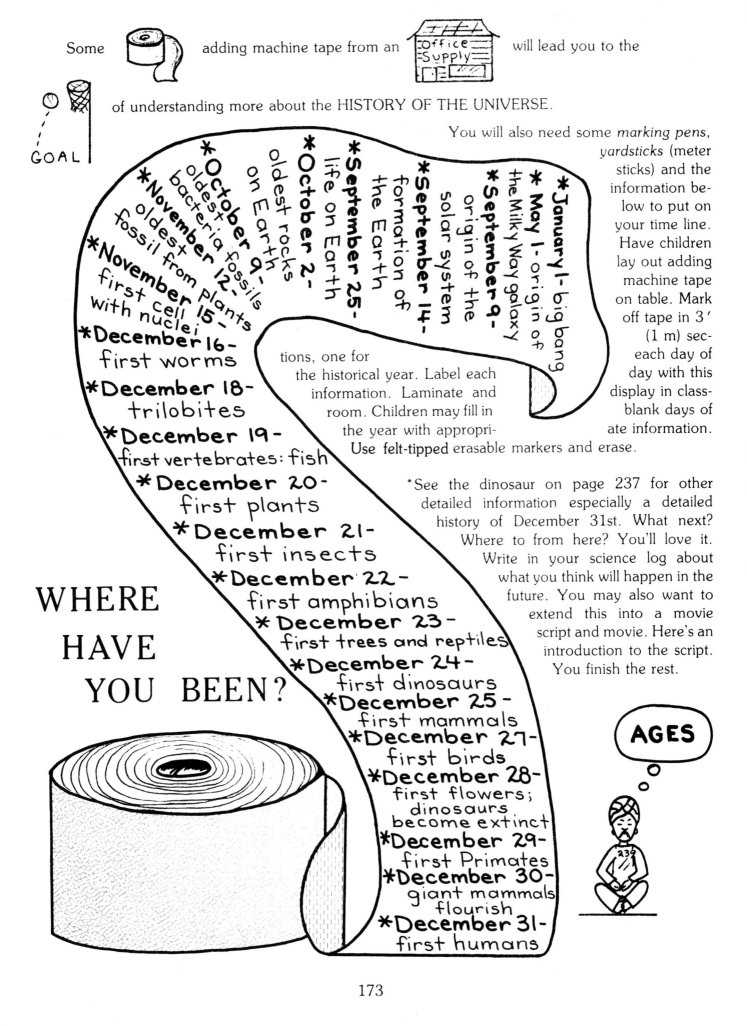 adding machine tape from an [office Supply] will lead you to the

GOAL

of understanding more about the HISTORY OF THE UNIVERSE.

You will also need some *marking pens, yardsticks* (meter sticks) and the information below to put on your time line. Have children lay out adding machine tape on table. Mark off tape in 3′ (1 m) sec- each day of day with this display in class- blank days of ate information.

* January 1 - big bang
* May 1 - origin of the Milky Way galaxy
* September 9 - origin of the solar system
* September 14 - formation of the Earth
* September 25 - life on Earth
* October 2 - oldest rocks on Earth
* October 9 - oldest fossils: bacteria
* October 12 - oldest bacteria fossils
* November 15 - oldest plants fossil from
* November 15 - first cell with nuclei
* December 16 - first worms
* December 18 - trilobites
* December 19 - first vertebrates: fish
* December 20 - first plants
* December 21 - first insects
* December 22 - first amphibians
* December 23 - first trees and reptiles
* December 24 - first dinosaurs
* December 25 - first mammals
* December 27 - first birds
* December 28 - first flowers; dinosaurs become extinct
* December 29 - first Primates
* December 30 - giant mammals flourish
* December 31 - first humans

tions, one for the historical year. Label each information. Laminate and room. Children may fill in the year with appropri- Use felt-tipped erasable markers and erase.

*See the dinosaur on page 237 for other detailed information especially a detailed history of December 31st. What next? Where to from here? You'll love it. Write in your science log about what you think will happen in the future. You may also want to extend this into a movie script and movie. Here's an introduction to the script. You finish the rest.

WHERE
HAVE
YOU BEEN?

AGES

Some computer print-out sheets from a  will lead you to the

of understanding the HISTORY

OF THE EARTH. You will also need some *marking pens, yardsticks* (meter sticks) and the information below.

Have children lay out computer print-out sheets on table. Allow 2 yards (meters) per one billion years and mark these sections with corresponding number of years. Make sketches of events on printout. Your history may include the information below. Display in your classroom and have children make a record in your science log books.

Event	Number of years ago	Event	Number of years ago
Earth formed	5 billion	First reptiles	320 million
Moon rocks	4.5 billion	Great Ice Age in	
Oldest rocks	3.3 billion	Southern Hemisphere	270 million
First known plants	3.2 billion	First mammals	225 million
First known animal	1.2 billion	Continents begin drifting	130 million
First fossils	600 million	First horse	60 million
First fish	500 million	Earliest elephants	40 million
First land plants and		First manlike animals	2 million
air-breathing animals	440 million	Beginning of Ice Age	1 million
First amphibians	400 million	Ice Age ends	10,000

GOOD OL' EARTH

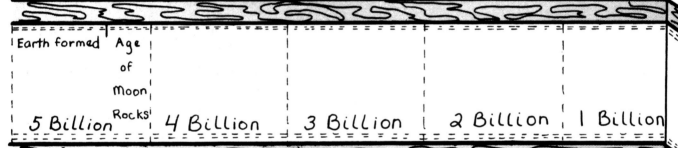

Earth formed   Age of Moon Rocks

5 Billion   4 Billion   3 Billion   2 Billion   1 Billion

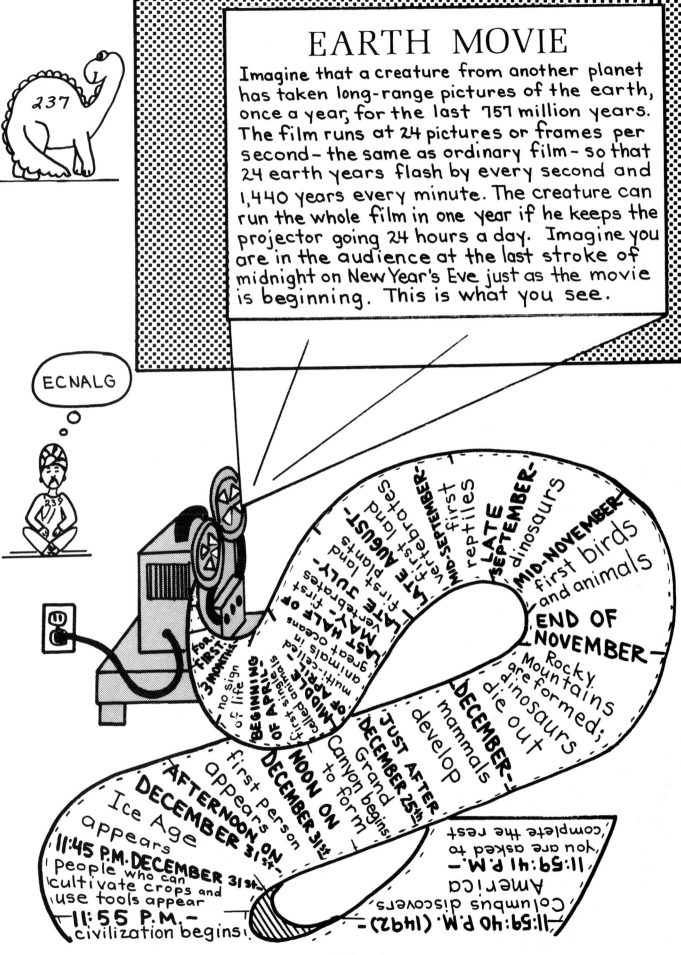

EARTH MOVIE

Imagine that a creature from another planet has taken long-range pictures of the earth, once a year, for the last 757 million years. The film runs at 24 pictures or frames per second—the same as ordinary film—so that 24 earth years flash by every second and 1,440 years every minute. The creature can run the whole film in one year if he keeps the projector going 24 hours a day. Imagine you are in the audience at the last stroke of midnight on New Year's Eve just as the movie is beginning. This is what you see.

ECNALG

237

239

FOR FIRST 3 MONTHS - no sign of life

BEGINNING OF APRIL - first single-celled animals

MIDDLE OF APRIL - multi-celled animals called animals

LAST HALF OF MAY - first vertebrates in great oceans

LATE JULY - first vertebrates

LATE AUGUST - first land plants

MID-SEPTEMBER - first land vertebrates

LATE SEPTEMBER - first reptiles

MID-NOVEMBER - dinosaurs

first birds and animals

END OF NOVEMBER - Rocky Mountains are formed; dinosaurs die out

DECEMBER - mammals develop

JUST AFTER DECEMBER 25th - Grand Canyon begins to form

NOON ON DECEMBER 31st - first person appears

AFTERNOON ON DECEMBER 31st - Ice Age appears

11:45 P.M. DECEMBER 31st - people who can cultivate crops and use tools appear

11:55 P.M. - civilization begins

11:59:40 P.M. (1492) - Columbus discovers America

11:59:41 P.M. - You are asked to complete the rest.

175

★ Some **Plaster of Paris** from a local **STORE** will help you reach the **GOAL**

of discovering how FOSSILS are formed by replacement. You will also need some *oil-based clay*, *water*, and *shell* or other object. Merely follow the path below and you'll end up with some interesting fossils. You will also a *table knife, pencil*, a *solution of soapy*

Fossils

1. Form a lump of clay into the shape of a box.
2. Cut the clay into two parts.
3. Score the end of one part so that the parts will not get mixed together.
4. Press a shell lengthwise into the middle of clay A.
5. Lay and press pencil into the clay next to the shell.
6. Put a coating of soapy solution on each part. (This makes it easier to get the two halves apart when the plaster is dried.)
7. Press B on top of A.
8. Carefully separate the two halves and remove the shell and pencil.
9. Make a mixture of plaster of Paris and water. (The mixture should be thin enough to run into the pencil hole, but not so thin that it will not harden.)
10. Pour plaster of Paris mixture into half of the mold. Do not overfill. Tap the clay gently to remove any air bubbles.
11. Now put the two halves together. Pour the plaster mixture into hole slowly. Tap again to remove any air bubbles.
12. Let dry 10-15 minutes. Separate the two halves carefully and you'll have an interesting fossil.

P.S. Heated liquid wax also works well if you want to make wax fossils.

176

A rock  from a field  will lead you to the  of **GOAL**

understanding YOURSELF and OTHERS in the world around you. Collect a bunch of different rocks and place on floor. Have each student choose a rock that matches his personality. Sit in circle. Have students carefully examine their rocks using their five senses. Close eyes. Pass rocks to the person next to you. Stop. Describe what your friend's rock feels like and how it might be like your friend or events in his life. Continue passing rocks until you find your rock. Open your eyes and check to see if it's really yours. Write a story about how you felt when you had to give up your rock and also when it was returned to you. This exercise helps students to describe their feelings about life when touching the rock. Use of the five senses is stressed throughout the exercise.

Read *Everyone Needs a Rock* and write a story about how this story relates to you and your life.

 construction paper from a  can lead you to the

of developing a feeling for PERCEPTION. You will need *a piece of red construction paper, white wall* or *movie screen*. Tape red piece of construction paper to white wall or movie screen. STARE AT CONSTRUCTION PAPER FOR 45 SECONDS. Shift eyes to the immediate right of construction paper. What do you see? How does this happen? Why? Now, allow a child to stand in front of the screen. Stare slightly above child's left shoulder. What do you see? Study auras and other forms of communication. Be sure to study the work of SEMYON KIRLIAN and the development of KIRLIAN photography in studying auras. Enter your results in your science log. Some people think that if you see these colors it means the following:

If you see Red—it means the color of high vitality

Orange—it means the color of stabilizing of emotions

Yellow—color of a people lover and thus the color of a teacher

Green—the color of peacefulness and healing

Blue—color of love which is demonstrated by blue jeans movement

Purple—color of aspiration

Violet—color of truth or being spiritual in nature

Gold—color of wisdom and great knowledge

White—encompasses all colors

Black—absence of light

What do you think the color of each aura means?

178

COMMUNICATION: ARE THERE OTHERS?

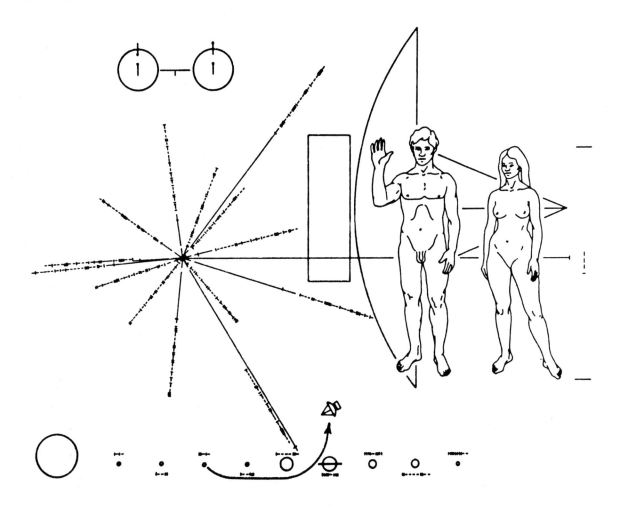

In an effort to expand fields of communication, this plaque was sent on *Pioneer 10* and *Pioneer 11*. The image is engraved on a 6″ (15 cm) by 9″ (23 cm) gold anodized aluminum plaque on which is etched drawings and configurations that will tell others about our planet and solar system. Find out what each symbol on the plaque means and the message you are sending to other possible civilizations. Then study how science fiction could help us communicate with others in distant places. Yes, there is a small chance that someone out there could be listening to your message. Do you believe that?

Some creative thinking will lead you to a Galaxy of Stars. You'll need to develop some good library, reading and writing skills before you take your trip. Research the people below and their contributions. Then, develop your own galaxy and write a story about what life would be like in the year 2050.

IS SCIENCE FICTION REALLY FICTION?

ROY BRADBURY - Fahrenheit 451; The Martian Chronicles

H.G. WELLS predicted lasers; gas warfare

FRANK HERBERT - Dune

HARLAN ELLISON - A Boy and His Dog

J.R.R. TOLKIEN The Hobbit; The Lord of the Rings

FREDERIK POHL - psychology of science fiction

JULES VERNE - hot air balloon; nautilus submarine

EDGAR RICE BURROUGHS - created Tarzan

ISAAC ASIMOV - 300 books, etc., including The Gods Themselves

ROBERT A. HEINLEIN, Rocket Ship Galileo

ARTHUR C. CLARK - A Space Odyssey; The Fountains of Paradise

FRANK KELLY FREAS - illustrates Analog

LARRY NIVEN - Lucifer's Hammer

KURT VONNEGUT, JR. Cat's Cradle

Here are some **SCIENCE FICTION TERMS** that will help you develop your own **Science Fiction Dictionary.** Use these words often in your science fiction writing in an effort to communicate with others on different galaxies.

CRYOGENICS
GRANDFATHER'S PARADOX
GROK
ROBOT
TACHYON
DOUBLESPEAK
LIGHT-SAIL
DYSON SPHERE
FTL
CRYONICS
RAMSCOOP
LIGHT YEAR
NEW WAVE
PSI

My Science Fiction Dictionary

HUGO
UTOPIA
SF
ICE NINE
HYPERSPACE
WALDO
PARALLEL WORLDS
NEBULA
BLACK HOLE
S & S
CYBORG
PAR-SEC
ENCOUNTERS

A LOOK TO THE 1990'S AND BEYOND!

What are people doing to find out if there is life in other solar systems? If you can decode Voyager's greetings below, you will be able to tell what some scientists are doing to find out more about themselves and others who by some small chance would be out there watching and listening. Decode the greetings. Then, make up your own coding system that would help you communicate with others in far-out distance places. Be sure to keep a record of your system in your science log.

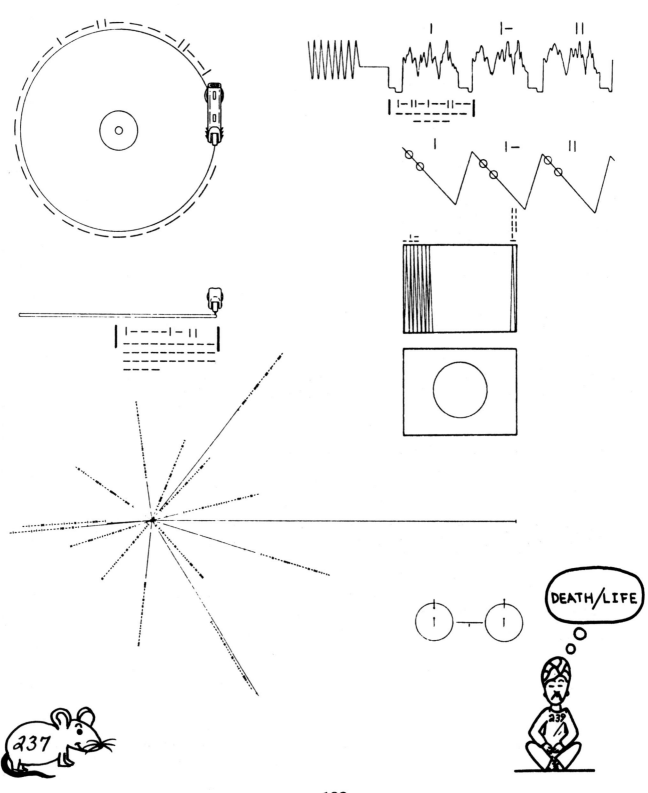

MY MINI BOOK

OF

SCIENCE ACTIVITIES

THIS MINI BOOK OF SCIENCE ACTIVITIES IS DEDICATED TO ME.

NAME_____

SCHOOL _____

IN THE HOPES THAT WHEN I'M BORED WITH LIFE AND HAVE

NOTHING TO DO, I WILL TRY MY HAND AT SOME OF THESE

ACTIVITIES THAT WILL MAKE LIFE MORE INTERESTING AND

MEANINGFUL.

- Paint nature scenes on clam shells.

- Develop a flower or plant arrangement suitable for the classroom and identify as many different species of flowers or plants that you can find.

- Develop a system whereby one flower or plant is studied per week in the classroom.

- Develop a vegetable or animal arrangement for the home or school. Identify each of the specimens in the arrangement.

- Make paperweights and jewelry by painting pebbles. Identify pebbles used.

- Develop a footprint collection of as many different animals as you can find.

- Design a flowerpot using an appropriate coating of putty and seashells.

- Make a bird calendar for the classroom or home.

- Write a nature diary keeping accurate records of observations, changes, etc., that have occurred for at least a month or so.

- Using a tape recorder, make a birdcall collection of as many different birdcalls as you can hear.

- Construct a beetle collection that has many different specimens.

- Make a shell collection that has a lot of different kinds of shells. Classify these shells.

- Look for 4-leaf clovers and then develop a clover leaf collection for the home or classroom.

- Make a feather collection which could also be used for making an actual bird on a poster. See page 156 for further feather activities.

- Make a bird on a poster using leaves from different trees.

- Develop a fern collection for the home or classroom.

- Make a poster of as many different kinds of weeds as you can find.

- Make a poster of how seeds travel.

- Make a poster of animal habitats and scenes.

- Photograph as many signs of murder in nature that you can find.

- Construct posters that show types of trees, leaves, bark, buds, and grains.

- Study an anthill for at least an hour or so.

- Go on a hike and note different types of berries. Identify each but do not eat.

- Make a model of a birch bark canoe.

- Make a list of new friends that you made on a hike including animals and insects.

- Go on a nature snoop for salamanders, toads and frogs.

- Make it rain by using a large jar and some ice cubes.

- Study plant geography giving the names of plant species for different areas in the United States.

- Identify as many different types of fish as you can find.

- Go outside for at least two hours and make a sketch of nature.

- Dig one square foot (four square decimeters) of ground and count all insects, worms and moving specks. Separate, list, and classify them.

- Do creative writing on nature subjects such as the wind, snow, rain, etc. Paint a picture of the wind.

- Study insects at a pond, brook, clump of flowers, wasp's nest, rotted log, or other center of activity. Photograph and make notes on what you see.

- In the field or, if this is impossible, from mounted specimens, identify to which order insects belong. Explain how you recognize each order of insects.

- Make a spreading board for insects. Then collect, mount, and label many different kinds of insects including those beneficial and harmful to man. Exhibit this collection.

- Find out something about the life histories and habits of insects. Learn where each is likely to be found, what each eats, the different stages of its life, how it sees, hears, smells feels, and what plants, animals, birds and other insects with which it is associated.

- Spend some time in each of two different kinds of natural habitats or at two different elevations (field or prairie, forest, marsh, etc.) and make a list of the different bird species found in each. Write a story about why all birds do not live in the same kind of habitat.

- Spend some time on each of five days near a wooded area and make a list of bird species you can identify by sound or sight. Tape-record the sounds.

- Recognize by sound alone as many birds as you can that are found in your backyard. Tape-record the sounds and play them to your classmates.

- From reading and talks with your teacher, make a list of the bird families usually found in your locality in the course of a year. Include at least one bird from the following families: Pigeons and Doves, Woodpeckers, Tyrant Flycatchers, Swallows, Crows-Magpies and Jays, Titmice-Bushtits, Wrens, Thrashers and Mockingbirds, Thrushes-Solitaries-Bluebirds, Wood Warblers, Weaver Finches, Blackbirds, Orioles, Meadowlarks, Finches, Sparrows, Grosbeaks, and Crossbills.

- From personal observation and reading, write the life history on one bird that nests in your locality. You may want to include photos of the bird in your story.

- Keep accurate records of birds observed on several field trips during one season.

- Watch a bird's nest for an hour a day for ten days and describe what you saw. See page 81 for other bird nest activities.

- Go on a Christmas census with a bird club. Make a list of birds that you observed.

- Visit a national, state, or private bird refuge and describe its purpose and how it is managed. Make a presentation to the class.

- Develop a background sanctuary by planting trees and shrubs for food and cover and describe what birds and animals you expect to attract and why.

- Build some bird feeders of different kinds and set them out. Keep them stocked with food in winter and describe what birds used them and what kinds of food these birds preferred.

- Build some nest boxes for different birds and set them out in appropriate places. Describe the birds that used them and tell how many young birds were raised in these boxes.

- Take some clear, sharp, recognizable photographs of different species of birds.

- Build a watering device for birds and keep it filled with water for an extended period of time. Tell what kinds of birds used it and describe any interesting things you saw.

- Select one species of bird (hawk, owl, heron, kingfisher, etc.) that eats other animals and give a talk to the class on its place in the world of nature. Keep a record of what birds your state pays a bounty, if any, and give your opinion on whether this is a valuable practice.

- Make a migration map of the United States. Name some of the birds that use each flyway, where they nest and where they winter. Describe bird banding, the technique used to develop the flyway idea.

- Make a list of the extinct or declining birds of the United States and describe the chief causes that are known for the extinction of these species. Take a poll of your classmates' views on endangered species.

- Identify and photograph different species of trees or wild shrubs in your area and tell their names and chief uses. Present your photographs to the class.

- Obtain wood samples of different trees and tell some of the uses of each kind of wood. Distinguish between hardwoods and softwoods and where each type of wood is found and used.

- Describe the value of forests in protecting soil and building fertility, regulating the flow of water, wildlife management, and as recreational areas. Tell the class about a watershed or other source where your community obtains its water.

- Develop a play that illustrates the part that forest products play in our everyday lives.

- Make a diameter tape or Biltmore stick. Show how to determine the height and diameter of trees. Estimate the board foot volume of these trees.

- Find and examine several stumps or logs that have variations in the rate of growth as shown by rings and list reasons for these variations. Cut a cross section of the log. Sand and varnish for lasting protection. See page 93 for other log activities.

- Develop a slide tape presentation to show what is meant by forest management.

- Working with your teacher, plan and carry out a forestry project that meets a need such as one of tree planting, seed collecting, range improvement, recreation area improvement, or forest wildlife management around your home or school.

- Photograph the damage to forests and watersheds, resulting from fire, insects, tree diseases, overgrazing, and unwise cutting practices. Tell the class what is being done to reduce this damage. Don't forget to note the damage caused by air pollution including acid rain.

- Tell your classmates what to do if a fire is discovered in woodlands or in your school.

- Take part in a forest fire prevention campaign at school with the assistance of your teacher, fire warden, *et. al.* Report to the class on your activity.

- Take a field trip to a wood-using industrial plant and observe what the raw material is, where it comes from, how the finished product is made, how products are used, and how waste materials are disposed. Note the presence or absence of pollution on your trip.

- Visit a managed farm, public or private forest area, or watershed with its owner or supervisor and observe how the area has managed to grow repeated crops of corn, etc., that provide other services and benefits. Report your findings to the class.

- Make field trips and observe wild plant life. Keep a record, based on field notes, of varieties of flowers found, with date, place, nature of locality (swamp, roadside, woods, meadow, etc.) and other observations such as seed pods, leaf arrangements, insect attraction. Include photographs and sketches to make your report to the class very interesting. Be sure not to pick any wild plant life.

- Identify from living specimens as many plant specimens as you can.

- Identify all parts of a perfect and complete flower. Explain how plants are pollenized and how ferns differ from flowering plants. See page 85 for other activities.

- Collect leaves or winter twigs of forest trees or shrubs. Mount them in a notebook, writing the name of each, where it grows in the United States, and the chief uses of such trees.

- Identify specimens of flowering plants and submit properly labeled specimens of such families to your teacher.

- Study what plants are rare in your community and what is being done or should be done to protect them. Take a poll of your friends to find out if they feel rare plants should be protected.

- Explain how plants use light, heat, water, oxygen, and carbon dioxide for the manufacture of their own food.

- Identify and collect a specimen of fungi, algae, lichens, and mosses for a class study of these.

- Develop a seed collection of as many seeds as you can find. Then germinate seeds and find out all you can about different varieties of seeds and how they are scattered.

- Find specimens of different species of flowering plants. Include leaf, stem, flower, and root. Mount neatly. Label both with common and scientific name including date, place found, and nature of locality. Be careful not to pick a rare plant.

- Make a study of plant life in an area for at least two months. Keep a record of species found, type of locality, insect attraction, seeds produced, etc.

- Raise a wild flower or fern garden. Learn both the common and scientific names of each and proper methods of transplanting and care.

- Tell your classmates how insects are different from all other animals. Show them the differences between insects, spiders, centipedes, and millipedes.

- Point out to the class the name and main parts of an insect. Obtain some mealworms from a pet shop and study their development.

- Collect and mount different species of insects. Include the orders and family for each. Label each with common and scientific names where possible and share with the class.

- Find some sow bugs and time how long it takes them to go a yard (meter).

- Show your collection of insects to your classmates. Act out what each insect does in its environment.

- Compare the life histories of a butterfly, moth, grasshopper and mosquito. Show the class how they are different.

188

- Raise a butterfly or moth from a caterpillar. Keep a diary of your experiences.

- Tell the class what makes social insects different from solitary insects.

- Identify species of insects helpful to man and tell the class how they are helpful. Also, identify species of insects harmful to man and tell the class how they can be controlled. Be sure to investigate chemicals used to control insects.

- Using several similar plants, study the growth rate of each when exposed to different colors of light, including white. Colored light bulbs and colored cellophane present two possibilities for controlling the light. Graph the heights. What other growth characteristics should be observed?

- Identify living organisms found in your home. Which are permanent residents and which are transient? Be sure to consider the complete range of living things including fungi. Are any of your groceries alive when you buy them? Are any insects caught on screens or in light fixtures? What weather conditions and room conditions are conducive to presence and abundance of various organisms? Save some specimens for display in the classroom.

- Find out whether exercise benefits the health of a caged family pet. Use mice, gerbils, or hamsters. Compare an animal in a cage with an exercise wheel with a control animal without the exercise wheel. Identify the factors that must be controlled? Does the animal with the wheel in fact exercise more than the other one? Report your results to the class.

- Make a key to the plants in your own backyard, vacant lot, or the trees in your block. Do a systematic survey and collect specimens. Observe distinguishing characteristics. Remember that a key does not need to follow family relationships, as long as it works in distinguishing reliably among the plants or animals in the group for which it is designed. Show your key to the class.

- Determine how long it would take various crawling animals like a beetle, caterpillar, earthworm, centipede, etc., to go a mile (kilometer) What is a snail's pace? A turtle's? Build a grooved path of dirt for the "racetrack" for the smaller animals. Discover what stimuli can be used to make them move. Do different stimuli result in different speeds? Be sure to try different amounts of light, heat, cold, etc. Record the results in a chart for all your classmates to see.

- Set up controlled experiments starting plants in different media such as water, moist paper towels, peat moss, vermiculite soil. Do your plants grow in all of them? Report your findings.

- Find out about Van Helmont's experiment. Try the same thing with a rapidly growing plant of your own. You will need at least several weeks. The soil must be dry for weighing before and after the plant grows in it. Weigh the plant, too. Where do you think the material came from to make the plant's tissues? Do your results mean soil is not important to plants? Explain your findings to the class. Then study hydroponics.

- Make a diagram of how insects fit into the food chains of other insects, fish, birds, and mammals. Study predator-prey relationships.

- Expose different types of food to air for a number of days. Make a daily record of weight, color, size, odor, texture, etc., on a large chart. Does fresh meat or cooked meat deteriorate more quickly? What is destroyed in fresh meat by cooking? Share your chart with the class.

- Set up several small aquaria with plants and fish. Make and record your regular observations of such things as appearance of the water, bottom cleanliness, activity of fish, etc. How do you interpret your observations? Are scavengers important to other living communities? Try to set up an aquarium in your classroom for others to see.

- Devise a homemade calorimeter and determine the amounts of energy produced by various foods. A major part of the problem will be to get foods to burn. They should be thoroughly dried. You may want to use some dehydrated foods and dry them even further in the oven. Do your findings seem to indicate more calories per gram in protein, fat, or carbohydrate food? You will want to check with appropriate sources of information. Find out what you can about "health foods."

- Determine various activities that affect the rate of human heartbeat. Your pulse rate might be checked before the activity, after two minutes of activity, after a longer period (perhaps ten minutes), and after ten minutes of rest. Children of different age, sex, weight, etc., might be asked to help you. Charts and graphs are useful. Study heart disease and how health and physical education habits like jogging are related to heart function and report your findings to the class.

- Determine what kind of ecological succession takes place in a grass-water mixture. You might make more than one mixture with dried grass from different places. Examine your mixture daily for two or three weeks or until you can no longer find any living organisms in it. Be sure to take one drop from the surface of the water, and others from other depths. Make a sketch of each type of organism, noting its size in comparison with others or with the total field of the microscope under low power. Find some way to record the abundance of each kind of organism each day.

- Study succession of a pond. What organisms are "pioneers"? Which ones take their place, and which ones follow them? Can you see any kinds of interaction taking place? Why do the populations change? Why do some species finally die out? How do you feel about endangered species?

- Determine how mealworms, sow bugs, or earthworms respond to various stimuli. Do those creatures prefer light or darkness, moisture or dryness? Find out their favorite temperature. Do they live in open spaces or physical contact? On an inclined plane, do they tend to crawl up or down? You might compare reactions of different organisms. Are their behaviors adaptive in their natural environments? Be sure to repeat each test a number of times and tally the responses you observe. Then share your results with the members of the class.

- Conduct a study on how different food materials affect the rate of growth. Do various amounts of chemicals such as salt, vinegar, lime powder, or plant fertilizer affect the processes of plant success? Find out the effect of sugar, salt, etc., on the human body.

- Sketch the face of the moon, indicating on it the locations of as many seas and craters as you can find. Identify these features and study how the moon may affect human emotions.

- Collect pictures of geometric shapes found in nature. Ask how you feel when you see these pictures. Then go outside and collect actual objects that have geometric shapes in them.

- Go outside and find evidence of pollution and bring back as many samples of such pollution as you can.

- Go outside and find a million of something and prove it. This will take you a-while. Can your friends help? Can you find a million pull tabs from pop and beer cans?

- Invent a way of communicating with an animal. Write a story of your attempts.

- Keep a record for a week of how many hours sleep you get each night. Also, keep a record of how many calories of food you eat each day. Find out if there is a relationship between hours slept and number of calories eaten.

- Find out a way that you could determine how many hairs are on a person's head.

- Find one object in the environment that begins with each letter of the alphabet.

- Classify all the animals in your home or school by different properties including legs, color, etc. Make a record of your results.

- Describe an object that you can see and one that you have never seen but only heard about. What is the effect of actually seeing an object on your description? How do blind people "see"? Study how blind people can discriminate between a one dollar bill and a five dollar bill.

- Find how different animals react to different stimuli, e.g., food, climate, etc. Keep a record of your findings.

- Study your family members at different times during the day for a period of time. What can you say about mood changes in family members. Does the weather affect family members' moods? Read *Body Weather* by Bruce Palmer.

- Go through your family's garbage and evaluate the life-style of your family. Compare with other families.

- Collect an assortment of objects. Take them to a body of water and see which float and which sink. Keep a record of your results.

- Using water, vinegar, and other household liquids, observe what happens when various powders such as sugar and salt are placed in the liquids. Keep an accurate record of your findings.

- Take a walk in your neighborhood and make a list of all the happy and sad things you see. Write a story about what makes you happy and sad.

- Play Twenty Questions with someone at home or in the class. Pick an object and have your friend try to identify it by asking questions which can be answered yes or no.

- Photograph or sketch all the happy experiences that you can find in school and your environment. Proudly display your photographs and sketches for all to see.

- List ten facial expressions seen by you on a trip to the forest. Sketch them.

- Draw a path from your house to your favorite place in nature. Then take a trip by following your path. Make a map of your route.

- Measure the distance from your bedroom to the kitchen using any part of your body. List other ways this could be done.

- Measure the length of your classroom using a leaf. How many leaves is it from ceiling to floor.

- Given red, yellow, green, and blue food coloring, find out the different colors you can make. Paint a picture using all your colors.

- Measure with your hands the height of everyone in the home or classroom. Make a graph illustrating the differences in each person.

- Take a walk, any distance. Write down everything you observe. Then look through a tube (empty paper towel roll) and write down all the things that you missed. Write a report on which trip was more interesting and why.

- Develop a commercial on drug addiction, pollution, or conservation. Find out the difference in a commercial that is purely propaganda or one that is completely straightforward and factual. What topics are the most important to mention in any commercial? Use a tape recorder or camera to improve your commercial.

- Find out how much air is polluted in your neighborhood. Obtain a large strip of white cotton felt or batting. Tack it to a board with another board. Each day uncover another 1/5 of the cotton. Observe how the visible impurities increase each day. Determine the apparent density of the polluting elements by examining each section of the cotton under a magnifying glass and comparing them. You could then make drawings of your findings at this point for further display.

- Identify the areas in your neighborhood that contribute to ecological problems. How would you solve these problems?

- After a snowstorm, collect surface snow from one square foot (four square decimeters) of surface, and, after allowing it to melt, filter it through a fine mesh cloth. Do this on several days. Compare the accumulation of polluting elements found in this study.

- Investigate any past periods of smog that have occurred in your locality. Take some photographs of things which cause the air to become polluted. Include chimney smoke, auto exhaust, rubbish fires, etc. Find out what PSI is and keep PSI records for at least a month.

- Find as many different ways as you can to measure a bush outside.

- Make a chart showing the chemical composition of air and air pollution in your community. Watch TV weather reports for pertinent information.

- Try to find out how your community compares with other communities and large cities in the country in the amount of air pollution. What are some possible explanations of the differences in these amounts of pollution? Find out what your community is doing about such pollution.

- Catch and measure the water from one leaky faucet in a given period of time. Then figure the amount that would be lost in one year if the faucet continued to leak at that rate. Make up other problems based on the assumption of a certain number of leaky faucets in your community. What is the cost? What methods were used in purifying and pumping the water to the houses? Do a water test of water found in your home.

- Tear five pictures that you like from a science magazine and make up a story as to why these pictures make you feel as you do.

- Hair is a remarkable substance. It is strong and flexible. Find a way to test its strength and flexibility.

- Find out what effects various colors of light have upon plants. Keep a record of such effects.

- Stake off a plot of land on the playground and observe the living/nonliving things you see in this area. Count and classify these things according to color, shape, size and living/nonliving.

- Collect as many different kinds of seeds as you can and classify them. Which plants grow near each other? What kinds of ground do the different plants grow on? What kind of animals live with plants? Write a story of your findings including illustrations.

- Observe any animal kept in the home or classroom. Make a graph to show how the animal changes. Observe its eating and mating habits.

- Choose a friend and keep a record of the friend's height, weight, feelings, etc. Graph your data accordingly.

- Take a magnifying glass outside to examine as many different objects that you can.

- Find things in the environment which have four dimensions or qualities of some type, e.g., 4 sides, 4 legs, etc. Make a record of your findings.

- Find things in the environment that make up a population, e.g., pop cans, cigarette butts, cars, and apartment buildings. Find out how population is controlled and think about whether you favor such population control.

- Find things in the environment that remind you of animals in a zoo. Texture, smell, looks should be considered.

- Measure the blacktop yard using as many different objects in your environment as you can.

- Take several different kinds of rocks either from a collection or from what you collect outside. Find as many different ways to classify them as possible.

- Fill pop bottles with various amounts of water. Hit the bottles with a spoon and create different sounds. Play a song using your pop bottles.

- Write a letter to a friend using only pictures of things found in the environment.

- Go outside and find the youngest and the oldest car, truck, bicycle, etc. Write a story about whether you like newness or oldness in objects. How do years affect the object?

- Make a poster of something that makes you feel good without using paper.

- Explore and discuss the properties of materials in a "touch kit" (blocks, cloth, sandpaper, steel wool, sponge, deflated balloon, etc.). Play a game that emphasizes the texture, thickness, etc., of the objects.

- Tape-record sounds that express different moods. Have a friend try to guess which mood is depicted in your sounds.

- Take apart an old clock or some household appliance. Make a drawing as to where each item fits. Then put the object back together again.

- Gather different materials such as wood, metal, plastic and glass. Expose them to heat such as a sunlamp or cold by using a freezer, etc. Keep a record of your findings.

- Use straws, small cans, Ivory Snow, glycerine (2-4 tsp. of glycerine per quart [liter] of soap solution) to make bubbles and observe their size and other properties. Use a pull tab from a pop can or a plastic six-pack ring for your bubble holder and blower.

- Using a long empty plastic tube as an inclined plane, let marbles roll down the tube onto the floor. Make observations, ask questions, and keep a record of your results.

- Make a shaker using either an aluminum or plastic container. Fill with peas, beans, rice, rocks, etc. Fill each shaker with different materials that can be classified by weight or sound.

- Make a balance using a yardstick (meter stick) and paper cups. Then weigh various objects found in your environment.

- Try to find out if hot water freezes more quickly than cold water. Some people believe it does, and there are instances in which that seems to be true. Set up a series of controlled experiments. In each separate experiment, only the temperature of the water should be different at the beginning of the experiment. Try different ways of cooling the water, different amounts, different types of containers, etc. Does hot water go through the stage of becoming cold water before it freezes? Consider such possibilities as how much evaporation occurs from a small amount of hot water in a flat pan that its volume becomes substantially less, cooling in ice compartment of refrigerator, melting of frost resulting in better contact with the cooling surface, possible changes in composition of tap water when heated, etc. The whole class might help you develop hypotheses and plan tests for the study.

- Find out what is the best way to make a string telephone. Try different kinds of strings and different ways of attaching the string to the cans. What are some other ways that you can think of? Test your telephone. Think of a way to be sure all telephones are tested by sounds for the same loudness, clearness, etc. Report your results to the class.

- Show attraction and repulsion in magnets. Make and use a simple electromagnet. Show the class how these work.

- Show in a simple drawing how you have made an electric bell and buzzer work. Make a report to the class on how your doorbell at home works.

- Explain why a fuse blows out. Tell how to find a blown fuse in your home. Show the class how to change it safely. Study circuit breakers and their function in the home and school.

- Explain what overloading an electric circuit means. Tell the class what you and your parents have done to make sure your home circuits aren't overloaded. Make a chart of rules for use of electricity.

- Join two pieces of insulated wire the correct way, or fix a bad wire on an appliance or a plug. Have your classmates do the same.

- Show how to save a person who is touching a live wire in the home. Show proper first aid procedures when a person is found unconscious from electrical shock. Study safety precautions taken during an electrical storm.

- Study how important simple machines are in your home? Make a search for simple machines in your home. For each one, decide what kind it is (lever, pulley, inclined plane, wedge, screw, or wheel and axle). Which ones gain force? Which ones gain speed? Remember, they can't gain force and speed at the same time. You might look for gear systems, too. Do they help you gain force or speed? Find some gears on machines that change the direction of the force. Record your results on a chart.

- Study how the construction of a bridge affects its strength. Make two or more model bridges of the same length using balsa wood or strips of cardboard, but using different designs, e.g., beam, truss, arch, suspension, etc. Compare the load limits of the bridges. Parts should be fastened together securely so there will be no breaking apart at the fastenings before the materials themselves bend or break. While checking load limit, support the center gently with your hand, in an effort to save the bridge when it first shows signs of collapse. Other than strength, what advantages might there be for different kinds of bridges? Where have you seen different kinds used? Take some photographs of different kinds of bridges. Identify each and report your findings to the class.

- Study how we keep track of time. Take apart an old clock, and try to figure out how each part works. Figure out the gear ratio of the wheels, and determine how many revolutions per second, or minute, or hour, must be made by each wheel. If you want to go further, investigate sundials and make one. On the subject of clocks, if you are really ambitious, find out how a sidereal clock is different, or how you could add a hand that would tell phases of the moon. What other time keepers can you find out about or devise? Make a report on your findings to your classmates.

- Make an electrical maze by laying strips of tape (plastic or other nonconductor) on a sheet of aluminum foil (conductor). Connect the foil in series with a lamp, battery, and nail. You must move the nail along the foil from start to finish without ever making the light go out. Set up learning experiments, recording errors and time to complete the task with each trial. Compare performance of your classmates. Graph the number of seconds for each trial. Keep accurate records of your results.

- Investigate the difference between direct current and alternating current. Tell the common uses of each. Show one way of finding which is found in an electric power line. An electrician may help you with your study.

- Make a detailed study of the types of electrical circuits found in your home. Develop a chart showing where electrical wiring and outlets are located. Make a list and diagram of what outlets are on what circuits in your home. Don't forget the furnace.

- Find out the benefits that have come from the space program. Make a list of products, such as Teflon, which have resulted from space research. Read about Sky Lab and the Space Shuttle and what products may result from this research. Are there any material objects that might be added to a display which help convey a message to your classmates? NOTE: Use other library research topics, such as UFO's or hurricanes, to enhance your project.

- Make a map of the home or classroom locating the position of desks, tables, etc., by any way you can. You may want to use the idea of longitude and latitude for your map.

- Go outside and find evidence of pollution and bring back samples of such pollution.

- Chart the movement of the moon and one planet for a few hours. Relate this movement to a point on the horizon.

- Chart the position of the moon on the days or nights you can see it for one month. Sketch the size, shape, and position of the moon as you see it. Be sure to include the area surrounding you for a reference point.

- Chart the positions of a number of constellations in relation to the North Star during an evening astronomy session. Share your chart with the class.

- Watch and report to the class on an eclipse of the moon, a meteor shower, or similar, future astronomical event such as the next occurrence of Haley's Comet.

- Tell your friends what factors keep the moon in orbit around the earth. Then design an experiment that would show these factors.

- Photograph or make a map of the sky that shows a planet at approximately weekly intervals at the same time of night for several weeks. Explain any changes noticed on the photographs or map.

- Find out when each of the visible planets will be observable in the evening sky during the next 12 months and compile this information in the form of a chart or table. This will be a handy reference for your future class activity in astronomy.

- In a sketch, show the position of Venus, Mars, or Jupiter in the sky at approximately weekly intervals at the same time for several weeks.

- Build a simple telescope or microscope. Then use it. Investigate the characteristics of various lenses and prisms.

- Using a compass, record the direction to the sun at sunset at approximately weekly intervals for several weeks in spring or fall or for 6 to 8 weeks in summer or winter. Find out why this takes longer in winter or summer and relate this information to the seasons of the earth.

- With the aid of diagrams and models show the class the relative positions of sun, earth, and moon at the times of lunar and solar eclipses and at the times of New, First Quarter, Full, and Last Quarter phases of the moon.

- Using the shadow made by a vertical pole in sunshine, lay out a true north-south line called a meridian. Then using the line and the pole on another day, measure the altitude of the noontime sun and determine your latitude. Share your results with the class.

- Identify in the sky as many constellations as you can including some which are in the zodiac. Identify conspicuous stars, some of which are the first magnitude. What makes a star a first magnitude star? What is the brightest star and how is its magnitude measured?

- Make a sketch of the position of the Big Dipper and its relation to the North Star and the horizon early some evening and again 6 hours later on the same night. Record the date and time of making each sketch. Compare your results.

- Explain what we see when we look at the Milky Way. How could our Milky Way Galaxy be different from other solar systems? Write a story about why you think they'd be different.

- Make a diagram of a real telescope if you have one and explain the difference between reflecting and refracting telescopes. Describe the basic purpose of a telescope and list several other instruments used with telescopes.

- Describe the composition of the sun, its relationship to other stars, and some effects of its radiation on the earth's weather. Define sunspots and describe some of the effects they may have on this radiation. Also, find out how astronomers measure sunspots.

- Identify at least one star that is red, one that is blue, and one that is yellow, and explain the meaning of these colors to the class.

- Visit a planetarium or observatory and submit a report to the class both on the activities occurring there and on the exhibits of instruments and other astronomical objects you observed.

- Spend several hours observing celestial objects through a telescope or with field glasses, and make a presentation to the class on what you observed.

- Identify a number of career opportunities in astronomy. Explain how to prepare for one of them. List elementary and high school experiences that would be useful in pursuing a career in astronomy.

- Imagine what it would have been like to live a thousand years ago. Then write a story of what you feel it was like.

- Get a topographic map of your area. Study it. Explain the important geological features shown on it. If you can't get a local map, study one of another place that you know. Air photos may also be used instead of a topographic map. Report your findings to the class.

- Prepare a report including maps or drawings of the geological features on or below the surface of your community.

- Visit your local water system. Describe the source, quality, and amount of water needed for your community. Present its relation to your community's geological features. Study the quality of water in your area.

- Describe how the soil in your community was formed. Make a slide tape presentation on the kinds of rock from which it came. Find out how soil tests are made.

- Describe the earth materials used in your home or a public building. Tell where they came from. Make a list of those which you use every day.

- Photograph different kinds of clouds and tell what atmospheric conditions existed while each kind of cloud was forming.

- Photograph conditions in the environment which come immediately before and during different kinds of precipitation.

- Can a homemade weather station yield accurate weather data? Build a homemade weather station. Record and graph weather data. You might compare your data with TV weather reports. Don't expect them to be identical, though, as you measured at a different location. See page 134 for more weather activities.

- Find out whether the weather has any effect on human emotions and moods. Record relative humidity, barometric pressure, and temperature for a period of time. For the same time periods, have a few friends report how they feel. Do the fluctuations of mood seem to have any connection with the weather? In order to come to any conclusions at all you will probably have to ask them to choose from a short list of words the one which best describes their feelings. Why is it so difficult to conduct a study of this type?

- Collect a cup of snow. Observe what happens as the cup sits at room temperature. Write a story that tells about snow and its qualities made from your observations.

- Soak a piece of paper or cloth in a cobalt chloride solution and dry it. Use ½ teaspoon of crystals in ½ glass of water. When thoroughly dry the material is blue, and when there is high humidity it turns pink. How closely does the indicator check with actual weather conditions? Keep a chart recording date and hour, color of the indicator, weather condition, and the relative humidity given by the Weather Service. Perhaps you can check by using a wet-dry bulb thermometer. You might expand this investigation by varying the strength of the cobalt chloride solution and by trying different kinds of materials, e.g., cotton, wool, rayon, blotting paper, writing paper, etc. What is the best way to make the indicator? What factors would you have to control in setting up these experiments? Share the results of your study with the class.

- Predict whether man will live for long periods of time on the moon and other planets. Write a story of your predictions.

- Go outside and find some small things that have been used by people in the past or are being used now or will be used in the future. Record your results.

- Get a soil map of your county. Then, collect soil samples from different parts of the county, and display samples connecting the samples with yarn to the places where they appear. Try to find out why the soils are different and how the differences are important to farming and other land use.

- Convert a topographic map into a relief model. You will want to display the original topographic map along with your model. Perhaps you will add some explanation of the procedures used, description of the area modeled, etc. Share your model with the class.

- Construct a working model of a seismograph. Observe the reaction of your instrument to truck vibrations, etc. Do some library research on earthquakes, and include information in the display. Find a way for the seismograph to record vibrations, and learn how to locate earthquakes from seismograph data.

- Examine rocks from various locations. Try to explain what changes each has undergone. It will be helpful to learn first how to classify your rocks as sedimentary, igneous, and metamorphic. Then you will know something about their story. Do you find any rocks that have been moved by water? Find out why so many surface rocks are different inside if you break them open. You might select several interesting rocks and let each one tell its story.

- Separate a metal from its ore. Study metallurgy.

- Grow crystals from a melted or dissolved substance. Make a display of your results.

- Research a streambank, a vacant lot, or an area that has been recently cleared for a construction project, or some other location where erosion is taking place. Develop a plan that would stop this erosion.

- Photograph and describe exposure of a rock stratum or strata. This can be at a road cut, an excavation, or at a natural canyon or gorge. Report your findings to the class.

- Photograph the changes in the looks of several different kinds of rocks or minerals after you break them and let them weather for a month or so.

- Develop a collection of different ores, rock-forming minerals, and fossils. Give names, uses, and age of each.

- Make a collection of different sedimentary, igneous, and metamorphic rocks. Name the important minerals found in each. Tell what use can be made of these rocks.

- Visit a mine, quarry, oil or gas field, a gravel, clay, sand, or shell pit. Explain the composition of the deposits. Tell the class how the product is removed, transported, sold, and used. What safety precautions and pollution standards are used to guarantee a safe environment.

- Clip a weather map from a local newspaper. Present to the class information on what constitutes a high-pressure system, low-pressure system, cold front, warm front, jet stream, isobar, and isotherm.

- Draw a cross section of the atmosphere showing its three main layers. Present your findings to the class.

- Distinguish between hurricanes, tornadoes, cyclones, squall lines, and blizzards. Inform the class of the safety precautions for thunderstorms and other severe weather patterns.

- Make a presentation on what types of storms affect your community and what safety precautions should be followed during each type of storm.

- Estimate the wind direction and velocity by its effect upon trees, flags, or like objects. Make a chart of your estimations and check them with a Beaufort Scale.

- Make a drawing showing the hydrologic cycle. Then, show the class this by using ice cubes, water and a teakettle.

- Identify clouds according to shape, color, and altitude. Tell the differences between cumulus and cumulonimbus, stratus, altostratus, and cirrostratus, stratocumulus and altocumulus clouds.

- Make a cloud in a large jar.

- Distinguish between drizzle, rain, freezing rain, sleet, hail and snow. Make a chart of these types of precipitation.

- Make a tape of the United States Weather Bureau forecast obtained from radio or television at the same time each day for several weeks. Also record a brief description of how the weather actually turned out. Count the number of times the tapes were in agreement and present your results to the class.

- Make a chart of the daily weather patterns for a month noting the following: dew or frost in the morning, wind direction, temperature, types of clouds, and precipitation.

- Report to the class how ocean waves are made. Point out the differences between the storm surge, tidal wave, and tidal bore. Also, show the difference between sea, swell, and surf. Develop an experiment to show how breakers are formed.

- Make a model of a typical cross section of underwater topography, illustrating what is meant by the terms (2) continental shelf, (b) continental slope, and (c) abyssal plains. Locate the following on your diagram: seamount, guyot, deep, rift valley, canyon, and trench. Compare the depths in the oceans with the heights of mountains. Identify the deepest oceans in the world.

- Obtain information about the climate (maximum and minimum temperatures, humidity, rainfall, wind) in your community and discuss its influence on industry, agriculture, clothing, transportation, housing, and recreation with the class.

- Find out what is meant by meteorology. Visit a weather bureau station at an airport. Explain the methods and devices that are used in taking observations. Describe the following instruments and tell how they are used in a weather study: wind vane, anemometer, barometer, thermometer, hygrometer, rain gauge.

- Report to the class on how radar, satellites, and electronic devices are used in forecasting or changing the weather.

- Make a list of the radio and television stations in your area and show the times they broadcast weather forecasts. Inform the class on when and how severe weather warnings are given.

- Use materials that are more dense than water to build something that will float.

- Develop an experiment that will show the freezing of salt water differs from the freezing of tap water.

- Research the fields of oceanography and then report on different ways that mankind is becoming more dependent upon knowledge of the oceans. Write a story on what it would be like to live under the ocean in the year 2000.

- Describe the effect of the oceans, including the effect of current circulation, on the weather and climate. Point out the similarities and differences between the general circulation of air and ocean currents.

- Construct a wave maker and demonstrate reflection and refraction of waves. Show how jetties and breakwaters affect these patterns. Compare this to a river or ocean in your community.

- Make a creative presentation to the class on any good book in the field of oceanography. Verify the book beforehand with your teacher who may have additional ideas for your presentation.

- Visit an oceanographic institute in your area and present a research report on an oceanographic research ship and its functions.

- Explain to the class "Why Oceanography Is Important" or "Career Opportunities in the Science of Oceanography." Before making your presentation, submit your written work to your teacher.

- List the principal gases and nutrients dissolved in seawater. Describe the importance of these substances to the life in the sea. Also describe how seawater may develop into a viable alternative to meet the future's energy demands especially through nuclear fusion.

- Research what is meant by the Dittmar's principle? Why is it so important to our everyday lives?

- Define photoplankton and zooplankton. Describe the importance of photoplankton as a primary producer of living material and of the position and importance of plankton in the food chain.

- Construct a plankton net. Tow the net alongside a pier or wade with it in shallow water. Preserve the sample. Examine the plankton under a microscope or high-power magnifying glass. Identify the most common types of plankton in the sample with appropriate drawings for a class presentation.

- Make a series of models using clay, plaster, or wood of a volcanic island, showing the growth cycle of an atoll from a fringing reef through a barrier reef. Describe the Darwinian theory of coral reef formation.

- Measure the water temperature 1 foot (30 cm) below the surface of a body of water or in a stream four times daily (8 a.m., 12 noon, 4 p.m., 8 p.m.) for a number of consecutive days. In addition, measure the air temperature and note the cloud cover and roughness of the water. Graph the data. Show how the water responds to changes in air temperature.

- Make a stream table showing inshore sediment movement by littoral currents, tidal movement, and wave action. Include such features as high and low waterlines, low tide terrace, cusps, beach scarp, and berm. Also, show how the offshore bars are built up and torn down in your stream table.

MY CHOICES

-
-
-
-
-
-

My Mini Book
Notes

100 SCIENCE IDEAS USING

FREE & INEXPENSIVE
MATERIALS

Space is premium when writing a book. Due to space limitations, all possible science activities could not be included. However, below is a listing of some additional science ideas and activities that you and your children may find interesting to do using free and inexpensive materials. In the example below, the activity is to build a planetarium. The material used is an old umbrella; the mini sketch shows a possible outcome. Many teachers have run off copies of these activities and put them on activity cards for children to use. Good luck in your work.

Ex: Build a planetarium that
       shows the constellations in
       the sky.   Old umbrella

Starter Idea or Activity	Main Material Used	Mini Sketch
1. Find out how far a mealworm, sow bug or snail travels in five minutes.	Adding machine tape that is calibrated and laminated	
2. Make a stream table to show geological features.	Aluminum foil pans	
3. Make a seed germinator that shows seed germination.	Aluminum foil pan with plastic lid	
4. Make a boat that will float with a full load of cargo.	Aluminum foil and pull-top tabs from pop cans	
5. Make a system of gears to study gear movement in machinery.	Bottle caps	
6. Musical rhythm instruments held on board of nails to study sound.	Bottle caps	
7. Make interesting designs in studying absorption.	Blotter paper and food coloring	

Starter Idea or Activity	Main Material Used	Mini Sketch
8. Build a balance beam to study center of gravity and three types of levers.	Scrap lumber	
9. Build wheels, axles, and pulleys.	Broom handles	
10. Study static electricity by rubbing balloon in hair.	Balloons	
11. Study gear ratios in machines.	Ten-speed bicycle	
12. Develop classification skills in children.	Buttons in hamburger containers	
13. Study knotty problems and types of knots.	Baler twine	
14. Study texture of various substances.	Mix cornstarch and water. Knead to form pliable mixture.	
15. Make a telephone.	Cigar boxes or tin cans, string, wire	
16. Puzzle/Mystery boxes	Leftover boxes from checks at bank	
17. Fish/Animal puzzles	Cardboard	

Starter Idea or Activity	Main Material Used	Mini Sketch
18. Study capillary action in plants.	Celery	
19. Make bird feeders.	Coffee cans	
20. Make pulleys for simple machines.	Coat hanger and spool	
21. Build structures and test strength of structures.	Cardboard ring or tube on coat hangers. Plastic golf club tubes also work well for this.	
22. Study atomic structure.	Coat hanger wire and construction paper for electrons	
23. Study plant growth under different light conditions.	Cellophane paper of different colors	
24. Study conduction of heat by metal and glass rods.	Metal, glass rods and candle	
25. Rod/Pencil holder	Clothespins	
26. Study electricity.	Clothespin bulb holder	
27. Build solar collector.	Car headlight frame and holder	

Starter Idea or Activity	Main Material Used	Mini Sketch
28. Make a cube to show cubic crystals.	Computer cards	
29. Identify and study poisonous plants.	Preserve in clear Con-Tact paper for display purposes.	
30. Study and improve senses.	Cloves, etc., in sealed white #10 envelopes. Identify by smell.	
31. Study properties of sound and static electricity.	Comb and bits of paper	
32. Gum and cigarette pack foil used to make electroscope. Rub comb through hair. Touch wire. What happens to leaves of foil?	Aluminum foil electroscope made from a pill bottle	
33. Study effects of water on plant growth.	Aspirators made from squeezable detergent bottles	
34. Study atomic reaction or chain reaction.	Dominoes	
35. Make magic markers to study color.	Deodorant bottles	
36. Classify fossils and shells and make collections of these.	Egg cartons	
37. Build a wind tunnel.	Electric fan and 6 mil plastic	
38. Study operation of anemometer and wind vane.	Electric fan	

Starter Idea or Activity	Main Material Used	Mini Sketch
39. Study simple machines.	Erector sets and Tinker Toys	
40. Study motion of pendulum.	Fishing corks and fishline	
41. Purification of water samples	Filter paper	
42. Study human/animal prints.	Fingers and water soluable ink	
43. Study principles of flight.	Fishline	
44. Study parts of science creatures.	Felt scraps and board	
45. Make bubbles and observe their sizes and properties.	Straws, small cans, Ivory Snow, glycerine (2-4 teaspoons of glycerine per quart of water)	
46. Study balance principles.	Pegboard scraps and golf tees	
47. Study circulation in fish tail.	Wet gauze wrapped around gills with tail of fish under microscope	
48. Study properties of water and propulsion of boats.	Gutters from a home	
49. Test for starch.	Iodine on potato	
50. Study properties of light.	Ice-cream container with cord socket and light bulb	
51. Study magnetic lines of force on overhead projector.	Iron filings, piece of glass and magnets	
52. Study heart recovery rate and breathing rates.	Jump ropes	

Starter Idea or Activity	Main Material Used	Mini Sketch
53. Investigate properties/attributes of an object(s).	Keys and locks	
54. Color spectrum	Old lenses and prisms	
55. Make a carpenter's level.	Soda straw and water	
56. Make a heart model.	One-gallon plastic jugs with various colors of yarn for veins and arteries	
57. Air pressure and what causes milk to go up straw into the mouth	Small milk carton with straw when children are having lunch or snack	
58. Study properties of light.	Old mirrors	
59. Splitting of the atom and nuclear power	Wooden matches and clay	
60. Study chemical and physical changes.	Magnifying glass and burn paper	
61. Study Newton's Third Law of Motion.	Marbles	
62. Study properties of paper when dry and wet.	Newspaper	
63. Study cells.	Onion skin under microscope	
64. Study viscosity of liquids by oil race.	Oils of various types and wax paper on inclined plane	
65. Pond scope	Pringle's can with wax paper over one end	
66. Science games, puzzles and spinner wheels	Pizza wheels	
67. How to read electric and gas meters	Four pizza wheels with appropriate markings	

211

Starter Idea or Activity	Main Material Used	Mini Sketch
68. Star and constellation finder	Pizza wheel	
69. Study air pressure.	Plunger	
70. Study air bubbles.	Pull tabs or plastic 6-pack holders from pop cans for bubble blowers	
71. Patterns in nature	Pinecones that show sequencing	
72. Study balance of nature in aquaria.	Plastic shoe boxes for aquaria	
73. Show properties of light.	Pencil in glass of water	
74. Study fossils and animal tracks.	Plaster of Paris	
75. Study Bernoulli's principle.	Ping-Pong ball and straw	
76. Make an electromagnet.	Dry cell, wire, nail and paper clips	
77. Make a switch work.	Cardboard, paper fasteners, dry cell, wire, light bulb	
78. Measure height of plants with plant pole marker.	Paper clips and adding machine tape with Popsicle stick for pole	
79. Study density and buoyancy of boats.	Paper clips make good cargo and weigh one gram.	
80. Study molecular structure.	Pipe cleaners	

Starter Idea or Activity	Main Material Used	Mini Sketch
81. Study resistor code in electronics.	Pipe cleaners of various colors	
82. Study water wheel or anemometer.	Panty hose container for cups	
83. Keep a record of science investigations and clip together with clips from newly purchased pants.	Pant clips	
84. Clean electical contacts on radios, computer games, etc.	Q-tips and carbon tetrachloride	
85. Develop a feeling for rocks.	Make paperweights, jewelry, pet rocks.	
86. Learn about supporting structures.	Old bed springs make excellent structures.	
87. Study simple machines. Make model of terrace and contour farming.	Screws	
88. Make rock sifter to study sizes of rocks and classify them.	Window screen	
89. Study types of sound waves.	Slinky	
90. Study energy conservation.	Styrofoam packaging material with hamburger containers	

Starter Idea or Activity	Main Material Used	Mini Sketch
91. Grow seeds.	Sponge	
92. Build super structures.	Straws and clay	
93. Study how sandpaper and glass are made.	Sand and glue	
94. Study air pressure and the principles of flight.	Spool and sheet of paper on top of spool. Blow through spool.	
95. Study force and acceleration.	Roller skates with bricks on incline plane	
96. Study dispersal rates of liquids.	Tray and water. Add drop of food coloring on bull's-eye. Time. Can use clear plastic dish on overhead to show this also.	
97. Study paths of projectiles.	Tree branch crotch makes good slingshot rocket launcher.	
98. Study how a volcano operates.	Vinegar, baking soda, liquid soap and food coloring	
99. Study the principles of flight or make a model solar system to scale.	Wire from telephone or electrical company	
100. Study bones of human body.	X-rays from doctor or dentist	
101. Your choice		

STRETCHING

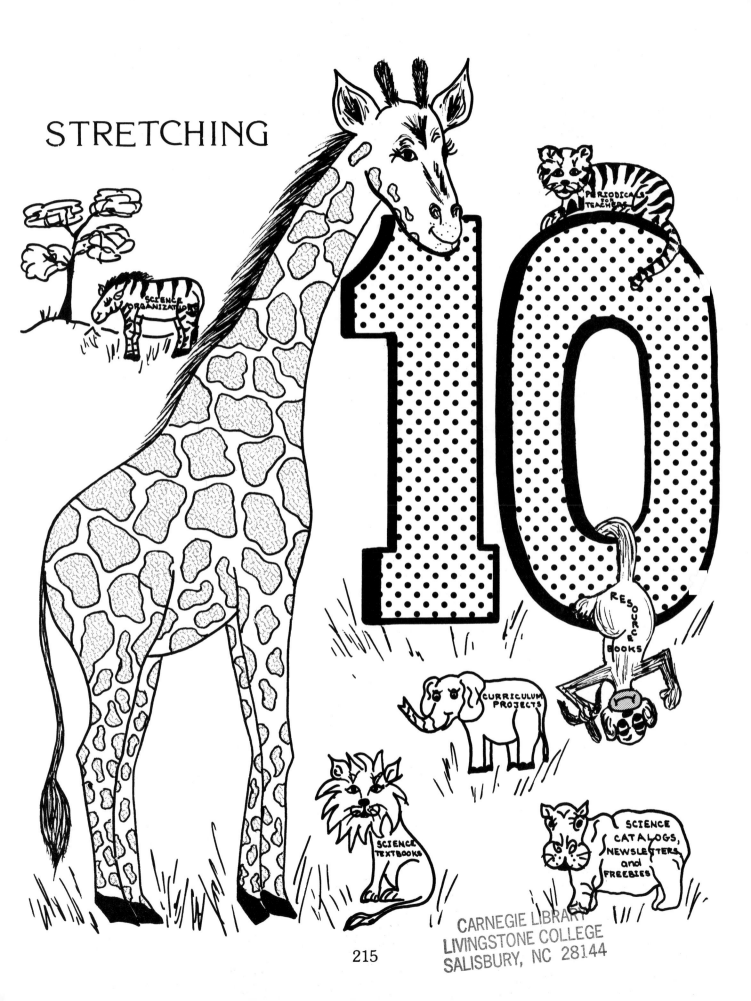

SCIENCE RELATED ORGANIZATIONS (O) AND PERIODICALS (P) FOR TEACHERS

	(O) American Association for the Advancement of Science 1333 H Street Washington, D.C. 20005	(O) Association for the Education of Teachers of Science Tennessee Technological University Cookeville, TN 38505
(O) National Association for Research in Science Teaching University of Cincinnati Cincinnati, OH 45221-0002	(O) National Geographic Society 17th and M Streets, N.W. Washington, D.C. 20036	(O) National Science Teachers Association 1742 Connecticut Avenue, N.W. Washington, D.C. 20009
(O) National Wildlife Federation 1412 Sixteenth Street, N.W. Washington, D.C. 20036	(O) School Science and Mathematics Association Bowling Green State University Bowling Green, OH 43403	(O) World Future Society 4916 St. Elmo Avenue (Bethesda) Washington, D.C. 20014
	(P) *The Good Apple Newspaper* Good Apple, Inc. Box 299 Carthage, IL 62321	(P) *Instructor* Instructor Publications, Inc. 757 Third Avenue New York, NY 10017
(P) *Learning* 530 University Avenue Palo Alto, CA 94301	(P) *National 4-H News* 7100 Connecticut Avenue Chevy Chase, MD 20815	(P) *National Wildlife* National Wildlife Federation 225 E. Michigan Avenue Milwaukee, WI 53202
(P) *Science Activities* Heldref Publications 4000 Albemarle Street, N.W. Room 504 Washington, D.C. 20016	(P) *Science and Children* National Science Teachers Association 1742 Connecticut Avenue, N.W. Washington, D.C. 20009	(P) *Science Education* John Wiley and Sons 605 Third Avenue New York, NY 10016
(P) *Science 86* American Association for the Advance of Science 1515 Massachusetts Avenue, N.W. Washington, D.C. 20005	(P) *Science News* 1719 N Street, N.W. Washington, D.C. 20036	(P) *The Science Teacher* National Science Teachers Association 1742 Connecticut Avenue, N.W. Washington, D.C. 20009
(P) *School Science and Mathematics* Bowling Green State University Bowling Green, OH 43403	(P) *Sky and Telescope* Sky Publishing Corporation 49 Bay State Road Cambridge, MA 02138	(P) *Science Scope* National Science Teachers Association 1742 Connecticut Avenue, N.W. Washington, D.C. 20009
(P) *Nature Scope* National Wildlife Federation 1412 16th Street, N.W. Washington, D.C. 20036	(P) *Oasis* Good Apple, Inc. Box 299 Carthage, IL 62321	(O) (P) Educational Resources Information Center (ERIC) The Ohio State University 1200 Chambers Road Columbus, OH 43212

RESOURCE BOOKS WITH SCIENCE IDEAS AND TIPS ON HOW TO TEACH SCIENCE

Below is a listing of a few of the many useful science books that will help you make science come alive for children. Your school, local library or university may have copies for you to borrow and use.

Abruscato, Joseph. *Children, Computers and Science Teachers: Butterflies and Bytes*. Englewood Cliffs, NJ: Prentice-Hall, Inc., 1986.

_____. *Teaching Children Science*. Englewood Cliffs, NJ: Prentice-Hall, Inc., 1982.

Abruscato, Joseph, and Jack Hassard. *Loving and Beyond, Science Teaching for the Humanistic Classroom*. Pacific Palisades, CA: Goodyear Publishing Company, Inc., 1976.

_____. *The Whole Cosmos: Catalog of Science Activities*. Santa Monica, CA: Goodyear Publishing Company, Inc., 1977.

_____. *The Earth People Activity Book*. Santa Monica, CA: Goodyear Publishing Company, Inc., 1979.

Alberti, Del, and Mary Laycock. *The Correlation of Activity-Centered Science and Mathematics*. Hayward, CA: Activity Resources Co., 1972.

American Association for the Advancement of Science. *Science: A Process Approach: Commentary for Teachers*. Washington, D.C.: American Association for the Advancement of Science, 1963.

Anastasiou, Clifford. *Teachers, Children and Things: Materials-Centered Science*. Minneapolis, MN: Mine Publications, Inc., 1972.

Anderson, Ronald, et al. *Developing Children's Thinking Through Science*. Englewood Cliffs, NJ: Prentice-Hall, Inc., 1970.

Bartholomew, Rolland B., and Frank E. Crawley. *Science Laboratory Techniques*. Menlo Park, CA: Addison-Wesley Publishing Co., 1980.

Blackwelder, Sheila Kyser. *Science for All Seasons*. Englewood Cliffs, NJ: Prentice-Hall, Inc., 1980.

Blough, Glenn O., and Julius Schwartz. *Elementary School Science and How to Teach It*. New York, NY: Holt, Rinehart and Winston, 1979.

Brandes, Louis Grant. *Science Can Be Fun*. Portland, ME: J. Weston Walch, 1979.

Brandwein, Paul, and Hy Ruchlis. *100 Invitations to Investigate*. New York, NY: Harcourt, Brace, and World, Inc., 1971.

Brown, Bob. *666 Science Tricks and Experiments*. Blue Ridge Summit, PA: Tab Books, 1978.

Butts, David P. *The Teaching of Science, A Self-Directed Planning Guide*. New York, NY: Harper & Row, 1974.

_____. *Teaching Science in the Elementary School*. New York, NY: The Free Press, 1973.

Butts, David P., and Gene E. Hall. *Children and Science: The Process of Teaching and Learning*. Englewood Cliffs, NJ: Prentice-Hall, Inc., 1975.

Bybee, Roger. *Personalizing Science Teaching*. Washington, D.C.: National Science Teachers Association, 1974.

Bybee, Roger, et al. *Teaching About Science and Society: Activities for Elementary and High School*. Columbus, OH: Charles E. Merrill Publishing Company, 1984.

Cain, Sandra E., and Jack M. Evans. *Sciencing: An Involvement Approach to Elementary Science Methods.* Columbus, OH: Charles E. Merrill Publishing Co., 1979.

Carin, Arthur, and Robert Sund. *Teaching Modern Science.* Columbus, OH: Charles E. Merrill Publishing Co., 1980.

_____. *Teaching Science Through Discovery.* Columbus, OH: Charles E. Merrill Publishing Co., 1985.

Craig, Gerald S. *Science for the Elementary School Teacher.* New York, NY: Ginn and Company, 1958.

DeBruin, Jerry. *Young Scientists Explore Light & Color.* Carthage, IL: Good Apple, Inc., 1986.

_____. *Young Scientists Explore Rocks & Minerals.* Carthage, IL: Good Apple, Inc., 1986.

_____. *Young Scientists Explore Nature.* Carthage, IL: Good Apple, Inc., 1986.

_____. *Young Scientists Explore The World of Water.* Carthage, IL: Good Apple, Inc., 1985.

_____. *Young Scientists Explore An Encyclopedia of Energy Activities.* Carthage, IL: Good Apple, Inc., 1985.

_____. *Young Scientists Explore Electricity & Magnetism.* Carthage, IL: Good Apple, Inc., 1985.

_____. *Young Scientists Explore Inner & Outer Space.* Carthage, IL: Good Apple, Inc., 1983.

_____. *Young Scientists Explore The Weather.* Carthage, IL: Good Apple, Inc., 1983.

_____. *Young Scientists Explore The Five Senses.* Carthage, IL: Good Apple, Inc., 1983.

_____. *Young Scientists Explore The Moon.* Carthage, IL: Good Apple, Inc., 1982.

_____. *Young Scientists Explore Animals.* Carthage, IL: Good Apple, Inc., 1982.

_____. *Young Scientists Explore The World Around Them.* Carthage, IL: Good Apple, Inc., 1982.

DeBruin, Jerry, et al. *Touching & Teaching Metrics: Duplicating Masters for the Primary Grades.* Carthage, IL: Good Apple, Inc., 1978.

_____. *Touching & Teaching Metrics: Duplicating Masters for the Intermediate Grades.* Carthage, IL: Good Apple, Inc., 1978.

DeBruin, Jerry, and Rita Sheperak. *Touching & Teaching Metrics.* Carthage, IL: Good Apple, Inc., 1977.

DeVito, Alfred. *Creative Wellsprings for Science Teaching.* West Lafayette, IN: Creative Ventures, Inc., 1984.

DeVito, Alfred, and Gerald H. Krockover. *Creative Sciencing, A Practical Approach.* Boston, MA: Little, Brown and Company, 1980.

_____. *Creative Sciencing, Ideas and Activities for Teachers and Children.* Boston, MA: Little, Brown and Company, 1980.

Elementary Science Study. *The ESS Reader.* Newton, MA: Educational Development Center, Inc., 1970.

Esler, William K. *Teaching Elementary Science.* Belmont, CA: Wadsworth Publishing Co., Inc., 1984.

Farmer, Walter A., and Margaret A. Farrell. *Systematic Instruction in Science for the Middle and High School Years.* Menlo Park, CA: Addison-Wesley Company, 1980.

Ferguson, A.R. *Science You Need.* Ontario, Canada: Thomas Nelson and Sons Ltd., 1979.

Friedl, Alfred E. *Teaching Science to Children: The Inquiry Approach Applied.* New York, NY: Random House, Inc., 1972.

Gega, Peter. *Science in Elementary Education.* New York, NY: John Wiley and Sons, Inc., 1986.

George, Kenneth D., et al. *Elementary School Science Why and How*. Lexington, MA: D.C. Heath and Company, 1974.

_____. *Science Investigations for Elementary School Teachers*. Lexington, MA: D.C. Heath and Company, 1974.

Good, Ronald G. *How Children Learn Science*. New York, NY: Macmillan Publishing Co., Inc., 1977.

Heller, Robert L. *Geology and Earth Sciences Sourcebook for Elementary and Secondary Schools*. New York, NY: Holt, Rinehart and Winston, 1970.

Henson, Kenneth, and Nelmar Janke. *Elementary Science Methods*. New York, NY: McGraw-Hill Book Company, 1984.

Hittle, David R., et al. *Sourcebook for Chemistry and Physics*. New York, NY: Macmillan Publishing Company, 1983.

Hone, Elizabeth B., et al. *A Sourcebook for Elementary Science*. New York, NY: Harcourt Brace Jovanovich, Inc., 1971.

Hubler H. Clark. *Science for Children*. New York, NY: Random House, Inc., 1974.

Hungerford, H., and A. Tomera. *Science in the Elementary School*. Champaign, IL: Stipes Publishing Company, 1977.

Ivany, J.W. George. *Science Teaching in the Elementary School: A Professional Approach*. Palo Alto, CA: Science Research Associates, Inc., 1975.

Jacobson, Willard J., and Abby B. Bergman. *Science Activities for Children*. Englewood Cliffs: Prentice-Hall, Inc., 1983.

Jacobson, Willard J. *Science for Children*. Englewood Cliffs, NJ: Prentice-Hall, Inc., 1980.

Joseph, A., et al. *A Sourcebook for the Physical Sciences*. New York, NY: Harcourt, Brace and World, 1961.

Kaplan, S.N., et al. *Change for Children*. Pacific Palisades, CA: Goodyear Publishing Company, 1973.

Kauchak, Donald, and Paul Eggen. *Exploring Science in the Elementary Schools*. Chicago, IL: Rand McNally College Publishing Co., 1980.

Kuslan, Louis I., and A. Harris Stone. *Teaching Children Science: An Inquiry Approach*. Belmont, CA: Wadsworth Publishing Company, Inc., 1972.

Lansdown, Brenda, Paul E. Blackwood, and Paul F. Brandwein. *Teaching Elementary Science Through Investigations and Colloquium*. New York, NY: Harcourt Brace Jovanovich, Inc., 1971.

Lewis, June E., and Irene C. Potter. *The Teaching of Science in the Elementary School*. Englewood Cliffs, NJ: Prentice-Hall, Inc., 1970.

Liem, Tik L. *Invitations to Science Inquiry*. Lexington, MA: Ginn Custom Publishing Co., 1981.

Lowery, Lawrence F. *The Everyday Science Sourcebook*. Boston, MA: Allyn & Bacon, Inc., 1978.

Lunetta, Vincent, and Shimson Novick. *Inquiring and Problem Solving in the Physical Sciences: A Sourcebook*. Dubuque, Iowa: Kendall/Hunt Publishing Company, 1982.

Mathews, Charles, et al. *Student-Structured Learning in Science*. Dubuque, IA: Kendall/Hunt Publishing Company, 1977.

McIntyre, Margaret. *Early Childhood and Science*. Washington, D.C.: National Science Teachers Association, 1984.

Moore, Shirley. *Science Projects Handbook*. Washington, D.C.: Science Service, 1960.

Morholt, E., et al. *A Sourcebook for the Biological Sciences*. New York, NY: Harcourt, Brace and World, 1966.

McGavack, John, and Donald P. LaSalle. *Crystals, Insects and Unknown Objects*. New York, NY: The John Day Company, 1971.

Munson, Howard R. *Science Activities with Simple Things*. Belmont, CA: Fearon Pitman Publishers, Inc., 1962.

Navarra, John G., and Joseph Zafforoni. *Science in the Elementary School*. Columbus, OH: Charles E. Merrill Publishing Company, 1975.

Nelson, Leslie W., and George C. Lorbeer. *Science Activities for Elementary Children*. Dubuque, IA: William C. Brown Publishers, 1976.

Nowak, Joseph D., and D. Bob Gowin. *Learning How to Learn*. Cambridge, MA: Cambridge University Press, 1984.

Orlich, Donald C., et al. *Teaching Strategies*. Lexington, MA: D.C. Heath and Company, 1985.

Penn, Linda. *Young Scientists Explore The Human Body*. Carthage, IL: Good Apple, Inc., 1986.

_____. *Young Scientists Explore Parks & Playgrounds*. Carthage, IL: Good Apple, Inc., 1986.

_____. *Young Scientists Explore Wild Plants & Animals*. Carthage, IL: Good Apple, Inc., 1986.

_____. *Young Scientists Explore Dinosaurs*. Carthage, IL: Good Apple, Inc., 1985.

_____. *Young Scientists Explore The Kingdom of Plants*. Carthage, IL: Good Apple, Inc., 1985.

_____. *Young Scientists Explore The Sun, Moon & Stars*. Carthage, IL: Good Apple, Inc., 1985.

_____. *Young Scientists Explore Animal Friends*. Carthage, IL: Good Apple, Inc., 1983.

_____. *Young Scientists Explore Butterflies & Moths*. Carthage, IL: Good Apple, Inc., 1983.

_____. *Young Scientists Explore Seasons*. Carthage, IL: Good Apple, Inc., 1983.

_____. *Young Scientists Explore Air, Land, & Water Life*. Carthage, IL: Good Apple, Inc., 1982.

_____. *Young Scientists Explore Insects*. Carthage, IL: Good Apple, Inc., 1982.

_____. *Young Scientists Explore The World of Nature*. Carthage, IL: Good Apple, Inc., 1982.

Piltz, Albert, and Robert Sund. *Creative Teaching of Science in the Elementary School*. Boston, MA: Allyn & Bacon, Inc., 1974.

Renner, John W., et al. *Teaching Science in the Elementary School*. New York, NY: Harper & Row, Publishers, 1973.

Romey, William D. *Inquiry Techniques for Teaching Science*. Englewood Cliffs, NJ: Prentice-Hall, Inc., 1968.

Rowe, Mary Budd. *Teaching Science as Continuous Inquiry*. New York, NY: McGraw-Hill Book Company, 1978.

Roy, Mary Massey. *Probe: A Handbook for Teachers of Elementary Science*. Stevensville, MI: Educational Service, Inc., 1962.

Schatz, Albert. *Teaching Science with Garbage*. Emmaus, PA: Rodale Press, Inc., 1971.

Schmidt, Victor, and Vern Rockcastle. *Teaching Science with Everyday Things*. New York, NY: McGraw-Hill Book Company, 1982.

Scott, John M. *The Everyday Living Approach to Teaching Elementary Science*. West Nyack, NY: Parker Publishing Company, Inc., 1970.

Selbert, Edith M., et al. *Discovering Science in the Elementary School*. Reading, MA: Addison-Wesley Publishing Co., Inc., 1970.

Simpson, Ronald D., and Norman D. Anderson. *Science, Students, and Schools: A Guide for the Middle and Secondary School Teacher.* New York, NY: John Wiley and Sons, 1981.

Smith, Walter. *Career Oriented Modules to Explore Topics in Science.* Washington, D.C.: National Science Teachers Association, 1984.

Stone, A. Harris, Fred Geis, and Louis Kuslan. *Experiences for Teaching Children Science.* Belmont, CA: Wadsworth Publishing Company, Inc., 1971.

Strongin, Herb. *Science on a Shoestring.* Reading, MA: Addison-Wesley Publishing Company, 1976.

Sund, Robert, and Leslie Trowbridge. *Teaching Science Through Inquiry.* Columbus, OH: Charles E. Merrill Publishing Company, 1974.

Sund, Robert, William Tillery, and Leslie Trowbridge. *Investigate and Discover: Elementary Science Lessons.* Boston, MA: Allyn & Bacon, Inc., 1975.

Sund, Robert, and Roger Bybee. *Becoming a Better Elementary Science Teacher.* Columbus, OH: Charles E. Merrill Publishing Company, 1973.

Sund, Robert B., et al. *Elementary Science Discovery Lessons: The Physical Science.* Boston, MA: Allyn & Bacon, Inc., 1970.

Tannenbaum, Harold E., et al. *Science Education for Elementary School Teachers.* Boston, MA: Allyn & Bacon, Inc., 1965.

Taylor, Frank D., et al. *Exploring Our Environment: Science Tasks.* Denver, CO: Love Publishing Company, 1973.

Thier, Herbert. *Teaching Elementary School Science.* Lexington, MA: D.C. Heath and Company, 1970.

Trojack, Doris A. *Science with Children.* New York, NY: McGraw-Hill Book Company, 1979.

Triensnberg, Henry. *Individualized Science: Like It Is.* Washington, D.C.: National Science Teachers Association, 1972.

UNESCO. *700 Science Experiments for Everyone.* Garden City, NY: Doubleday and Company, 1962.

_____. *New UNESCO Sourcebook for Science Teaching.* New York, NY: UNIPUB, Inc., 345 Park Avenue South, 1976.

Utgard, Russel O., et al. *Sourcebook for Earth Sciences and Astronomy.* New York, NY: The Macmillan Company, 1972.

Van Deman, Barry, and Ed McDonald. *Nuts and Bolts: A Matter of Fact Guide to Science Fairs.* Harwood Heights, IL: The Science Man Press, 1980.

Vergara, William. *Science in the World Around Us.* New York, NY: Bantam Books, 1971.

Waston, Nathan. *Teaching Science in Elementary and Middle Schools.* New York, NY: David McKay Company, Inc., 1974.

Waters, Barbara W. *Science Can Be Elementary: Discovery-Action Programs for K-3.* New York, NY: Citation Press, 1973.

Wolfinger, Donna M. *Teaching Science in the Elementary School.* Boston, MA: Little, Brown and Company, 1984.

SCIENTIFIC COMPANIES THAT PUBLISH HANDY SCIENCE CATALOGS, NEWSLETTERS AND OTHER FREEBIES

NOTE: Order your handy science catalogs, newsletters and other free and inexpensive materials from the following companies. A short letter on school stationery will yield some neat materials including the most recent ideas in scientific discoveries and complete ordering information.

NAME AND ADDRESS OF COMPANY	NOTES ON MATERIALS TO ORDER
Bausch and Lomb 1400 N. Goodman Street Rochester, NY 14602 (716) 338-6000	Has educational microscopes for the elementary school.
Carolina Biological Supply Co. 2700 York Road Burlington, NC 27215 (919) 584-0381	Biology materials, live specimens. Be sure to have name put on mailing list and receive free monthly newsletter, *Carolina Tips*, to improve your content background.
Central Scientific Company (Cenco) 11222 Melrose Avenue Franklin Park, IL 60131 (312) 451-0150	Has general science materials and equipment.
Creative Publications, Inc. P.O. Box 238 Palo Alto, CA 94302	Creative math and science manipulative materials. Be sure to have your name placed on the mailing list for this handy catalog.
Curriculum Innovations, Inc. 3500 Western Avenue Highland Park, IL 60035 (312) 432-2700	Educational periodicals for classroom use.
Dale Seymour Publications Box 10888 Palo Alto, CA 94303 (800) USA-1100 or (800) ABC-0766	Excellent science books including English series *Using Your Environment*, *Science 5/13*, and *Teaching Primary Science*.
Delta Education, Inc. P.O. Box M Nashua, NH 03061-6012 (800) 258-1302	Has Science Curriculum Improvement Study (SCIS) (SCIS II) and Elementary Science Study (ESS) kit materials and manuals. Also SAPA II, OBIS, ISIS and ISCP materials. Supplies kits for textbooks also.
Eastman Kodak Company 343 State Street Rochester, NY 14560 (716) 724-3667	Publishes helpful pamphlets *Science Fairs* and *Astrophotography* for tips on photographing star trails, comets, meteors, aurorae, satellites, and the moon. See local photo dealer or send for information from the company for other science and photography related materials.
Educational Activities, Inc. P.O. Box 392 Freeport, NY 11520 (800) 645-3739	Microcomputer programs for science.
Edmund Scientific Company 7789 Edscorp Building Barrington, NJ 08007 1-800-282-0224	Catalog contains excellent materials. Ask to be placed on mailing list for free issues of the *Astronomy News* which contain valuable astronomy information including monthly sky charts. Excellent source for diffraction grating material for spectroscopes (see page 155) and has star, moon, and planet finders.

NAME AND ADDRESS OF COMPANY	NOTES ON MATERIALS TO ORDER
Estes Industries Dept. 169S Penrose, CO 81240 (303) 372-6565	Includes up-to-date materials and information on model rocketry. Excellent publications on how to build a wind tunnel and rocket engines.
Field Enterprise Merchandise Mart Plaza Chicago, IL 60654 (312) 245-3456	Has excellent free reprints from World Book Encyclopedia (see page 64). Also publishes *Science Year* among other useful science books.
Fisher Scientific Company Educational Materials Division 4901 W. LeMoyne Street Chicago, IL 60651 (800) 621-4769	Has excellent materials for science education.
Forestry Suppliers, Inc. 205 West Rankin Street P.O. Box 8397 Jackson, MS 39204 (601) 354-3565	Interesting catalog that contains information on forestry, engineering and environmental equipment. A handy catalog to have for your classroom.
Good Apple, Inc. Box 299 Carthage, IL 62321 1-800-435-7234	Publishes a variety of classroom teaching materials including *The Good Apple Newspaper*, a bimonthly publication featuring a wealth of teaching ideas. See page 248 in this book for other Good Apple products.
Hayes School Publishing Company, Inc. 321 Penwood Avenue Wilkinsburg, PA 15221 (412) 371-2373	Produces science duplicating masters and other science related printed materials.
Hubbard Scientific Company 1946 Raymond Drive Northbrook, IL 60062 (312) 272-7810	Has science media and materials available.
Jewel Industries, Inc. P.O. Box 104 1946 Raymond Drive Northbrook, IL 60062 (800) 323-8368	Has salt water aquaria, animal cages, including live specimens.
Lab-Aids, Inc. 130 Wilbur Place P.O. Box 158 Bohemia, NY 11716 (516) 567-6120	Features general science equipment and materials.
Learning Things, Inc. 68A Broadway P.O. Box 436 Arlington, MA 02174 (617) 646-0093	K-12 science/mathematics, technology and complete line of cardboard carpentry materials.
Mineral of the Month Club 13057-NS California Street Yucaipa, CA 92399 (714) 797-1650	Excellent rock and mineral materials. Use in conjunction with activities on page 172.

NAME AND ADDRESS OF COMPANY	NOTES ON MATERIALS TO ORDER
NASCO 901 Janesville Avenue Fort Atkinson, WI 53538 (414) 563-2446	Excellent catalog includes materials for all levels offering teaching aids and supplies. Has both living and preserved specimens. Wide variety of science books at all levels.

National Aeronautics and Space
   Administration
Lewis Research Center
21000 Brookpark Road
Cleveland, OH 44135
     or
Community Services and Education Branch
   (LFG-9)
Washington, D.C. 20546
(202) 453-1000
	Be sure to ask to have name put on free *Report to Educators* newsletter mailing list. Contains helpful astronomy related information for educators of all levels. Has Space Shuttle and space probe information available.

National Science Teachers Association 1742 Connecticut Avenue, N.W. Washington, D.C. 20009 (202) 328-5800	Publishes a variety of science teaching materials. Ask to have name placed on mailing list for free newsletters and announcements of important and upcoming programs and events.
OHAUS Scale Corporation 29 Hanover Road Florham Park, NJ 07932 (201) 377-9000	Has wide variety of mathematics and science equipment and materials.
Radio Shack/Ed. Division 1400 One Tandy Center Fort Worth, TX 76102 (817) 390-3832	Computer software programs. Wide variety of science kits and booklets for children.
Sargent-Welch Scientific Company 7300 N. Linder Avenue Skokie, IL 60077 (312) 677-0600	Wide variety of science materials available including chemicals, preserved specimens, prepared microscope slides and computer software.
The Science Man Company 4738 N. Harlem Avenue Harwood Hts., IL 60656 (312) 867-4441	Has general science materials and equipment.
Science Kit, Inc. 777 E. Park Drive Tonawanda, NY 14150 (716) 874-6020	Has a wide variety of general science materials and equipment available.
Science Research Associates, Inc. 155 N. Wacker Drive Chicago, IL 60606 (800) 621-0664	Publisher of Inquiry Development Program (IDP) materials and film loops.
Toys 'n Things 906 North Dale St. Paul, MN 55103 (612) 488-7284	Produces excellent book entitled *Teachables from Trashables: Homemade Toys That Teach*. Be sure to have your name put on mailing list.
Tops Learning Systems 10978 S. Mulino Road Canby, OR 97013 (503) 266-8550	Send for information on ordering these interesting, fairly inexpensive modules, activity cards, and teachers' guides. Good, open-ended activities included in a variety of science areas.

NAME AND ADDRESS OF COMPANY	NOTES ON MATERIALS TO ORDER
Turtox, Inc. 5000 W. 128th Place Alsip, IL 60658 (312) 371-5500	Biology materials. Be sure to have name placed on list for excellent Turtox science leaflets to help you set up aquaria and terraria, on page 78, in your classroom.
Ward's Natural Science Establishment, Inc. 5100 W. Henrietta Road P.O. Box 92912 Rochester, NY 14692 (716) 359-2502	Has general science materials and live specimens available for purchase.
Webster Division/McGraw-Hill Company 1221 Avenue of the Americas New York, NY 10020 (212) 997-4585	Has complete line of ESS kits and manuals.
Science Service 1719 North Street, N.W. Washington, D.C. (202) 785-2255	Produces handy, inexpensive small kits of materials; each kit features a related science topic. Order from Things of Science, RD#1, Box 1305, Newtown, PA 18940.
Xerox Education Publications 245 Long Hill Road Middletown, CT 06457 (203) 347-7251	Publishes SAPA II kits and modules.

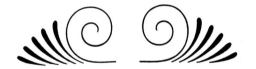

SOME NATIONAL ELEMENTARY AND MIDDLE SCHOOL SCIENCE CURRICULUM PROJECTS

The following includes a listing of some elementary and middle school science curriculum projects that were developed in the late 1960's and 1970's and continue to be prevalent to some extent in the 1980's. You may want to contact these project leaders and commercial publishers for additional information and science ideas.

Project Title	Address	Overview	Commercial Publisher
Adapting Science Materials for the Blind (ASMB)	Lawrence Hall of Science U. of California Berkeley, CA 94720	This Science Curriculum Improvement Study (SCIS) program isadapted for visually impaired students. This is a K-6 program that allows visually impaired and sighted students to work together with minimal assistance.	None
Conceptually Oriented Program in Science (COPES)	4 Washington Place New York, NY 10003	A spirally constructed program volves a series of learning experiences leading to an understanding of five major conceptual schemes. COPES features a hands-on curriculum involving active exploration in the learning of concepts, a nonreading program (no materials other than work sheets have been written for children), and low-priced, readily available materials. The curriculum is presented in the form of Teacher's Guides; each contains materials for assessing a child's understanding of the concepts.	None
Elementary Science Study (ESS)	Edu. Development Ctr. 55 Chapel Street Newton, MA 02160	A hands-on "discovery" based approach. Children are able to the physical world directly "hands-on" science activities. correlated well with interdisciplinary science study. (K-9)	McGraw-Hill Book Co. 1221 Ave. of the Americas New York, NY 10020 or Webster Division McGraw-Hill Company Manchester Road Manchester, MO 63011
Intermediate Science Curriculum Study (ISCS)	ISCS Project 415 N. Monroe Street Room 705 Florida State U. Tallahassee, FL 32301	This project has been designed children from 12 thru 15 years The level 1 materials would be appropriate for students in the upper grades (5 + 6) and jr. high school. The project materials allow the students to progress through various instructional pathways. The ISCS materials include independent study, laboratory investigations, discussion sessions, and self-pacing materials. (5-12)	Silver Burdett Company 250 James Street CN Morristown, NJ 07960-1918

Project Title	Address	Overview	Commercial Publisher
Individualized Science Instructional System	ISIS Project 1415 N. Monroe Street Florida State University Tallahassee, FL 32301	Series of individualized, in-minicourses covering topics of practical significance.	Ginn and Company 191 Spring Street Lexington, MA 02173
Minnesota School Mathematics and Science Center (MINNEMAST)	Minnesota Center University of Minnesota 148 Peik Hall Minneapolis, MN 55455	Math and science coordinated for kindergarten and primary grades. Lessons rely on co-ordination of math and science. Concepts are presented in an activity, data-gathering format. (K-3)	None
Schools Council and Nuffield Science 5/13 Project	Raintree Publishers, Ltd. 205 W. Highland Milwaukee, WI 53203	A series of elementary science booklets and materials for chil-Avenue

Originally developed in England. | Raintree Publishers, Ltd. 205 W. Highland Milwaukee, WI 53203 dren ages 5 through 13. |
Outdoor Biology Instructional (OBIS)	Lawrence Hall of Science University of California Berkeley, CA 94720	Helping children learn how to make intelligent decisions about the use of the environment is a principal focus of this project. The activities and materials of the OBIS project can be used with children aged 10 through 15.	Delta Education, Inc. Box M Nashua, NH 03061-6012
Science—A Process Approach II (SAPA) or (AAAS)	American Association for the Advancement of Science 1776 Massachusetts Ave. NW Washington, D.C. 20036	SAPA II, a revision of the 191 Spring Street activity-oriented curriculum. Its 105 modules are structured around the various processes of science. There are (1) instructional booklets for teachers (objectives, possible teaching sequences and activities, evaluation measures), (2) kit materials, and (3) storage units. (K-6)	Ginn and Company Lexington, MA 02173
Science Curriculum Improvement Study (SCIS)	Lawrence Hall of Sci. U. of California Berkeley, CA 94720	Ungraded, sequential physical and life science programs. Developed and evaluated by staff, originated by scientists, and adapted to elementary school children's needs. Challenging investigations using a laboratory approach. Scientific literacy is stressed. (K-6)	Rand McNally & Company Box 7600 Chicago, IL 60680

Project Title	Address	Overview	Commercial Publisher
Unified Science and Mathematics for Elementary Schools (USMES)	USMES, Education Development Center 55 Chapel Street Newton, MA 02160	Interdisciplinary program that challenges students to solve real problems from their school and community environment. There are no "right" solutions. Students are required to use their own ideas. The problems are "big" enough to require many class activities for effective solutions. (K-8)	Moore Publishing Co. P.O. Box 3036 West Durham Station Durham, NC 27705
University of Illinois Astronomy Program (UIAP)	U. of Illinois Dept. of Astronomy Urbana, IL 61801	Sequential development of the basic understanding of astronomy through a series of modules. Generally applicable science skills (processes) are practiced in unusual and interesting classroom astronomy activities. (5-8)	Harper & Row Publishers 10 East 53rd Street New York, NY 10022

*For a more detailed listing of all curriculum projects, see International Clearinghouse for Science & Mathematics Curricula, J. D. Lockard, ed., University of Maryland, College Park, Maryland 20742.

SOME ELEMENTARY SCIENCE TEXTBOOK SERIES

Below is a chart of some of the major elementary science texbook series used in elementary schools today. You may find your own series in the list. The materials in *Creative, Hands-on Science Experiences* can be used to complement, supplement, and expand upon basic concepts found in your series and hopefully will help you and your children stretch a bit further.

Publisher's Name and Address	Textbook Series	Date	Grade Level	Teacher's Notes
Addison-Wesley Publishing Co. 2725 Sand Hill Road Menlo Park, CA 94024 (415) 854-0300	Addison-Wesley Science	1980	K-6	
Cambridge Book Company 828 Seventh Avenue New York, NY 10019 (212) 957-5300	Cambridge Science Work-A-Texts	1977	1-6	
D.C. Heath and Company 125 Spring Street Lexington, MA 02173 (800) 225-1149	Heath Science	1985	K-6	
Ginn and Company 191 Spring Street Lexington, MA 02173 (617) 861-1670	Elementary Science	1982	K-6	
Globe Book Company, Inc. 50 West 23rd Street New York, NY 10010 (800) 221-7994	The Globe Science Series	1986	6-9	
Harcourt Brace Jovanovich, Inc. 6277 Sea Harbor Drive Orlando, FL 32887 (305) 345-2000	Concepts in Science: Curie Edition ALSO HBJ Science	1980 1985	K-9 K-6	
Holt, Rinehart and Winston 383 Madison Avenue New York, NY 10017 (212) 872-2000	Holt Science	1980	K-6	

Publisher's Name and Address	Textbook Series	Date	Grade Level	Teacher's Notes
Houghton Mifflin Company One Beacon Street Boston, MA 02107 (617) 725-5000	Houghton Mifflin Science	1979	K-6	
Laidlaw Brothers, A Division of Doubleday & Company, Inc. Thatcher and Madison River Forest, IL 60305 (312) 366-5320	The New Exploring Science Program	1976	K-6	
McGraw-Hill Webster Division 1221 Avenue of the Americas New York, NY 10020 (212) 997-4585	Gateways to Science	1979	K-6	
Charles E. Merrill Publishing Co. 1300 Alum Creek Drive Columbus, OH 43216 (614) 890-1111	Accent on Science	1985	K-6	
Rand McNally & Company P.O. Box 7600 Chicago, IL 60680 (312) 267-6868	SCIIS	1978	K-6	
Raintree Publishers Group 205 W. Highland Avenue Milwaukee, WI 53203 (414) 273-0873	Schools Council and Nuffield Science 5-13 Basic Set and Using the Environment	1974	K-8	
Scott, Foresman and Company 1900 E. Lake Avenue Glenview, IL 60025 (312) 729-3000	Scott, Foresman Science	1984	K-6	
Silver Burdett Company 250 James Street, CN 1918 Morristown, NJ 07960-1918 (201) 285-7740	Silver Burdett Science	1985	K-6	

TIPS ON HOW TO EVALUATE AN ELEMENTARY SCIENCE PROGRAM

The following information may assist teachers, administrators and parents who are evaluating their elementary science programs and considering the adoption of new materials. It is important to remember that you should have a strong program in science. This can be accomplished by:

(1) Involving teachers, administrators (from all levels), parents, and students in the selection process.

(2) Study and adapt what is now available rather than reinventing the wheel once again.

(3) Select a program that features hands-on activities that will get children interested in science.

(4) Try out different types of programs on a pilot basis. Visit other places that have these programs. Then select the one that meets your needs. Go slowly.

(5) Provide in-service training sessions for all concerned.

(6) Constantly monitor and evaluate your program's effectiveness.

(7) Run off the following evaluation form when considering a new science program. Then use these pages frequently to help you decide the type of science text or materials you will need.

ELEMENTARY SCIENCE PROGRAM EVALUATION

I. Preliminary Information

Subject Area _____Elementary Science_____ Copyright Date _____

Grade Level _____ Publisher_____

Name of Rater _____ Book Title _____

II. Criteria for Evaluation. Rate the following subheadings on the basis of one (lowest) to five (highest).

A. PROGRAM UP-TO-DATE
Do the books in the program have a recent copyright date?   1   2   3   4   5

B. AUTHORSHIP
Do the authors and consultants have actual classroom teaching experience?
1   2   3   4   5

Do the authors have experience in teaching training in science education?
1   2   3   4   5

C. RESEARCH

Is the program based on the latest research in science and science teaching?
1 2 3 4 5

Have the program and its materials been field-tested in the classroom to incorporate the suggestions and ideas of teachers and pupils?   1 2 3 4 5

Is the program acceptable to this community?   1 2 3 4 5

Is the program consistent with the philosophy of education in the school and community?   1 2 3 4 5

Does the publisher have a successful background and experience in publishing science materials?   1 2 3 4 5

Does the publisher provide consultants for demonstration teaching?   1 2 3 4 5

Does the publisher provide consultants to discuss the program's books and materials?
1 2 3 4 5

Will the publisher provide consultants and/or funds for in-service training?
1 2 3 4 5

D. PHYSICAL CHARACTERISTICS

Do the materials have strong durability?   1 2 3 4 5

Are the books attractive and eye-appealing?   1 2 3 4 5

Are manipulative materials plentiful and durable?   1 2 3 4 5

E. SUBJECT MATTER CONTENT

Does each level of the program include a balanced coverage of the life sciences, the physical sciences, and the earth and space sciences?   1 2 3 4 5

Is the content appropriate for the pupils' level of maturity at each level?
1 2 3 4 5

Does the program have accurate, up-to-date content?   1 2 3 4 5

Does the program include substantial coverage of the environment, energy and other contemporary topics?   1 2 3 4 5

Does the program include a listing or chart of concepts and generalizations to be taught?   1 2 3 4 5

Does the program include interdisciplinary activities?   1 2 3 4 5

Are metric measurements used throughout the program?   1 2 3 4 5

Are various science careers emphasized in the program?   1 2 3 4 5

F. READABILITY

Does it appear that pupils can read the books and materials with ease and understanding? 1 2 3 4 5

Does the program use a student-centered approach that speaks directly to the student?
1 2 3 4 5

Are questions above the recall level built into the content and illustrations to involve and interest pupils? 1 2 3 4 5

Are in-text definitions and phonetic spellings given for new or different words?
1 2 3 4 5

Do the pages have an open, easy-to-follow organization and consistent, clear placement of headings? 1 2 3 4 5

Is the size of print appropriate for each level? 1 2 3 4 5

G. ILLUSTRATIONS

Does each book in the program have full-color illustrations that are functional and help pupils learn? 1 2 3 4 5

Does the program provide for the interpretation of charts, graphs and tables?
1 2 3 4 5

H. TEACHABILITY

Are consumable booklets available, with simple hands-on activities, log sheets and notes to parents to involve them in their children's studies? 1 2 3 4 5

Do the textbooks have a flexible unit, chapter, and section organization that is easily adaptable to individual classroom needs? 1 2 3 4 5

Do the unit introductions capture pupils' interest through colorful illustrations and thought-provoking questions? 1 2 3 4 5

Does each chapter begin with a colorfully illustrated page that introduces the chapter topic and asks questions that encourage pupils to think? 1 2 3 4 5

Are special activities built into each chapter to stimulate pupil involvement?
1 2 3 4 5

Does each textbook offer a variety of hands-on activities that can be carried out with easily obtained inexpensive materials? 1 2 3 4 5

Does each book have extending or optional activities? 1 2 3 4 5

Do the textbooks have provisions for involving pupils in making value judgments and decisions? 1 2 3 4 5

Are suggestions given for involving pupils in science-related research?
1 2 3 4 5

Are chapter reviews and evaluation instruments provided at the end of each unit?
1 2 3 4 5

Is there a complete Glossary, Index, and Table of Contents in each book for pupil reference? 1 2 3 4 5

I . TEACHER'S GUIDE

Does the program have complete Teachers' Editions that are easy to use?
1 2 3 4 5

Does the Teacher's Edition have full-size, full-color pupil pages with annotated answers in the margins? 1 2 3 4 5

Do the pupil pages of the Teacher's Edition have teaching aids conveniently located in extended margins, including the following:

1. A rationale for teaching specific concepts? 1 2 3 4 5

2. Suggestions for introducing each unit? 1 2 3 4 5

3. Main concepts of each chapter? 1 2 3 4 5

4. Objectives? 1 2 3 4 5

5. Important science terms? 1 2 3 4 5

6. Teaching helps for the hands-on activities? 1 2 3 4 5

7. Suggestions for pupil activity, discussion, and research? 1 2 3 4 5

8. Sample answers? 1 2 3 4 5

Does the Teacher's Edition include a complete professional manual that contains:

1. An overview of the entire program? 1 2 3 4 5

2. Science background information? 1 2 3 4 5

3. Information necessary for effective use of the textbook and the Teacher's Edition?
   1 2 3 4 5

4. A bibliography of additional instructional materials including activities, scrounge-ables and related activities? 1 2 3 4 5

5. Unit evaluation instruments with answers? 1 2 3 4 5

J . TOTAL POINTS

K. RATER NOTES

L. OVERALL RATING

All criteria considered, I feel this program is:

UNACCEPTABLE		ACCEPTABLE		OUTSTANDING
1	2	3	4	5

SIGNED _____

DATE _____

NOTES

1. H	4. M	7. O	10. T	13. F	16. Q	19. X
2. R	5. P	8. C	11. E	14. B	17. Y	20. I
3. J	6. N	9. S	12. A	15. L	18. D	

An exercise similar to this and further extending activities are found in SAPA II (AAAS) Module 17 *Change*, published by Ginn and Company, Lexington, MA 02173, 1974.

This activity is based on a chapter in David Weitzman's book *Eggs and Peanut Butter* although an earlier version can be found elsewhere. *Eggs and Peanut Butter* is published by Word Wheel Books, Inc., Menlo Park, CA 94025, 1975. Used with permission.

See the work of Judith and Bruce Bergum in the *Bulletin of the Psychonomic Society*, Vol. 14, Nos. 1 and 5.

For a comprehensive guide to science safety, order this handy publication "Safety in the Elementary Science Classroom" published by the National Science Teachers Association, Washington, D.C. 20009. Stock #471 14750. $2.00 but well worth it.

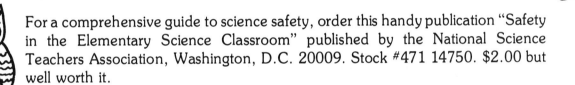

Guidebook to Constructing Inexpensive Science Teaching Equipment. Vol. 1 *Biology*, Vol. 2 *Chemistry*, Vol. 3 *Physics*. Inexpensive Science Teaching Equipment Project, University of Maryland, College Park, MD 20740, 1972.

New UNESCO Sourcebook for Science Teaching. UNIPUB, Inc., 650 First Avenue, New York, NY 10017.

Teachables from Trashables. Toys and Things Training and Resource Center, Inc., 906 North Dale, St. Paul, MN 55103.

Exploring Science in Your Home Laboratory. The Four Winds Press, Division of Scholastic Magazines, New York, NY, 1963.

Science Equipment in the Elementary School. Mountain View Center for Environmental Education, University of Colorado, Boulder, CO 30302, 1975.

Educator's Guide to Free Science Materials. Educational Progress Services, Inc., Randolph, WI 53956.

Contact the Creative Recycling Center, 4614 Liberty Avenue, Bloomfield, Pittsburgh, PA 15224.

See *Science and Children*, November-December 1979, published by the National Science Teachers Association, 1742 Connecticut Ave., N.W., Washington, D.C. 20009. Original source is NOAA and EDIS, 1977.

This is a takeoff idea on the original *Guinness Book of Records* by Norris McWhirter and published by Sterling Publishing Co., Inc., 2 Park Avenue, New York, NY 10016.

This is a takeoff idea on *Consumer Reports* published by the Consumer's Union of U.S. Inc., 256 Washington Street, Mt. Vernon, NY 10550.

A helpful publication entitled "Hucksters in the Classroom" cautions the users of free and inexpensive material and may be obtained from the Center for Study of Responsive Law, P.O. Box 19367, Washington, D.C. 20036. The price is $20 to corporations, $10 to educators and others.

A similar idea is found in *World Book Reprint on the Heart,* published by Field Enterprises, Inc., Merchandise Mart Plaza, Chicago, IL 60654. Used with permission.

For related Piagetian diagnostic activities, *see Piaget for the Classroom Teacher* by Barry J. Wadsworth, published by Longman Inc., New York, NY 10036, 1978.

Related activities can be found in various manuals published by the Boy Scouts of America, North Brunswick, NJ 08901, 1962.

Helpful information on the setting up of aquaria and terraria can be found in *Turtox Leaflets* published by Turtox/Cambosco, Chicago, IL 60620.

Jonathan Livingston Seagull by Richard Bach. Published by the Macmillan Company, New York, NY 10022, 1970.

Extending activities can be found in *Bones Teachers Guide, Bones and Chicken Skeleton* published by the Elementary Science Study, 55 Chapel Street, Newton, MA, now available from McGraw-Hill Book Company, Manchester Road, Manchester, MO 63011.

A delightful children's book that shows this process is *The Wonderful Egg* by G. Warren Schoat published by Charles Scribner's Sons, New York, NY 10017, 1952.

This activity is related to an activity found in *Consumer Product Testing* by Unified Sciences and Mathematics in the Elementary School (USMES) now published commercially by Moore Publishing Company, P.O. Box 3036, West Durham Station, Durham, NC 27705.

See "Glue Critters" originally written by the author and published in *Science and Children*, National Science Teachers Association, 1742 Connecticut Ave., N.W., Washington, D.C. 20009, January, 1978.

For related activities see *Colored Solutions* published by the Elementary Science Study, 55 Chapel Street, Newton, MA now available from McGraw-Hill Book Company, Manchester Road, Manchester, MO 63011.

For related activities see *Batteries and Bulbs I, II* published by the Elementary Science Study, 55 Chapel Street, Newton, MA now available from McGraw-Hill Book Company, Manchester Road, Manchester, MO 63011.

Many scientific supply companies have diffraction grating material. One such source is Edmund Scientific Company, 7789 Edscorp Building, Barrington, NJ 08007.

For related feather activities see *The Colors of My Rainbow* by Joe Wayman published by Good Apple, Inc., Box 299, Carthage, IL 62321.

Handy book for any rock collector is *The Golden Guide to Rocks and Minerals* by Herbert Zim published by Golden Press, New York, NY 1957.

Big Blue Marble
Dear Pen Pal
P.O. Box 4054
Santa Barbara, CA 93103

Project Pen Pal
P.O. Box 3773
318 McGill Avenue
Ventura, CA 93006   U.S.A.

For teachers helping teachers exchange information, etc., acquire a copy of the *Teacher's Desk Catalog* published by R.M. Educational Service, Inc., 27022 Mallorca Lane, Mission Viejo, CA 92691.

For a detailed history of December 31st, etc., see *Dragons of Eden* by Carl Sagan published by Random House, Inc., New York, NY 10022, 1977.

A delightful children's book to read with this activity is *Everybody Needs a Rock* by Bryd Baylor published by Charles Scribner's Sons, New York, NY 10017, 1974.

From *Murmurs of the Earth: The Voyager Interstellar Record* by Carl Sagan with F.D. Drake, Ann Druyan, Timothy Ferris, Jon Lomberg, and Linda Salzman Sagan, 1978 by Carl Sagan. Represented by permission of Random House, Inc.

ANSWERS TO MEDITATORS

Preface viii / Just Between You and Me

TEXT PAGE # / Answer

15 / Knockdown

14 / SHUT UP

27 / Misunderstanding Between Two Friends

30 / Argue over It

53 / HURRY UP

54 / I Understand

55 / SIDE BY SIDE

57 / Pain in the Neck

63 / Countdown

73 / TENANTS

83 / Eggs Over Easy

86 / Two Feet Under Ground

67 / Dark Circles Under Eyes

103 / I'm Underwater

104 / ONE on ONE

107 / WATERFALL

239

SCIENCE DIARY & LOG

Sketches · Silly Doodles · Dreams · Fantasies · Insights · Ideas

SCIENCE LOG by

THIS IS MY STORY INCLUDING PICTURES...

I THINK THIS HAPPENED BECAUSE...

THIS EXPERIENCE MAKES ME FEEL...

PERIODIC TABLE OF THE ELEMENTS

KEY

42 — ATOMIC NUMBER
95.94 — ATOMIC WEIGHT
Mo — SYMBOL
Molybdenum — NAME
2-8-18-13-1 — ELECTRON CONFIGURATION

PERIOD	Group I-A	II-A	III-B	IV-B	V-B	VI-B	VII-B	VIII			I-B	II-B	III-A	IV-A	V-A	VI-A	VII-A	INERT GASES
1	1 1.008 **H** Hydrogen 1																	2 4.003 **He** Helium 2
2	3 6.939 **Li** Lithium 2-1	4 9.012 **Be** Beryllium 2-2											5 10.811 **B** Boron 2-3	6 12.011 **C** Carbon 2-4	7 14.007 **N** Nitrogen 2-5	8 15.999 **O** Oxygen 2-6	9 18.998 **F** Fluorine 2-7	10 20.179 **Ne** Neon 2-8
3	11 22.99 **Na** Sodium 2-8-1	12 24.305 **Mg** Magnesium 2-8-2											13 26.982 **Al** Aluminum 2-8-3	14 28.086 **Si** Silicon 2-8-4	15 30.974 **P** Phosphorus 2-8-5	16 32.064 **S** Sulfur 2-8-6	17 35.453 **Cl** Chlorine 2-8-7	18 39.948 **Ar** Argon 2-8-8
4	19 39.102 **K** Potassium 2-8-8-1	20 40.08 **Ca** Calcium 2-8-8-2	21 44.956 **Sc** Scandium 2-8-9-2	22 47.90 **Ti** Titanium 2-8-10-2	23 50.942 **V** Vanadium 2-8-11-2	24 51.996 **Cr** Chromium 2-8-13-1	25 54.938 **Mn** Manganese 2-8-13-2	26 55.847 **Fe** Iron 2-8-14-2	27 58.933 **Co** Cobalt 2-8-15-2	28 58.71 **Ni** Nickel 2-8-16-2	29 63.546 **Cu** Copper 2-8-18-1	30 65.37 **Zn** Zinc 2-8-18-2	31 69.72 **Ga** Gallium 2-8-18-3	32 72.59 **Ge** Germanium 2-8-18-4	33 74.922 **As** Arsenic 2-8-18-5	34 78.96 **Se** Selenium 2-8-18-6	35 79.904 **Br** Bromine 2-8-18-7	36 83.80 **Kr** Krypton 2-8-18-8
5	37 85.47 **Rb** Rubidium 2-8-18-8-1	38 87.62 **Sr** Strontium 2-8-18-8-2	39 88.905 **Y** Yttrium 2-8-18-9-2	40 91.22 **Zr** Zirconium 2-8-18-10-2	41 92.906 **Nb** Niobium 2-8-18-12-1	42 95.94 **Mo** Molybdenum 2-8-18-13-1	43 (99) **Tc** Technetium 2-8-18-13-1	44 101.07 **Ru** Ruthenium 2-8-18-15-1	45 102.905 **Rh** Rhodium 2-8-18-16-1	46 106.4 **Pd** Palladium 2-8-18-18	47 107.868 **Ag** Silver 2-8-18-18-1	48 112.40 **Cd** Cadmium 2-8-18-18-2	49 114.82 **In** Indium 2-8-18-18-3	50 118.69 **Sn** Tin 2-8-18-18-4	51 121.75 **Sb** Antimony 2-8-18-18-5	52 127.60 **Te** Tellurium 2-8-18-18-6	53 126.90 **I** Iodine 2-8-18-18-7	54 131.30 **Xe** Xenon 2-8-18-18-8
6	55 132.905 **Cs** Cesium 2-8-18-18-8-1	56 137.34 **Ba** Barium 2-8-18-18-8-2	57 ★ 138.91 **La** Lanthanum 2-8-18-18-9-2	72 178.49 **Hf** Hafnium 2-8-18-32-10-2	73 180.948 **Ta** Tantalum 2-8-18-32-11-2	74 183.85 **W** Tungsten 2-8-18-32-12-2	75 186.2 **Re** Rhenium 2-8-18-32-13-2	76 190.2 **Os** Osmium 2-8-18-32-14-2	77 192.2 **Ir** Iridium 2-8-18-32-17	78 195.09 **Pt** Platinum 2-8-18-32-17-1	79 196.967 **Au** Gold 2-8-18-32-18-1	80 200.59 **Hg** Mercury 2-8-18-32-18-2	81 204.37 **Tl** Thallium 2-8-18-32-18-3	82 207.19 **Pb** Lead 2-8-18-32-18-4	83 208.98 **Bi** Bismuth 2-8-18-32-18-5	84 (210) **Po** Polonium 2-8-18-32-18-6	85 (210) **At** Astatine 2-8-18-32-18-7	86 (222) **Rn** Radon 2-8-18-32-18-8
7	87 (223) **Fr** Francium 2-8-18-32-18-8-1	88 (226) **Ra** Radium 2-8-18-32-18-8-2	89 ★★ (227) **Ac** Actinium 2-8-18-32-18-9-2															

★ Lanthanide Series — 6

58 140.12 **Ce** Cerium 2-8-18-19-9-2	59 140.91 **Pr** Praseodymium 2-8-18-20-9-2	60 144.24 **Nd** Neodymium 2-8-18-22-8-2	61 (147) **Pm** Promethium 2-8-18-23-8-2	62 150.35 **Sm** Samarium 2-8-18-24-8-2	63 151.96 **Eu** Europium 2-8-18-25-8-2	64 157.25 **Gd** Gadolinium 2-8-18-25-9-2	65 158.924 **Tb** Terbium 2-8-18-26-9-2	66 162.50 **Dy** Dysprosium 2-8-18-28-8-2	67 164.93 **Ho** Holmium 2-8-18-29-8-2	68 167.26 **Er** Erbium 2-8-18-30-8-2	69 168.934 **Tm** Thulium 2-8-18-31-8-2	70 173.04 **Yb** Ytterbium 2-8-18-32-8-2	71 174.97 **Lu** Lutetium 2-8-...-32-9-2

★★ Actinide Series — 7

90 232.04 **Th** Thorium 2-8-18-32-18-9-2	91 (231) **Pa** Protactinium 2-8-18-32-20-9-2	92 238.03 **U** Uranium 2-8-18-32-21-9-2	93 (237) **Np** Neptunium 2-8-18-32-22-9-2	94 (244) **Pu** Plutonium 2-8-18-32-23-9-2	95 (243) **Am** Americium 2-8-18-32-24-9-2	96 (247) **Cm** Curium 2-8-18-32-25-9-2	97 (247) **Bk** Berkelium 2-8-18-32-26-9-2	98 (252) **Cf** Californium 2-8-18-32-27-9-2	99 (254) **Es** Einsteinium 2-8-18-32-29-8-2	100 (257) **Fm** Fermium 2-8-18-32-30-8-2	101 (257) **Md** Mendelevium 2-8-18-32-31-8-2	102 (255) **No** Nobelium 2-8-18-32-32-8-2	103 (256) **(Lw)** (Lawrencium)

HANDY METRIC/CUSTOMARY CONVERSION CHART

When You Know This	Symbol	Multiply by This	To Find This	Symbol
LENGTH				
millimeters	mm	0.04	inches	in
centimeters	cm	0.4	inches	in
meters	m	3.3	feet	ft
meters	m	1.1	yards	yd
kilometers	km	0.6	miles	mi
AREA				
square centimeters	cm²	0.16	square inches	in²
square meters	m²	1.2	square yards	yd²
square kilometers	km²	0.4	square miles	mi²
hectares (10,000 m²)	ha	2.5	acres	
MASS (WEIGHT)				
grams	g	0.035	ounce	oz
kilograms	kg	2.2	pounds	lb
tons (1000 kg)	t	1.1	short tons	
VOLUME				
milliliters	mL	0.03	fluid ounces	fl oz
liters	l	2.1	pints	pt
liters	l	1.06	quarts	qt
liters	l	0.26	gallons	gal
cubic meters	m³	35	cubic feet	ft³
cubic yards	m³	1.3	cubic yards	yd³
TEMPERATURE				
Celsius temp.	°C	(⅘ C) + 32	Fahrenheit temp.	°F
TEMPERATURE TO METRIC				
Fahrenheit temp.	°F	5/9 (°F − 32) of remainder	Celsius temp.	°C
LENGTH				
inches	in	2.54	centimeters	cm
feet	ft	30	centimeters	cm
yards	ys	0.9	meters	m
miles	mi	1.6	kilometers	km
AREA				
square inches	in²	6.5	sq. centimeters	cm²
square feet	ft²	0.09	square meters	m²
square yards	yd²	0.8	square meters	m²
square miles	mi²	2.6	sq. kilometers	km²
acres		0.4	hectares	ha
MASS (WEIGHT)				
ounces	oz	28	grams	g
pounds	lb	0.45	kilograms	kg
short tons (2000 lb)		0.9	tonnes	t
VOLUME				
teaspoons	tsp	5	milliliters	mL
tablespoons	tbsp	15	milliliters	mL
fluid ounces	fl oz	30	milliliters	mL
cups	c	0.24	liters	l
pints	pt	0.47	liters	l
quarts	qt	0.95	liters	l
gallons	gal	3.8	liters	l
cubic feet	ft³	0.03	cubic meters	m³
cubic yards	yd³	0.76	cubic meters	m³

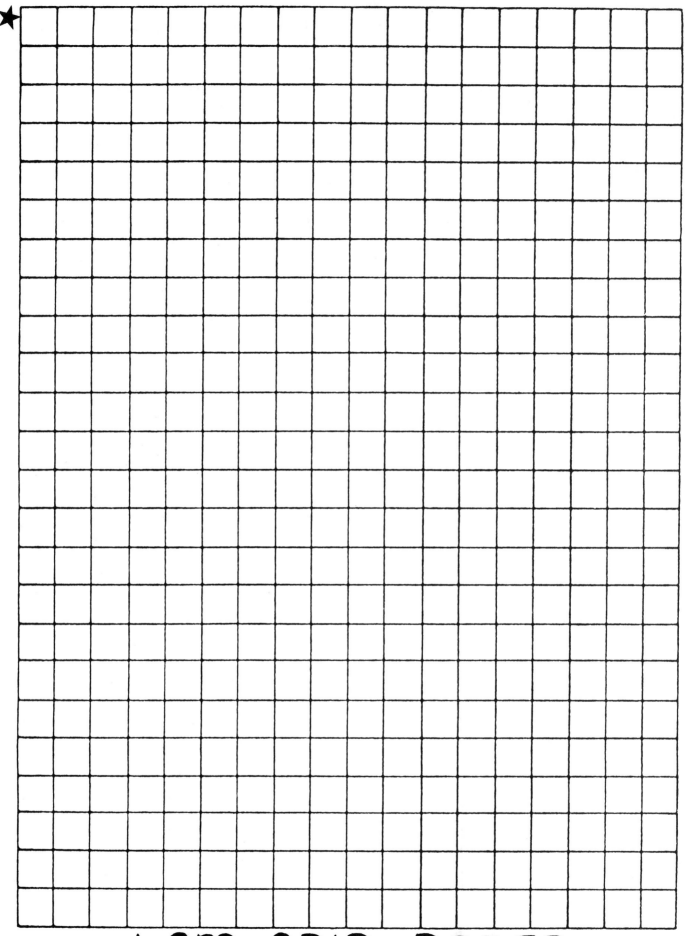

I CM GRID PAPER

244

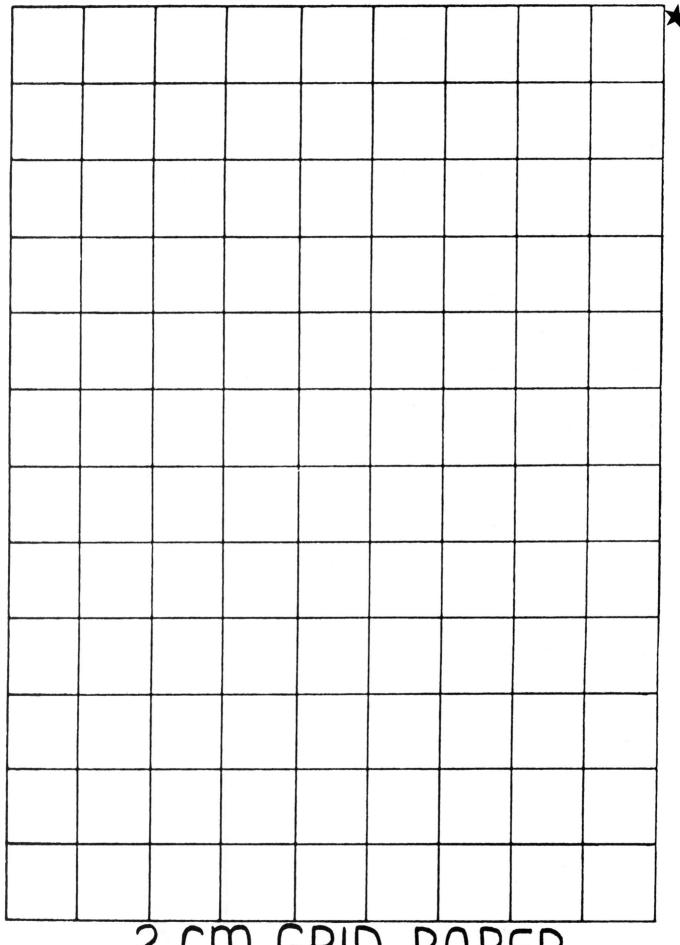

2 CM GRID PAPER

245

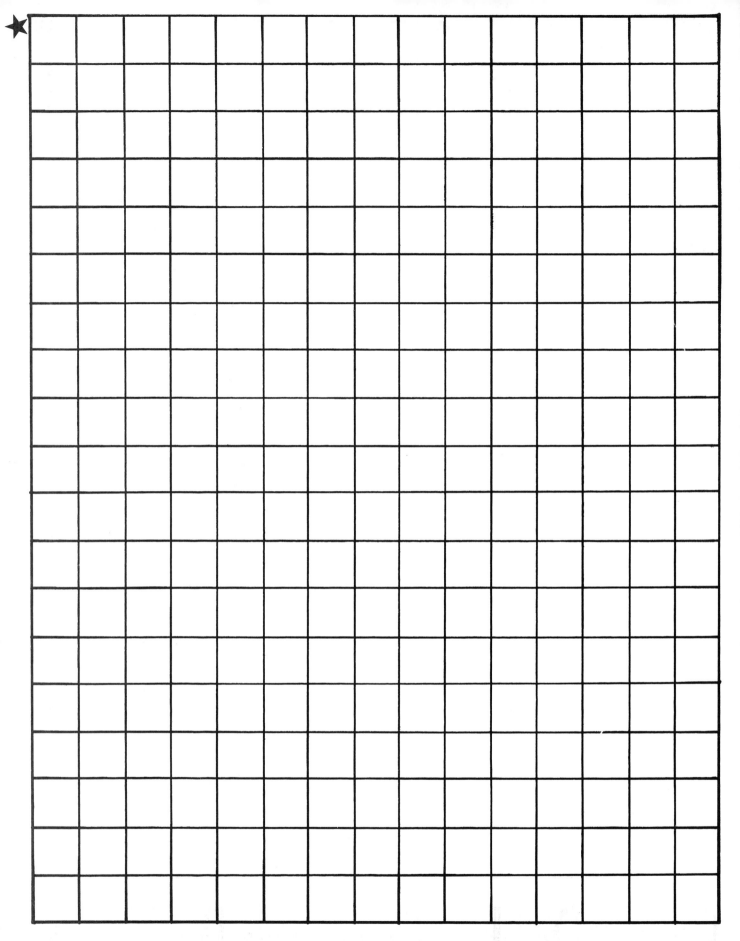

ONE-HALF SQUARE INCH GRID PAPER